FIFTY KEY JEWISH THINKERS

First published 1997
by Routledge
11 New Fetter Lane, London EC4P 4EE

Simultaneously published in the USA and Canada
by Routledge
29 West 35th Street, New York, NY 10001

Typeset in Times Ten by Florencetype Ltd, Stoodleigh, Devon
Printed and bound in Great Britain by
TJ Press (Padstow) Ltd, Padstow, Cornwall

British Library Cataloguing in Publication Data
A catalogue record for this book is available from the British Library

Library of Congress Cataloging in Publication Data
Cohn-Sherbok, Dan.
  Fifty key Jewish thinkers
      p.   cm.
  Includes bibliographical references.
      1. Rabbis–Biography. 2. Jewish scholars–Biography.
  3. Jewish philosophers–Biography. 4. Zionists–Biography.   I. Title.
  BM750.C57   1996
  296'.092'2—dc20   96-7554
  [B]   CIP

ISBN 0-415-12627-4
ISBN 0-415-12628-2 (pbk)

For Lavinia

CONTENTS

CONTENTS

PREFACE

For more than twenty years I have taught courses dealing with the history of Jewish thought at the University of Kent in Canterbury, England. During this time I have frequently directed students to such multi-volume encyclopedias of Judaism as the *Jewish Encyclopedia* and the *Encyclopedia Judaica*. These vast repositories of material provide a wealth of information about key thinkers in the history of the Jewish faith. Nonetheless, very often students find these works overwhelming as well as difficult to gain access to if they are much in demand in the library.

Aware of these difficulties, I suggested they look at a number of single-volume encyclopedias and dictionaries as well as specialized monographs dealing with Jewish thought. Many of these works, however, failed to meet their needs: they were either far too brief or overly detailed. Increasingly I came to see that what was needed was a single-volume survey of major Jewish thinkers. Such a handy reference book would not take the place of either multi-volume reference works or studies of individual thinkers; rather, it could serve as a first point of entry into the fascinating world of Jewish thought.

This book, *Fifty Key Jewish Thinkers*, was thus designed to fill a gap in the types of introductory books available to students as well as to teachers and more general readers. Inevitably such an overview of Jewish thought must be highly selective, and many important figures have been omitted. Yet, the aim of this survey is to introduce readers to some of the most important thinkers in the history of Judaism from post-biblical times to the present day. My intention has been to provide the type of general information most commonly sought by students who wish to explore the richness of Jewish philosophical, theological and mystical reflection as it developed through the centuries.

ACKNOWLEDGEMENTS

In writing this book I would like to acknowledge my indebtedness to a number of important books from which I have obtained information and source material: C. Sirat, *A History of Jewish Philosophy in the Middle Ages*, Cambridge, 1995; *Encyclopedia Judaica*, Jerusalem, 1971; I. Husik, *A History of Medieval Jewish Philosophy*, New York, 1966; W. Jacobs, *Judaism Through Christian Eyes*, Cincinnati, Ohio, 1974; R. Seltzer, *Jewish People, Jewish Thought*, New York, 1980; an important reader of Jewish mystical writings: L. Jacobs, *Jewish Mystical Testimonies*, New York, 1978; and two excellent studies and readers of Zionist thought: S. Avineri, *The Making of Modern Zionism*, New York, 1981 and A. Hertzberg, *The Zionist Idea: A Historical Analysis and Reader*, New York, 1969. Those who wish to discover more information about the writers covered in this volume – including philosophers, theologians, kabbalists and Zionists – are encouraged to consult these books as well as those listed throughout this study. For all Jewish thinkers I have provided brief biographical details and a concise description of some central features of their writing; at the end of each entry I have supplied a list of significant works as well as secondary literature. I would also like to thank Richard Stoneman of Routledge for his encouragement and Kieron Corless of Routledge for his help with this book.

CHRONOLOGICAL TABLE

Patriarchal period	*c.* 1900–1600 BCE
Exodus from Egypt	*c.* 1250–1230 BCE
Period of the Judges	*c.* 1200–1000 BCE
Period of the United Monarchy	*c.* 1030–930 BCE
Division of the Kingdoms	*c.* 930 BCE
Destruction of the Northern Kingdom	722 BCE
Destruction of the Southern Kingdom	586 BCE
Babylonian exile	586–538 BCE
Return of the exiles	538 BCE
Rebuilding of the Temple	*c.* 520–515 BCE
Second Temple period	*c.* 515 BCE–70 CE
Philo	20 BCE–50 CE
Jewish rebellion against Rome	66–70 CE
Destruction of the Second Temple	70 CE
Roman period	*c.* 146 BCE–400 CE
Mishnah compiled	*c.* 200 CE
Jerusalem Talmud compiled	*c.* 5th century
Babylonian Talmud compiled	*c.* 6th century
Period of the Geonim	*c.* 600–1300
Karaism founded	*c.* 760
Saadiah ben Joseph Gaon	882–942
Solomon ibn Gabirol	1020–1057
Bahya ibn Pakuda	1050–1120
Judah Halevi	1075–1141
Crusades	1095–1291
Abraham ibn Daud	1110–1180
Maimonides	1135–1204
Nahmanides	1194–1270
Establishment of the Inquisition	*c.* 1230
Gersonides	1288–1344
Hasdai Crescas	1340–1412
Joseph Albo	1380–1445
Disputation of Tortosa	1413–1415
Isaac Abrabanel	1437–1508
Expulsion of the Jews from Spain	1492
Isaac Luria	1534–1572

Hayyim Vital	1542–1620
Early Modern period	*c.* 1550–1700
Baruch Spinoza	1632–1677
Modern period	*c.* 1700–present
Baal Shem Tov	1700–1760
Moses Hayyim Luzzatto	1707–1746
Dov Baer of Mezhirich	1710–1772
Moses Mendelssohn	1729–1786
Solomon Maimon	1753–1800
Nahman of Bratslav	1772–1811
Reform Movement founded	*c.* 1850
Solomon Ludwig Steinheim	1789–1866
Zevi Hirsch Kalischer	1795–1874
Solomon Formstecher	1808–1888
Samson Raphael Hirsch	1808–1874
Abraham Geiger	1810–1875
Moses Hess	1812–1875
Samuel Hirsch	1815–1889
Heinrich Graetz	1817–1891
Leon Pinsker	1821–1891
Hermann Cohen	1842–1918
Conservative Movement founded	*c.* 1895
First Zionist Congress	1897
Aharon David Gordon	1856–1922
Ahad Ha-Am	1856–1927
Claude Montefiore	1858–1938
Theodor Herzl	1860–1904
Modern Orthodoxy founded	*c.* 1905
Abraham Isaac Kook	1865–1935
Leo Baeck	1873–1956
Reconstructionist Movement founded	*c.* 1935
The Holocaust	1942–1945
Founding of the State of Israel	1948
Martin Buber	1878–1965
Vladimir Jabotinsky	1880–1940
Ber Borochov	1881–1917
Mordecai Kaplan	1881–1983
Franz Rosenzweig	1886–1929
Ignaz Maybaum	1897–1976
Eliezer Berkovits	1900–1992
Abraham Joshua Heschel	1907–1972
Emil Fackenheim	1917–
Richard Rubenstein	1924–
Elie Wiesel	1928–
Arthur A. Cohen	1928–1986
Sherwin Wine	1928–

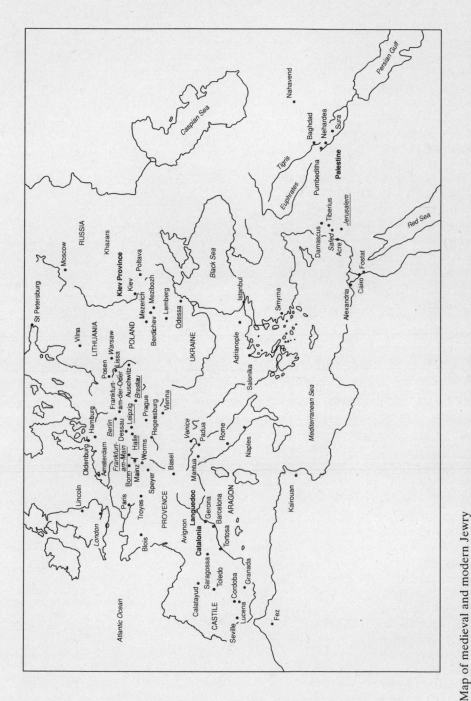

Map of medieval and modern Jewry

All the places listed are relevant to two or more thinkers; for those in *italics*, a Jewish seminary or centre is referred to in the text; for those <u>under-lined</u>, the university is referred to; countries and regions are shown in **bold**.

through the unanimous consent of several persons rather than the irresponsible will of only one individual. In this light continuity can be assured through the government of a succession of leaders as long as they are aware that they must provide an account of their actions. Regarding absolute power, Abrabanel insists that this is not a necessity. Furthermore, collective decision-making is advocated by the Torah. Turning to existing states, he asserts that government by elected judges, as found in Venice, Florence and Genoa, is far superior to monarchical rule.

As far as Israel is concerned, Abrabanel stresses that its true guide must be the God of the Jewish nation. It does not need a king, and experience has proved that monarchy is a disastrous institution. The judges, however, were faithful servants of the Lord. The best form of government is thus that of an elite group of judges who are guided in their decisions by the will of God. The Messiah, he continues, will not be a king, but a judge and prophet. In this respect, Abrabanel antici-pated the revolution in political thinking brought about by the Renaissance even though he resembles other thinkers of the Middle Ages in terms of his philosophical and theological ideas.

Abrabanel's major writings

Isaac Abrabanel, *Principles of Faith* (trans. M.M. Kellner), London and Toronto, 1982

See also in this book

Gersonides, Hasdai Crescas, Maimonides

Further reading

M.M. Kellner, 'Rabbi Isaac Abravanel on Maimonides' Principles of Faith', *Tradition* 18, 1980
E. Mihaly, 'Isaac Abravanel on the Principles of Faith', *Hebrew Union College Annual*, Cincinnati, OH 26, 1955
B. Natanyahu, *Don Isaac Abravanel, Statesman and Philosopher*, Philadelphia, 1953

A.J. Reines, *Maimonides and Abrabanel on Prophecy*, Cincinnati, OH, 1970
J. Sarachek, *Don Isaac Abravanel*, New York, 1938

ABRAHAM IBN DAUD

Born in Cordoba in 1110, Abraham Ben David Halevi ibn Daud lived in Spain until his death in 1180. Initially he received a religious and secular education including Arabic poetry, literature and philosophy. Fleeing Cordoba before the Almohad conquest, he settled in Toledo where he collaborated in translating texts from Arabic into Latin; subsequently these works were further translated into the vernacular in collaboration with other scholars. Among the texts translated in this way was the *Fountain of Life* by Solomon ibn Gabirol. Like most philosophers, ibn Daud was both a physician and an astronomer; in addition, he worked as an historian producing *Sefer ha-Kabbalah* (Book of the Tradition).

Ibn Daud's most important philosophical work, the *Exalted Faith* (*Emunah Ramah*), was composed in 1160–1; although the orig-inal text is not extant, Hebrew translations of the work dating from the fourteenth century were made by Samuel ibn Motot at the suggestion of Isaac ben Sheset. The *Exalted Faith* had little influence on those medieval philosophers who did not know Arabic, and was later overshadowed by Maimonides' *Guide of the Perplexed* written some years later.

In the introduction ibn Daud states that he wrote this work to resolve the difficulties connected with determinism and free will; in his view, this issue can only be dealt with in a broader context. Hence the book is structured in two parts: the first deals with physics, which he calls philosophy, including proofs for the existence of a Prime Mover; the second is devoted to revealed religion. For ibn Daud these topics are in fact the same since scientific truths are found in all sacred texts. Philosophical demonstration, he argues, must always be perfected by demonstrating that the Bible alludes to such philosophical proof. In particular, when passages appear to conflict with such demonstration or contradict one another, they need to be interpreted according to the intellect – this is because many verses are directed to the common people and do not reveal their deeper meaning on a superficial reading. The purpose of the *Exalted Faith* is to illustrate that Scripture is in accord with Aristotelian philosophy:

> When someone is just beginning his study of the sciences, he is perplexed about what he knows from the point of view of the traditional knowledge because he has not attained in science the degree where he could state the Truth in the questions which are not clear. Accordingly, this book will be very useful to him for it will acquaint him with many points of Science which we have built on the principles of religion. (ibn Daud, 1982, 2–4)

Like Moses Maimonides, ibn Daud composed this treatise because beginners in philosophy were unable to harmonize the Bible with science; as a result they were inclined to reject either biblical teaching or Aristotelianism:

> The first (reason) is that the Torah and philosophy are in flagrant contradiction when they attempt to describe the divine essence; for the philosophers, the incorporeal God is in no way capable of alteration; the Torah, on the contrary, narrates God's movements, his feelings . . . . Given that philosophy and the Torah are in opposition on this subject, we are in the situation of a man with two masters, one great and the other not small; he cannot please the first without opposing the opinion of the second. (Ibid., 82)

To alleviate such difficulty, ibn Daud explains that the biblical text should be understood in a rational sense. In the first part of this work, ibn Daud begins each chapter with an exposition of philosophical ideas; this is followed by supporting scriptural verses. The first chapter commences with a discussion of substance and accident – this is followed by a treatment of substance, infinite length and breadth, movement, the soul and the spheres. The second part of the *Exalted Faith* continues with an exposition of what ibn Daud regards as the principles of the Jewish faith. Beginning with the concept of religious commitment, he attempts to answer the question: what is faith? Ibn Daud contends that it is not the faith of popular belief which is of concern. The common people assume that what is not matter does not exist; thus they do not believe in an incorporeal God. When such individuals advance in their understanding, they believe in the tradition of the sages – yet there remains the danger that they will not know how to deal with confusion and doubt.

Regarding the faith of the rabbis, it is based on a knowledge of God's activities – it is to this type of religious conviction that the Torah directs the common people. However, such true belief grounded in a perception of God's acts does not prove that God is incorporeal: he could be either a sphere or a star. The true sages among the philosophers predicate their belief on the demonstration that God is the Prime Mover. At this stage in the argument, ibn Daud attempts to prove that the Prime Mover exists by demonstrating that such a being is unique and non-material. A second proof of the necessity of a unique and incorporeal God is based on cause and effect. The existence of all beings, ibn Daud argues, is contingent; a necessary being, however, can cause them to exist, creating them *ex nihilo*. Eternal beings, like angels, do not come into existence from the state of non-being; rather, their existence is derived from another than themselves, and ultimately from God himself.

After discussing the concept of God's unity, ibn Daud turns to the divine attributes.

In his opinion, the only true attributes are negative in character. This discussion is followed by a consideration of the nature of angels. The existence of angels is certain, he argues, because the human soul is initially *in potentia*, and then *in actu*. The transition from one state to the other involves movement: all movement is caused by a mover, and the Active Intellect is the motive power for such change. Another proof concerns the course of the stars: in ibn Daud's view, such a phenomenon is explicable only through incorporeal intermediaries and a unique God. It is this unique God who produces the material world. Multiplicity does not emanate directly from God since only One can come from One. Instead, multiplicity accompanies the First Being issuing directly from God – this First Being is what the philosophers call Intellect and the Torah calls Angel. In comparison with God, it is imperfect since it receives its being from something other than itself. Duality is therefore at its very root. From this first Intellect emerge three beings: a Second Intellect which is less perfect than the first because it does not arise directly from God but from a being outside the divine realm; the soul of the sphere; and its matter.

Ibn Daud goes on to explain that the soul of the sphere of the fixed stars and the matter of the sphere of the fixed stars emanate from the Second Intellect. Hence from intellect to intellect, we reach the Final Intellect, that which presides over the lower world which gives forms to all sublunary beings. It is this which makes our intellect pass from potentiality to actuality and serves as the source of prophecy. Concerning prophetic apprehension, ibn Daud maintains that there are three types of prophetic state: true dreams; visions that take place in an unconscious state; and visions that occur while the prophet is awake and conscious. Describing the highest degree of prophecy, he writes:

> Divine providence on behalf of His creatures is already evident to all those who meditate, but since these are few in number, the perfect goodness of God makes it still more evident by making it repose on those men who are of perfect conduct and irreproachable morals, so that, as it were, they become intermediaries between God and his creatures. He elevates them to such a point that they have a power comparable to that of the eminent substances which incline towards them in prophecy.... Only perfect and pure souls can attain such a level. This perfection and this purity are sometimes in a man from the beginning of his formation, and also moral perfection, but study is of great utility, as is the society of virtuous men.... (Ibid., 73–4)

In ibn Daud's view, although prophecy is a natural phenomenon, only Israel has the gift of attaining this highest state of perfection. Hence the biblical text, which is the fruit of prophecy, should not be understood as depicting God in corporeal form. To interpret anthropomorphic expressions in Scripture literally is to commit an act of heresy. In this light, ibn Daud criticizes his co-religionists who have misinterpreted the biblical text in contrast with those Christians and Muslims who read Scripture correctly:

> The other, non-Jewish, religious communities have not wished to belittle God by attributing to him these vile details unworthy of him, thus, the Christians have translated the verses: God said, God descended, by: the Lord said, the Lord appeared; thus the Moslems have never claimed that God spoke to the prophets or appeared to them ... while among our co-religionists certain have so little discernment that they are not satisfied with attributing to God change and movement, they go so far as to attribute to him more transformations than to any of his creatures. (Ibid., 90–1)

Before concluding with a discussion of the divine commandments, ibn Daud returns to the problem of free will. Free will, he believes, consists in keeping God's commandments – if there were no such choice, the notion of reward and punishment would have no place in Jewish teaching. Citing 1 Samuel 26:10, ibn Daud illustrates that there are three major causes of human events: divine, natural and accidental causes. The fourth cause – free will – is exemplified by a description of the flight from Keilah. This event was an episode in the conflict between David and Saul in 1 Samuel 23. From this example, human events are described as determined by divine, natural and accidental causes, but the wise person who hears the divine word can foresee future events and take precautions. Free will thus consists in the liberty to follow God's law and purify one's soul – when this occurs, God's providence watches over those who are faithful to him.

References/ibn Daud's major writings

Abraham ibn Daud, *Sefer ha-Kabalah* (trans. G.D. Cohen), London, 1969
Abraham ibn Daud, *Emunah Ramah*, Frankfurt-am-Main, 1982

See also in this book

Maimonides, Solomon ibn Gabirol

Further reading

J. Guggenheimer, *Die Religionsphilosophie des Abraham b. David ha-Levi*, 1850
S. Horovitz, 'Die Psychologie des Aristotelikers Abraham Ibn Daud', *Jahresberichte des jüdisch-theologischen Seminars*, Breslau, 1912
I. Husik, *A History of Medieval Jewish Philosophy*, New York, 1966
C. Sirat, *A History of Jewish Philosophy in the Middle Ages*, Cambridge, 1955

AHAD HA-AM

Born in Skvira in Kiev province (now in the Ukraine) in 1856, Asher Hirsch Ginsberg (later known as Ahad Ha-Am) was preoccupied with the spiritual regeneration of the Jewish people. He received a typical Jewish education, but in 1868 his family moved to an estate leased by his father, where he studied medieval Jewish philosophy as well as the writers of the Enlightenment. At the age of twenty he was exposed to French and German literature as well as philosophy. Subsequently he unsuccessfully attempted to pursue his studies in various European capitals. In 1884 he settled in Odessa where he began to publish essays dealing with modern Jewish life.

His first essay, 'Wrong Way', appeared in 1889, setting the stage for his role within the *Hovevei Zion* (Lovers of Zion) movement. In this work he encourages the restoration of Zion although he is critical of several aspects of the movement. In a later essay, 'The Jewish State and the Jewish problem', which was written after his return from the first Zionist Congress, he discusses Max Nordau's opening address to the congress. For Nordau, the central problem facing Eastern European Jewry is economic misery, whereas Jews in Western countries are confronted by the failure of the Emancipation to provide a framework for Jewish identity in the contemporary world. According to Nordau, these dilemmas illustrate the need for the creation of a Jewish state in Palestine.

In Ahad Ha-Am's view, however, the situation is more complex. Assuming that such a homeland were established, what would occur when the Jewish state absorbed the first wave of immigrants? Would this solve the Jewish problem? Clearly not all Jews throughout the world could settle in Palestine. What would be the result if only a small segment of the world Jewish population emigrated to Palestine? Ahad Ha-Am argues that the economic difficulties facing

Eastern European Jewry would not be over-come for those who remained behind. Hence the major problem faced by Zionism is how to resolve the spiritual perplexities of Jews living in the diaspora.

In Ahad Ha-Am's opinion, Zionism is able to solve the problems of Western Jewry more readily than it can ameliorate the conditions of Jews living in Eastern Europe. The Jew in the West is separated from Jewish culture as well as alienated from the society in which he lives. The establishment of a Jewish state would enable him to resolve the problems of national identity, thereby compensating him for his lack of integration into the culture of the country in which he resides:

If a Jewish state were re-established [in Palestine], a state arranged after the pattern of other states, then he [the Western Jew] could live a full, complete life among his own people, and find at home all that he now sees outside, dangled before his eyes, but out of reach. Of course, not all the Jews will be able to take wing and go to their state; but the very existence of the Jewish state will raise the prestige of those who remain in exile, and their fellow citizens will no more despise them and keep them at arm's length as though they were ignoble slaves, dependent entirely on the hospitality of others. (Ha'am, 1962, 74–5)

Such an ideal would be able to cure the Jew in the West of his social unease – the consciousness of his inferiority in lands where he is regarded as an alien.

In Eastern Europe, on the other hand, such a solution is inadequate. With the disappearance of the ghetto, Judaism has lost its hold on the Jewish people. In the past, Jews were able to ensure the survival of the tradition through common practice. Yet, the passing of this closed society has led to the collapse of Jewish learning. Thus for Ahad Ha-Am, it is impossible for Eastern European Jews to return to the traditional religious system of the ghetto. What is required now is the creation of a new Jewish social identity in Israel:

Judaism needs at present but little. It needs not an independent state, but only the creation in its native land of conditions favourable to its development: a good sized settlement of Jews working without hindrance in every branch of culture, from agriculture and handicrafts to science and literature. This Jewish settlement, which will be a gradual growth, will become in the course of time the centre of the nation, wherein its spirit will find pure expression and develop in all its aspects up to the highest degree of perfection of which it is capable. Then from the centre the spirit of Judaism will go forth to the great circum-ference, to all the communities of the dias-pora, and will breathe new life into them and preserve their unity; and when our national culture in Palestine has attained that level, we may be confident that it will produce men in the country who will be able, on a favourable opportunity, to estab-lish a state which will be truly a Jewish state, and not merely a state of Jews. (Ibid., 78–9)

Israel, therefore, is to be a state infused with Jewish values. It should not simply be a homeland for world Jewry. Rather, it must embody the religious and cultural ideals of the past. The strength of Judaism, Ahad Ha-Am argues, resides in the prophetic emphasis on spiritual values. A Jewish state which is devoid of such an orientation is doomed – a secular state is not viable, he maintains, because 'a political ideal which does not rest on the national culture is apt to seduce us from our loyalty to spiritual greatness, and to beget in us a tendency to find the path of glory breaking the thread that unites us with the past, and undermining our historical basis.' (Ibid., 80)

Without such spiritual ideals, political power can become an end in itself. To illustrate this point, Ahad Ha-Am uses the example of Judea under Herod the Great:

History teaches us that in the days of the Herodian house Palestine was indeed a Jewish state, but the national culture was despised and persecuted, and the ruling house did everything in its power to implant Roman culture in the country, and frittered away the national resources in the building of heathen temples and amphitheatres, and so forth. Such a Jewish state would spell death and utter degradation for our people. Such a Jewish state ... would not be able to give us a feeling of national glory; and the national culture, in which we might have sought and found our glory, would not be implanted in our state and would not be the principle of its life. (Ibid., 80–1)

After visiting Jewish settlements in Palestine, Ahad Ha-am wrote 'Truth from the Land of Israel', an essay filled with his impressions of the country. Condemning land speculation, he calls on the *Hovevei Zion* to intercede. Further, he focuses on the problems faced by Zionism arising from the existence of a large Arab population. This people, he states, must be dealt with by those wishing to settle in the land. As early as 1891 he recognized that the Arab community would in all likelihood press for the creation of a national movement. It is an error to believe that Palestine lacks a native people:

We tend to believe abroad that Palestine is nowadays almost completely deserted, a non-cultivated wilderness, and that anyone can come there and buy as much land as his heart desires. But in reality this is not the case. It is difficult to find anywhere in the country Arab land which lies fallow. (in Avineri, 1981, 122)

What is required then is a sense of realism. Jews should not see themselves as superior to their Arab neighbours; instead they should acknowledge that the Arabs are proud and determined:

We tend to believe abroad that all Arabs are desert barbarians, an asinine people

who do not see or understand what is going on around them. This is a cardinal mistake. .... The Arabs, and especially the city dwellers, understand very well what we want and what we do in the country; but they behave as if they do not notice it because at present they do not see any danger for themselves or their future in what we are doing and are therefore trying to turn to their benefit these new guests. But the day will come in which the life of our people in the land of Israel will develop to such a degree that they will push aside the local population by little or much, then it will not easily give up its place. (Ibid., 123)

So that they will be able to flourish in the land of their ancestors, Jews should act with love and compassion for those Arabs in their midst.

Even though Ahad Ha-Am's conception of the return to the Holy Land was not based on messianic longing, his idealization of the spiritual, religious and cultural dimensions of Judaism and their embodiment in a Jewish state was rooted in Jewish messianism. For Ahad Ha-Am, it would not be a divinely appointed Messiah who would bring about God's kingdom on earth – rather this would be accomplished by the Jewish people themselves. Through the creation of a Jewish state, the spiritual values of Judaism are to materialize in the Holy Land.

References

Ahad Ha'am, *Nationalism and the Jewish Ethic*, New York, 1962
Shlomo Avineri, *The Making of Modern Zionism: The Intellectual Origins of the Jewish State*, New York, 1981

Ha'Am's major writings

Ahad Ha'Am, *Selected Essays* (trans. L. Simon), Philadelphia, 1912
L. Simon, *Ahad Ha-Am, Essays, Letters, Memoirs*, Oxford, 1946

Further reading

S. Avineri, *The Making of Modern Zionism*, New York, 1981

N. Bentwich, *Ahad Ha'am and his Philosophy*, Jerusalem, 1927

D. Cohn-Sherbok, *Israel: The History of an Idea*, London, 1992

J. Fraenkel, *Dubnow, Herzl, and Ahad Ha-Am*, London, 1963

L. Simon, *Ahad Ha'am-Asher Ginzberg: A Biography*, Philadelphia, 1960

L. Simon, *Ahad Ha-Am, the Lover of Zion*, London, 1961

JOSEPH ALBO

Born in 1380, Joseph Albo was a Spanish philosopher and preacher who played a prominent role in the Disputation of Tortosa and San Mateo in 1413–14 as a representative of the Jewish community of Daroca, a province of Saragossa. Albo's most important work, the *Book of Principles* (*Sefer ha-Ikkarim*), is a treatise on the central principles of the Jewish faith. Written as a response to the decline of religious commitment among his co-religionists, the *Book of Principles* was designed to restore confidence in Judaism by providing a rational presentation of the Jewish faith. Drawing on the Islamic philosophical tradition, Latin Christian scholasticism, and the writings of his teacher, Hasdai Crescas, Albo offers a presentation of the central beliefs of Judaism.

In this work, Albo argues that an unbeliever should be defined as one who knows the Torah lays down a principle but denies its truth. Such rebellion against the teaching of the tradition constitutes unbelief. But a person who, upholding the law of Moses and believing in the cardinal principles of the faith,

> when he undertakes to investigate these matters with his reason and scrutinizes the texts, is misled by his speculation and interprets a given principle otherwise than it is taken to mean at first sight; or denies the principle because he thinks that it does not represent a sound theory which the Torah obliges us to believe; or erroneously denies that a given belief is a fundamental principle, which however he believes as he believes the other dogmas of the Torah which are not fundamental principles; or entertains a certain notion in relation to one of the miracles of the Torah because he thinks that he is not thereby denying any of the doctrines which is obligatory upon us to believe by the authority of the Torah – a person of this sort is not an unbeliever; his sin is due to error and requires atonement. (Jacobs, 1988, 21)

The *Sefer ha-Ikkarim* begins in Part I with a critique of earlier attempts by philosophers (primarily Maimonides and Crescas) to formulate the underlying principles of the Jewish faith. In Albo's view, Maimonides failed to offer any specific criterion by which such selection could be made; further, he questions whether Crescas' list of six criteria actually furnishes a basis for determining the general principles of divine law. In contrast with these writers, Albo was anxious to explain the principles without which it is not possible to conceive of a divine law. Albo then goes on to formulate three essential principles of divine law:

1 the existence of God;
2 divine revelation; and
3 reward and punishment.

Previously these three fundamental beliefs had been proposed by Simeon ben Zemah Duran – arguably, both Duran and Albo adopted this system from Averroes' Fasl al-Maqal where they are specified as examples of the principles of revealed law.

In explaining the nature of these three fundamental principles of the faith, Albo points out that the three benedictions incorporated in the Additional Service for New Year – Kingdoms, Memorials and Trumpets – represent these beliefs. According to Albo, these three blessings were ordained in order to direct one's attention to the basic beliefs of the Jewish religion at the beginning of the year (the traditional period of divine judgment) so that by properly believing in these principles together with the dogmas derived from them it would be possible to win a favourable verdict in the divine judgment.

Averroes' influence on Albo is reflected in the distinction Albo draws between a person who denies these three principles of the faith, and the individual who, holding to erroneous interpretations of Scripture, denies other articles of Judaism. Hence the sage Hillel who maintained that Jews can expect no Messianic deliverance in the future was guilty of not believing in the coming of the Messiah, yet he was not a heretic. This is because the belief in the Messiah is not a fundamental principle of the Jewish religion, but one of the six dogmas which should be conceived as branches issuing from the principles. In all likelihood, the relegation of belief in the Messiah to this secondary position was designed to refute the Christian faith which had made belief in the Messiah a fundamental tenet of the faith. In this connection, at the Tortosa Disputation, Albo declared that even if it could be proved that the Messiah had already come, he would not consider himself less faithful a Jew.

Albo concludes his discussion of the principles of Judaism by contending that there are eight derivative principles which branch out from the three major principles of the faith. Together with the belief in the existence of God, divine revelation, and reward and punishment, these derivative beliefs constitute the indispensable elements of the divine law. Four of these derivative principles pertain to the existence of God:

1 divine unity;
2 divine incorporeality;
3 God's independence from time; and
4 divine perfection.

Three other derivative principles are related to revelation:

5 God's knowledge as embracing the terrestrial world;
6 prophecy; and
7 the authenticity of divine messengers proclaiming the law.

Finally, the eighth derivative principle is concerned with the notion of reward and punishment:

8 providence.

In addition to these central beliefs (the three essential, and the eight derivative, principles), Albo states that there are six dogmas which everyone who professes the law of Moses is obliged to accept – anyone who denies them is a heretic who has no share in the world to come. However, they are not referred to as principles of the faith since, in Albo's opinion, the only beliefs entitled to be designated as fundamental principles are those without which the Jewish faith is inconceivable. These six further beliefs, or dogmas, are:

1 *creatio ex nihilo*;
2 the superiority of Moses' prophecy;
3 the immutability of the Torah;
4 human perfection can be attained by fulfilling even one of the commandments of the Torah; .
5 the resurrection of the dead; and
6 the Messiah.

In formulating this list of the central beliefs of Judaism, Albo was preoccupied with the concept of divine law. Previous Jewish, Christian and Muslim philosophers had drawn a distinction between conventional and divine law; Albo, however, argues that there are three major types of law:

1 natural law;
2 conventional law; and
3 divine law.

In Albo's view, the superiority of divine law over natural and conventional law derives from its aim to guide human beings to the attainment of true felicity. While natural law is designed to order society, and conventional law seeks to improve the social order, divine law regulates conduct and belief. As a consequence, it is perfect, restoring the soul. In presenting this thesis, Albo interprets Psalm 19 as illustrating the supremacy of divine law over conventional and natural laws.

After its appearance, Albo's *Sefer ha-Ikkarim* attained considerable popularity within the Jewish community. Following his death in 1445, it appeared in a large number of printed editions after the *editio princeps* by Joshua Solomon Soncino in 1485. In the next century it was commented upon by Jacob Koppelmann of Brest and in the seventeenth century by Gedaliah ben Solomon Lipschuetz of Lublin. In 1884 a German translation by W. Schlesinger with a scholarly introduction by L. Schlesinger appeared in Frankfurt, and a critical edition of the text, accompanied by an English translation and notes, was published by I. Husik in 1929–30. Within Christian circles, a number of theologians including Hugo Grotius and Richard Simon regarded the work with favour; other theologians viewed Albo's writing as a powerful defence of Judaism and thereby a potential threat to Christian teaching.

References

Louis Jacobs, *Principles of the Jewish Faith*, Northvale, NJ, 1988

See also in this book

Hasdai Crescas, Maimonides

Albo's major writings

Joseph Albo, *Sefer ha-Ikkarim* (*Book of Principles*, trans. I. Husik), Philadelphia, 1929

Further Reading

W.Z. Harvey, 'Albo's Discussion of Time', *Jewish Quarterly Review*, 70, 1980
I. Husik, 'Joseph Albo, the Last of the Jewish Philosophers', *Proceedings of the American Academy of Jewish Research* 1, 1930
E. Schweid, 'Joseph Albo's System of Dogmas as Distinct from that of Maimonides', *Tarbiz* 33, 1964

BAAL SHEM TOV

Known as the Baal Shem Tov (Master of the Good Name) (Besht), Israel ben Eliezer was the founder and leader of the Hasidic movement in eastern Europe. Born in 1700 in Okop in Podolia (now south-west Ukraine) to a poor family, he was orphaned as a child. At first he earned a living as an assistant teacher in a *heder* (Jewish elementary school), later working as a watchman at a synagogue. While working as a teacher he befriended Meir ben Zevi Hirsch Margolioth who subsequently became a well-known talmudic scholar. According to tradition, Israel went into hiding in the Carpathian Mountains in his twenties accompanied by his second wife Hannah, his first wife having died shortly after their marriage. There he worked as a digger of clay, which his wife sold in town. Subsequently he became an innkeeper together with his wife. In about 1730 he moved to Tluste.

In the mid-1730s Israel revealed himself as a healer and spiritual leader, attracting a wide circle of followers. Owing to his ability to perform miracles, many Jews accepted his leadership and teaching. For a number of years Israel undertook journeys in order to effect cures, expel demons and evil spirits, as well as to gain influence. Later Hasidic traditions after his death in 1760, however, sought to minimize such activity, emphasizing instead his charismatic personality.

For the Baal Shem Tov, prayer served as the central mystic approach to God as opposed to study and scholarship. At particular moments he was able to attain a state of mystical exaltation. Both future events and figures from the past were disclosed to him in dreams. In Hasidic lore he is portrayed as conversing with individuals and groups rather than preaching in the synagogue: usually he is depicted as having a pipe in his hand or mouth. In his discourses there is little evidence of talmudic scholarship, and his adversaries criticized him for his lack of learning and his concern with healing, his making amulets and his discussions with simple people.

Both Israel and his disciples were conscious of their leader's mission. A number of his dreams and visions from on high are related to the actual difficulties of everyday existence. Emphasizing the importance of charity, the Baal Shem Tov sought to ransom captives and prisoners. In his teaching, he stressed that devotional joy is the proper attitude for Jews to adopt in every moment of their lives, particularly during prayer. Opposed to the preoccupation with ascetic fasting, he was also critical of admonitory preaching. In time his personality became the inspiration for generations of *Hasidim* who sought to live a godly life.

As far as the Baal Shem's teaching is concerned, he was conscious of his special mission. In a letter to his brother-in-law, Abraham of Kutow, he gives a vivid account of his mystical experiences in relation to his divinely appointed role as God's messenger:

On the day of the New Year of the year 5507 (1746 CE), I engaged in an ascent of the soul, as you know I do, and I saw wondrous things in that vision that I had never before seen since the day I had attained to maturity. That which I saw and learned in my ascent it is impossible to describe or to relate even from mouth to mouth. But as I returned to the lower Garden of Eden I saw many souls, both of the living and of the dead, those known to me and those unknown. They were more than could be counted and they ran to and fro from world to world through the path provided by that column known to the adepts in the hidden science. They were all

in such a rapture that the mouth would be worn out if it attempted to describe it and the physical ear too indelicate to hear it. Many of the wicked repented of their sins and were pardoned, for it was a time of much grace . . . . They also enjoyed much rapture and ascended. All of them entreated me to my embarrassment, saying: 'The Lord has given your honour great understanding to grasp these matters. Ascend together with us, therefore, so as to help us and assist us.' Their rapture was so great that I resolved to ascend together with them. (in Jacobs, 1978, 149–50)

The Besht recounted that in a vision he saw Samael act as an accuser. Filled with dread, he requested that his teacher accompany him in the ascent:

I went higher step by step until I entered the palace of the Messiah wherein the Messiah studies the Torah together with all the tannaim and the saints and souls with the Seven Shepherds. There I witnessed great rejoicing and could not fathom the reason for it so I thought that, God forbid, the rejoicing was over my own departure from the world. But I was afterwards informed that I was not yet to die since they took great delight on high when, through their Torah, I performed unifications here below. (Ibid, 150).

Performing unifications meant meditating on the letters of God's name to bring about the unification of the universes.

On this ascent the Besht confronted the Messiah and asked him when he would come. In reply the Messiah declared that it will occur when the Besht's teaching is revealed to the world and others will be able to perform unifications and have ascents of the soul. Then, he stated, all the *kellipot* (powers of evil) will be consumed and it will be a time of grace and salvation. Although the Besht was dismayed at the length of time this might take, he was told of special charms and holy names which would facilitate such heavenly ascent.

> I thought to myself it is possible by this means for all my colleagues to attain the stages and categories to which I have attained, that is to say, they too will be able to engage in ascents of the soul and learn to comprehend as I have done. (Ibid., 151)

Although he was not allowed to reveal this secret, the Besht gave advice as to the correct procedure to follow when studying and praying:

> Whenever you offer your prayers and whenever you study, have the intention of unifying a divine name in every word and with every utterance of your lips, for there are worlds, souls and divinity in every letter. These ascend to become united one with the other and then the letters are combined in order to form a word so that there is complete unification with the divine. Allow your soul to be embraced by them at each of the above stages. Thus all worlds became united and they ascend so that immeasurable rapture and the greatest delight is experienced. (Ibid.)

In the wake of the Baal Shem Tov's influence, the growth of this new movement engendered considerable hostility on the part of rabbinic authorities. In particular the rabbinic leadership of Vilna issued an act of excommunication: the *Hasidim* were charged with permissiveness in their observance of the commandments, laxity in the study of the Torah, excess in prayer, and preference for the Lurianic rather than the Ashkenazic prayerbook. In subsequent years *Hasidim* and their opponents (*Mitnagdim*) bitterly denounced one another. Relations deteriorated further when Jacob Joseph of Polonnoye published a book critical of the rabbinate; his work was burned and in 1781 the *Mitnagdim* ordered that all relations with the *Hasidim* cease.

Despite such opposition, Hasidism exerted a profound change in Jewish religious pietism. Following the teaching of the Baal Shem Tov, hasidic teachers emphasized the omnipresence of God. In their view, there is no place where God is absent. As the Besht explained: 'In every one of man's troubles, physical and spiritual, even in that trouble God himself is there.' For some *Hasidim*, cleaving to God (*devekut*) in prayer was understood as the annihilation of selfhood and the ascent of the soul to divine light. In this context they stressed the Besht's emphasis on joy, humility, gratitude and spontaneity. The central obstacles to concentration in prayer, they maintained, are distracting thoughts. According to Hasidism, such sinful intentions contain a divine spark which can be released.

In this regard, the traditional kabbalistic stress on theological speculation was replaced by a preoccupation with mystical psychology in which inner bliss was conceived as the highest aim rather than repair (*tikkun*) of the comos. For the Beshtian *Hasidim*, it was also possible to achieve *devekut* in daily activities including eating, drinking, business affairs and sex. Such ordinary acts become religious if in performing them one cleaves to God, and *devekut* is thus attainable by all Jews rather than by a scholarly elite alone. Unlike the earlier mystical tradition, Hasidism provided a means by which ordinary Jews could reach a state of spiritual ecstasy. Hasidic worship embraced singing, dancing, and joyful devotion in anticipation of the period of messianic redemption.

Another central feature of this new movement was the institution of the *zaddik* or *rebbe*, a notion based on the Besht's teaching about spiritual leadership. According to Hasidism, the *zaddikim* were spiritually superior individuals who had attained the highest level of *devekut*. The goal of the *zaddik* was to elevate the souls of his flock to the divine light; his tasks including pleading to God for his people, immersing himself in their daily affairs, and counselling and strengthening them. As an authoritarian figure, the *zaddik* was seen by his followers as possessing miraculous power to ascend to the divine realm.

References

L. Jacobs, *Jewish Mystical Testimonies*, New York, 1978

Baal Shem Tov's major writings

A. Kahana, 'Ben Porat Yosef' in *Sefer ha-Hasidut*, Warsaw, 1922

See also in this book

Luria

Further reading

D. ben Amos and J.R. Mintz, *In Praise of the Ba'al Shem Tov*, Bloomington, IN, 1970
M. Buber, *Jewish Mysticism and the Legends of the Baalshem* (trans. L. Cohen), London, 1931
M. Buber, *The Legend of the Baal Shem* (trans. M. Friedman), New York, 1969
I.J. Klapholz, *Tales of the Baal-Shem-Tov* (trans. A. Nadav), Bnei Brak, Israel, 1970
E. Steinman, *Rabbi Yisrael Ba'al Shem Tov*, Jerusalem, 1960
H. Zeitlin, *Rabbi Yisrael Ba'al Shem Tov*, Warsaw, 1910

LEO BAECK

Born in Lissa (now Leszno), Poland in 1873, Leo Baeck was the son of Rabbi Samuel Baeck. After studying at the Conservative Jewish Theological Seminary of Breslau (Wrocław), he enrolled at the *Hochschule für die Wissenschaft des Judentums* in Berlin. Simultaneously he studied philosophy at the universities of Breslau and Berlin. After serving as a rabbi in Oppeln from 1897 to 1907, he was a rabbi in Düsseldorf until 1912, and then in Berlin. During this latter period he taught midrashic literature and homiletics at the *Hochschule*.

As a member of the committee of the *Central-Verein Deutscher Staatsbuerger jüdischen Glaubens*, he published various articles in its journal as well as in the periodical, *Der Morgen*; he also served as a non-Zionist member of the Jewish Agency, and contributed to the German Zionist weekly. From 1933 he served as president of the *Reichsvertretung*, the representative body of German Jews. During this period he refused all invitations to serve as either a rabbi or professor outside Germany – instead he devoted himself to the welfare of German Jewry. After being deported to Theresienstadt concentration camp in 1943, he continued to work for the benefit of his co-religionists. He survived and, after the war, he moved to London where he became president of the Council of Jews from Germany and chairman of the World Union for Progressive Judaism. Until his death in 1956, he taught intermittently at the Hebrew Union College, Cincinnati, Ohio.

Baeck's first and most important book, *The Essence of Judaism*, was published in 1905 as a polemic against Adolf von Harnack's critique of Judaism in his *The Essence of Christianity*. In this work Harnack offers a liberal interpretation of Jesus and a humanistic account of early Christianity. Baeck was critical of Harnack's work for ignoring rabbinic literature in his evaluation of first-century Judaism. In his study of the nature of the Jewish faith, Baeck offers a modern evaluation of the tradition. In his view, Judaism represents the clearest example of the classical type of religion, characterized by an ethical system which is both optimistic and in touch with the realities of everyday life.

Subsequently Baeck published other works dealing with various aspects of the Christian faith. In many of these studies he sought to illuminate the Jewish background to the New Testament as well as chart a path of reconciliation. This, he argues, is of vital importance since for nineteen centuries Jews and Christians have regarded one another with hostility and contempt:

The usual, and inevitable, result of any talk was an increase in the feeling, on the Christian side, of being uncompromisingly rejected by the Jew, and on the Jewish side, of being forcibly summoned and violently accused by the Christian – let alone the fact of the restrictions and burdens imposed on the Jew, or on behalf of, the Church. (Baeck, 1954, 102)

In the modern world, however, new opportunities for religious encounter have arisen, and Baeck emphasizes that it is now crucial for both communities to take advantage of these opportunities. Unlike previous centuries when Jews and Christians engaged in heated disputation, such dialogue can be conducted with respect and tolerance.

In exploring the nature of Judaism, Baeck drew attention to those features which distinguish it from Christianity. According to Baeck, Judaism does not need the sort of dogmatic formulations found in the Christian tradition:

In it [Judaism] there was no need for a constant, inviolable formula; this is necessary only in those religions at the heart of which lies a mystical consecrating faith – an act which alone can open the door to salvation and which therefore requires a definite conceptual image to be handed down from age to age. Such acts of salvation and gifts of grace are alien to Judaism; it does not pretend to be able to bring heaven to earth. It has always maintained a certain sobriety and severity, demanding even more than it gives. This is why it adopted so many commandments, and refused sacraments and mysteries. (Baeck, 1948, 13)

Elaborating this theme, Baeck contends that the romantic feature inherent in Christianity originated with Paul who integrated Oriental mystery cults into the nascent Christian faith. As this new religion grew, it became increasingly passive. For Baeck such an orientation has profoundly influenced Western civiliza-

tion: it led to the notion of the 'finished man', a person who believes he possesses absolute truth:

Since the end of the ancient world, the intellectual life of the Occident has in many ways been determined by this notion. It has established that orientation in which the answer precedes every question. (Baeck, 1958, 206)

In the medieval world such a conception dominated the age, and was hardly affected by the Reformation. It was only with the French Revolution and the growth of the Enlightenment that free thought became dominant. Yet despite this development, it is only classical religion as represented by Judaism (in contrast with 'romantic religion') which fosters a spirit of optimism and respect for human freedom.

In his writings Baeck was also preoccupied with Christian origins. In *The Gospel as a Document of the History of the Jewish Faith*, he examines the Jewish background of the New Testament. In this study Baeck seeks to strip the Gospels of later accretions so as to reconstruct the original documents. In Baeck's view the Gospels were derived from oral traditions that were later written down. Those who wrote the gospels were like Jewish sages who recorded oral traditions:

These men, too, experienced everything in terms of the Bible, and the words of Scripture directed, commanded, and exerted an inner compulsion. For these men, too, a fixed content, a fixed religious doctrine, was there to begin with and was most vividly real and the whole truth. For them, too, and for those who had received the tradition from them, their master's lot and fate had long been revealed and always preordained . . . . The tradition of the Gospel is, first of all, in every one of these respects, simply a part of the Jewish tradition of that time. (Ibid., 63)

Subsequently, however, the world view of Hellenism influenced the Christian vision and led to substantial changes in the transmission of the Gospel. Nonetheless it is possible, Baeck believes, to discover Jesus' original teaching:

On the whole it is nevertheless possible to get back to the original tradition. If one notes the special characteristics of each of the three authors and, so to say, eliminates them, the procedure and method to be followed after that can be shown quite clearly . . . . The following, on the other hand, must be part of the old original tradition: whatever is completely different from the tendencies and purposes of the generations which came after the first generation of disciples; whatever contradicts the tenets which later became part of the faith; whatever is different from, or even opposed to, the intellectual, psychic, and political climate in which these later generations gradually found themselves; whatever, in other words, exemplifies the way of life and the social structure, the climate of thought and feeling, the way of speaking and the style of Jesus' own environment and time. In all this we are confronted with the words and deeds of Jesus. (Ibid., 99f)

On this account the original Gospel was a thoroughly Jewish book, firmly standing within the Jewish heritage. Baeck hence reclaims Jesus for the Jewish people; in his view, the Jesus of history was fully Jewish. The Christ of faith, on the other hand, was a creation of the Graeco-Roman world. Jewish history should therefore not pass Jesus by; instead he should be understood as a Jewish figure firmly rooted in the traditions of his own time.

Turning to Paul, Baeck maintains that he was the person most responsible for this shift in Christian thought. Deeply influenced by Hellenistic ideas of his native Tarsus as well as the mystery religions of Asia Minor, he introduced foreign elements into the early Christian movement. 'This man, Paul from Tarsus', he states, 'joined the congregation of Jesus' adherents; and one day he began to preach and spread his own new faith and a new theology. What found its place here was not the doctrine of Jesus, but a doctrine about him, not his own faith which he had communicated to his disciples but faith in him' (Ibid., 72). Such a vision radically altered the character of Christian belief and the history of the Church. As a consequence of Paul's ministry, the theo-centric faith of Jesus was superseded by a Christ-centred faith: this change initiated a fundamental parting of the ways between Judaism and Christianity. According to Baeck, later Church history consists of a struggle between the Jewish elements of the Christian faith and the Pauline aspects of the Christian tradition.

In his treatment of Christianity then, Baeck was anxious to uncover the foundations of this new faith. His presentation of the Jewishness of Jesus was a quest to reclaim him as an authentic Jewish figure of the past. By this means he sought to encourage the Jewish community to discover common ground with Christians. Yet his discussion of the ways in which the original Christian message was reinterpreted by Paul, and subsequently through Graeco-Roman categories of thought, illustrates his conviction that the Church misconstrued Jesus' message. For Baeck, Christianity as it developed through the ages degenerated into a 'romantic religion' – in this respect it has been incapable of attaining the spiritual purity of the 'classical religion' from which it issued forth.

References/Baeck's major writings

Leo Baeck, 'Judaism in the Church', *Hebrew Union College Annual*, Cincinnati, OH, 1925

Leo Baeck, *The Essence of Judaism*, New York, 1948

Leo Baeck, 'Some Questions to the Christian Church from the Jewish Point of View', in Göte Hedenquist (ed.), *The Church and the Jewish People*, London, 1954

Leo Baeck, *Judaism and Christianity*, Philadelphia, 1958

Further reading

F. Bamberger in *Studies of the Leo Baeck Institute*, New York, 1967
E.H. Boehm, *We Survived*, New Haven, CN, 1949
A.H. Friedlander, *Leo Baeck, Teacher of Theresienstadt*, New York, 1968

BAHYA IBN PAKUDA

Little is known about Bahya ben Joseph ibn Pakuda other than that, in all likelihood, he was born *c.* 1050 and lived in Saragossa in the second half of the eleventh century, dying there in 1120. In addition to religious poetry, he composed a philosophical tract, *Duties of the Heart*, in about 1090; this was translated into Hebrew by Judah ibn Tibbon in 1161 and subsequently became immensely popular, profoundly influencing Jewish pietistic literature. A second translation was undertaken by Joseph Kimhi, and other versions followed in Arabic, Spanish, Portuguese, Italian and Yiddish. Later this work was translated into English, German and French. Although Pakuda's writing draws on Muslim mysticism and Arabic Neoplatonism, *Duties of the Heart* is Jewish in character. Throughout Bahya calls upon his readers to remain faithful to inner experience. Divided into ten chapters, the book progressively leads the faithful to the love of God.

In the introduction, Bahya divides human obligations into two types:

1 duties of the members of the body – these obligations involve overt action; and
2 duties of the heart – these comprise inner responsiblities.

The first category includes ritual and ethical practices which are prescribed by the Torah such as Sabbath regulations, prayer and charity; the second type consists of beliefs such as the conviction that there is one God, the need for love and fear of the Deity, the importance of repentance, and the centrality of ethical prohibitions (such as bearing a grudge or taking revenge). Bahya goes on to explain that he composed this treatise because such inner obligations had been largely neglected by previous thinkers as well as by his contemporaries who concentrated instead on outward acts. To redress this imbalance, Bahya seeks to supply a work which would complement the halakhic compendia which had been written for pious Jews.

The structure of Bahya's treatise was borrowed from Arab mystical tracts which lead the reader through ascending stages of man's inner life toward spiritual perfection and, ultimately, union with the Divine. Each of its ten chapters is devoted to a particular duty; the subjects treated include the unity of God, the nature of the world which reveals God's handiwork, divine worship, trust in God, sincerity of purpose, humility, repentance, self-examination, asceticism and the love of God.

The starting point of this spiritual journey is an awareness of God's unity; this belief, Bahya insists, is the fundamental principle of the faith:

When we inquired as to what is the most necessary among the fundamental principles of our religion, we found that the wholehearted acceptance of the Unity of God – the root and foundation of Judaism – is the first of the gates of the Torah. By the acceptance of the Unity of God, the believer is distinguished from the infidel. It is the head and front of religious truth. Whoever has deviated from it will neither practise any duty properly nor retain any creed permanently. (ibn Pakuda, 1962, 17)

Beginning with God's unity, Bahya argues that the Deity is neither substance nor accident – thus we cannot know God as He is in Himself. Rather, it is only through His creatures that we can gain an apprehension of the Divine. Here Bahya follows the same method as Saadiah Gaon and the *kalam*, proving the existence of the Creator on the basis of order in the cosmos. According to Bahya, God created the universe *ex nihilo*. From this observation, Bahya goes on to discuss God's nature. In his view, the unity of God is not undermined by the ascription to Him of divine attributes. In this context Bahya distinguishes between essential attributes which are the permanent attributes of God – existence, unity and eternity – and those attributes which are ascribed to God because of His action in the world. For Bahya, the essential attributes should be conceived as negative in character; they deny their opposites. The outcome of this discussion is that only two kinds of attributes are applicable to God: negative attributes and those which we can infer from God's activity as manifest in history.

This theological investigation provides the metaphysical background to Bahya's examination of the duties of the heart. To recognize God's unity with full devotion involves the quest to prove His existence and unity. On this basis, the pious can direct their hearts and minds to put such knowledge into action. Intellectual ascent to propositions about the Divine is therefore not of primary importance; rather, what matters is the translation of such understanding into concrete deeds. Study of the Active Attributes, then, is a precondition for living the religious life. It is one's duty to investigate the natural world so as to gain an appreciation of God's wisdom and goodness.

In Bahya's view, the variety of natural phenomena and the laws underpinning the order of the world exhibit God's providential will. Above all this is humanity, the highest of all creatures. In the laws and ordinances given to human beings it is possible to discover God's beneficence. In this context Bahya points out that all of us have a duty of gratitude to those who have been of assistance; how much the more is the duty to appreciate God's favours which He has bestowed upon all persons. The only way in which we can repay God for His kindness is

by submitting to His will and performing those acts which draw us near to Him. To accomplish this, each individual must abstain from too much eating, drinking and idleness; the quest for pleasure leads one from following God's laws. Similarly we must refrain from the quest for power.

In realizing their religious duty, human beings are not simply to follow the promptings of reason; rather, we possess a positive law which is designed to regulate human conduct. In presenting this interpretation of one's duty to God, Bahya differentiates between body and spirit. Bodily functions are located in the lower, earthly domain whereas spirit functions in the higher realms. The role of divine legislation is to nourish the spirit by restraining bodily appetites – this can be achieved through prayer, fasting and charity.

For Bahya, positive law is necessary because it encourages the middle course between asceticism and self-indulgence, regulating and defining human conduct. Further, it encourages new occasions for worship and thanksgiving as God continually bestows benefits to His chosen people. The law also prescribes actions which are not deducible by reason alone. These are the traditional, as opposed to the rational, commandments. In Bahya's view, positive law is necessary for the young, women and those of limited intellectual capacities. To worship God – not because the law prescribes such activity but because it is demanded by reason – constitutes a spiritual advance, and is reserved only for those of a prophetic or pious disposition.

Bahya stresses that one of the major duties of the heart is to trust in God. Leaving aside biblical injunctions, human reflection can lead one to such an attitude since in God alone are found the conditions necessary for such confidence. Only God has the power to protect and aid us – He is kind, generous and loving. Trust in God, he continues, is religiously advantageous – it leads to peace of mind and independence. In addition, by trusting in God a person can attain the freedom to devote himself to the service of God without being overwhelmed by worldly cares. It might be objected, however, that the suffering of the good and the prosperity of the wicked illustrate that such trust is misplaced. Although Bahya does not offer a solution to the problem of evil, he stresses that there are some possible explanations for this seeming discrepancy. The righteous may suffer because of a sin committed; alternatively, such suffering may simply occur so as to demonstrate the virtues of patience; or a good person may be punished because he has not rebuked evildoers. Conversely, it is possible to account for the fact that the wicked flourish on different grounds.

Turning to the notion of personal sincerity, Bahya states that the duties of the limbs are imperfect unless they are accompanied by the intention of the heart. Motives must be sincere, and a person's aim should not be to obtain the favour of others or to gain honour. Instead, the observance of the commandments must be motivated by regard for God. In order to act in this way a person must have a sincere concept of God's unity, an appreciation of His acts in nature, a willingness to submit to His will, and an indifference to the opinions of society.

Humility, too, is of vital importance in human conduct. True humility, Bahya explains, is an attitude of total dedication, manifesting itself in a quiet spirit and modest behaviour. A humble person practises patience and forgiveness, and is intent on doing good to all people. Such an individual is able to endure hardship with resignation, and is unmoved by praise or blame. Yet Bahya notes that humility is compatible with a certain type of pride: that which leads to gratitude for the gifts that have been bestowed by God. According to Bahya, such humility before God is a necessary condition for true repentance; this can be achieved only by returning to God, expressing regret, discontinuing the sinful act, confessing one's failing, and promising not to repeat the action. In all this Bahya encourages the

faithful to love God – this is the highest stage of human development and the goal of the religious life.

ibn Pakuda's major writings

Bahya ben Joseph ibn Pakuda, *Duties of the Heart* (trans. M. Hyamson), Jerusalem, 1962
Bahya ben Joseph ibn Pakuda, *The Book of Direction to the Duties of the Heart* (trans. M. Mansoor with S. Arenson), London, 1973

See also in this book

Saadiah Gaon

Further reading

Y. Eisenberg, 'Reason and Emotion' in '*Duties of the Heart*', *Daat* 7, 1981
M. Goldberger, *A Practical Guide to the Mitzvah of Bitochon*, Staten Island, NY, 1982
G. Vajda, 'La théologie ascétique de Bahya Ibn Paquda', *Cahiers de la Société Asiatique* 7, Paris, 1947
G. Vajda, 'La dialogue de l'âme et de la raison dans les *Devoirs des Coeurs* de Bahya Ibn Paquda', *Revue des études juives* 102, 1937

ELIEZER BERKOVITS

Born in 1900 in Oradea, Transylvania, Eliezer Berkovits was ordained at the Hildesheimer Rabbinical Seminary in 1934. After serving as a rabbi in Berlin, he left Germany for England in 1939 where he was a rabbi in Leeds from 1940 to 1946. He was then a rabbi in Sydney, Australia until 1950, when he moved to the United States to officiate as a rabbi in Boston until 1958. He then became Chairman of the department of Jewish philosophy at the Hebrew Theological College in Chicago. In a number of works, Berkovits seeks to provide a theological response to the religious challenge of the Holocaust.

In his most important writing about the Holocaust, *Faith after the Holocaust*,

Berkovits maintains that after the nightmare of the Holocaust, it is still possible to believe in an all-powerful and beneficent God. Reflecting on the theological dilemmas raised by the events of the Nazi era, Berkovits argues that the problem of faith must be confronted in the agony of one's soul. After the Holocaust, Jews have the responsibility to reason with God, and if need be to wrestle with Him. Such an attitude is not blasphemous; it is simply impossible to pass over such horror in silence. This questioning of God stands out as a guidepost at the very beginning of Jewish history when Abraham struggled with God over the fate of the inhabitants of Sodom and Gomorrah. In a similar fashion, Job debated with God over the justice of his misfortune. Hence the quest to comprehend God's providence in the death camps is consonant with this ancient tradition.

According to Berkovits, the history of the Jewish people has been marred by calamity: the Temple was destroyed twice; the Jewish people were compelled to go into exile; Spanish Jewry was devastated; mass murder occurred during the Crusades as well as in later centuries. The problem of sustaining faith in God was as acute then as in this century. Although the horrors of the death camps surpassed all previous tragedies, the impact of these events was no less intense. Hence, the problem of Jewish suffering is as old as Judaism itself.

In the talmudic period, Jewish sages attempted to resolve this dilemma by appealing to God's silence. In biblical terminology, this concept is expressed by the Hebrew phrase *Hester Panim* (the Hiding of the Face). When disaster occurs, God hides His face from human evil. Berkovits cites an example of *Hester Panim* in Psalm 44, verses 17 to 26:

> All this is come upon us; yet have we not
>   forgotten Thee,
> Neither have we been false to Thy
>   covenant.
> Our heart is not turned back,
> Neither have our steps declined from
>   Thy path;
> Though thou hast crushed us into a place
>   of jackals,
> And covered us with the shadow of
>   death.
> If we had forgotten the name of our
>   God,
> Or spread forth our hands to a strange
>   god;
> Would not God search this out?
> For He knoweth the secrets of the heart.
> Nay, but for Thy sake are we killed all
>   the day;
> We are accounted as sheep for the
>   slaughter.
> Awake, why sleepest Thou, O Lord?
> Arouse Thyself, cast us not off for ever.
> Wherefore hidest Thou Thy face,
> And forgettest our affliction and our
>   oppression?
> For our soul is bowed down to the dust;
> Our belly cleaveth to the earth.
> Arise for our help,
> And redeem us for Thy mercy's sake.

Here God is depicted as distant from human tribulation – He hides Himself mysteriously from the cry of the afflicted.

Through the centuries Jews struggled against God's seeming indifference to tragedy, yet rabbinic Judaism insists that God is present in His silence. He does not hide His face because of divine indifference; rather, His aim is to create space for human freedom. God did not decree that one person be righteous and another evil – instead He created the possibility for each person to act as a moral agent. God is all-good, but human beings have the ability to strive to act morally. This means that freedom of choice is a necessity, and man's freedom must not be restricted even by God Himself. If God did not respect such freedom, not only would morality be abolished but men and women would cease to be human. Freedom and responsiblity are the very essence of humanity; if human beings are to exist, they must be granted the capacity to choose the course of their lives. Hence although God is longsuffering, the wicked will go about their evil ways. There is no alternative: if human beings are to act freely without being overwhelmed by divine supremacy, God must absent Himself. The God of history is therefore both absent and present simultaneously. He is absent without being inaccessible.

Human beings therefore can have free will because God renounces the use of His power in history. The mightiness of God consists in shackling His omnipotence. Yet God has revealed Himself in Israel's survival. Berkovits stresses that there is no other witness that God is present in history than the endurance of this tiny, beleaguered nation. According to Berkovits, the Jewish people who bear witness to the presence of God are His suffering servant. In the suffering of His chosen people, God is not indifferent; instead He has simply allowed scope for human decision-making. The question after the Holocaust is therefore not how God could have tolerated so much evil, but whether the Jewish people can continue to testify to His elusive presence. In Berkovits' view, Jewish survival through the ages – and in the ingathering of the exiles into the Holy Land – proclaims God's presence at the very heart of His inscrutable hiddenness.

In a later book, *With God in Hell*, Berkovits returns to the theme of Jewish witness to God in the concentration camps. Here he illustrates the faith that sustained Jews as they faced torture and death. Thousands of Jews walked to the mass graves and gas chambers trusting in the Lord. Through their deaths they testified to God's hidden presence. In Auschwitz, for example, there were many pious Jews who sought to keep God's commandments. One of those who survived tells of a Jew who stubbornly refused to work on the Sabbath and Festivals: 'At first we thought he was mentally disturbed. In the course of years, however, we learned to appreciate that his "madness"

was a manifestation of a strong personality and an exalted faith' (Berkovits, 1979, 3).

Prayer services were a frequent occurrence in the camps: Jews usually said prayers which they knew by heart, but at times individual prayers or complete prayer books were written by hand. Some Jews were even able to use *tefillin* (phylacteries). Frequently Jews were determined to study Torah; although there were no volumes of the Talmud in the camps, many Jews knew passages by heart. Such faithfulness to the Jewish tradition also applied to the dietary laws. Through starved for food, a number of Jews rose above their deprivation by placing the requirements of Jewish law above the demands of their bodies. Yet the problem of legally permitted food at Passover was especially acute. In normal circumstances all unleavened bread was forbidden, but what was one to do in the camps? Pious Jews who ate the leavened bread given to them prayed that God would understand their dilemma and grant them strength:

> Our Father in Heaven! It is open and known before You that it is our will to do Your will to celebrate the festival of *Pesah* [Passover] by eating *matzah* [unleavened bread] and refraining from leavened bread. With aching heart we must realise that our slavery prevents us from such celebration. Since we find ourselves in a situation of danger to our lives, we are prepared and ready to fulfil Your commandment, 'And thou shalt live by them, but not die by them.' Therefore we pray to You that You maintain us in life and hasten to redeem us that we may observe Your statutes and do Your will and serve You with a perfect heart. Amen! (Ibid., 32)

These Jews were sustained by the belief in a providential God in the face of terror. Remaining steadfast in their faith, they glimpsed God's abiding presence in the camps. They marched to their deaths trusting in the God of Israel and the future of the Jewish people. With complete assurance, they were convinced that the Nazis would eventually be overcome. Despite the nightmare of the death camps, they rose early in the morning to put on *tefillin*, sought opportunities to pray and study, celebrated the festivals, and remained loyal to the religion of their ancestors. In spite of the monstrosities of what they experienced, they lived by the covenant. Standing in the presence of God with all generations of the Jewish past, they heard God's voice in His silence. Modern Jews, Berkovits argues, can gain some notion of the mystery of the Jewish faith and the destiny of God's chosen people by empathizing with these heroic figures of the Nazi era.

Death-of-God theologians pass over the faith of these Jewish martyrs in silence, yet what these writers ignore is that, in the concentration camps, God was present with His holy people. As *El Mistater* (the Hidden God) He was manifest in their agony. Those Jews who died in the camps with God's name on their lips glimpsed His abiding presence in their suffering. In the impenetrable darkness they remained firm in their dedication to the Lord of history. Jews today must model their response to the Holocaust on their example. Though the inexplicable cannot be explained, it can become a positive influence in the formulation of what is to be acknowledged. The sorrow will stay, but it can be blessed with the promise of God's faithfulness despite the tragedies of earthly existence.

References/Berkovits' major writings

Eliezer Berkovits, *Faith after the Holocaust*, New York, 1973
Eliezer Berkovits, *With God in Hell*, New York, 1979

Further reading

D. Cohn-Sherbok, *Holocaust Theology*, London, 1989
S. Katz, *Post-Holocaust Dialogues: Critical Studies in Modern Jewish Thought*, New York, 1983

DOV BER BOROCHOV

Born in Zolotonosha, Ukraine in 1881, Ber Borochov was raised in Poltava where he was educated at a Russian high school. Denied entry to a Russian university, he was self-educated. He joined the Russian Social Democratic Party, but he gradually became engaged by Jewish social problems leading him to create the Zionist Socialist Workers Union at Yekaterinoslav (now Dnepropetrovsk) in 1901 – this body actively engaged in Jewish self-defence and promoted the interests of Jewish workers. When the Uganda scheme for Jewish settlement was being debated, Borochov strongly advocated the creation of a Palestinian state, co-operating with Menahem Ussishkin and other leaders of the *Zion* Zionist group.

In 1905 Borochov was a delegate to the Seventh Zionist Congress, and in the following year oversaw the ideological and organizational development of the Jewish Workers' Social Democratic Party *Po'alei Zion*. In 1906 at the Eighth Zionist Congress in The Hague, Borochov participated in the establishment of the World Union of *Po'alei Zion* as a separate union of the World Zionist Organization. Subsequently Borochov urged the withdrawal of the Russian *Po'alei Zion* from the Zionist Organization in order to ensure the independence of Socialist Zionism.

From 1907 until the outbreak of the First World War, Borochov worked as a publicist of the World Union of *Po'alei Zion* in western and central Europe. In 1914 he travelled from Vienna to the United States where he served as a spokesman for the American *Po'alei Zion* as well as the World and American Jewish Congress movements. In addition, he became editor of the New York Yiddish daily, *Di Warheit*. At the outbreak of the Russian Revolution, Borochov returned to Russia; *en route* he stayed in Stockholm where he joined the *Po'alei Zion* delegation to a session of an international Socialist Commission of neutral countries. Arriving in Russia, he became embroiled in political activity prior to the October Revolution. In August 1917 he pleaded for the creation of a socialist settlement in Palestine at the Russian *Po'alei Zion* Conference. While on a speaking tour he contracted pneumonia and died in Kiev in 1917.

Borochov's defence of Socialist Zionism was expressed in his first major study, *The National Question and the Class Struggle*, published in 1903. In this work Borochov maintains that Marx's own thinking on the national question was more complex than generally assumed. In Borochov's view, both Marx and Engels were concerned with national struggle. Such an interpretation of Marxism enabled Borochov to establish his concept of a horizontal dimension within society in addition to a vertical division into classes. These groups were divided into socio-economic organisms: tribes, families, peoples, nations. In his view, the class struggle always takes place within the horizontal groupings. When class struggle is integrated into a nation's struggle, this creates important consequences: if an entire class is overwhelmed by another, the conquering group attempts to impose its own structure on the vanquished group. The conquered nation is therefore oppressed as a class by the bourgeoisie of the victorious group, and culturally subjugated. When this occurs, nationalism among the oppressed peoples appears in a particular form:

These oppressed peoples constantly exist under abnormal conditions of production ... such abnormal conditions bring the varying interests of all individuals of the nation into harmonious agreement. It is due to external pressure, which hinders and disorganizes the influence of the conditions of production, that the relations of production and the class struggle itself are hindered in their development. For the proper course of the mode of production

is thus hindered, class antagonisms become abnormally dulled, and national solidarity derives greater strength. (Borochov, 1935, 42–3)

Out of these circumstances the national struggle evolves into a social stuggle of the exploited classes against the exploiting classes of the oppressing national group:

All feel and all comprehend that the pressure is a national one. It has its origin in a foreign nation and is directed against their own nationality as such ... the national question of an oppressed people becomes sharply divided from the connection it normally has with its basis – with the material conditions of its productive life. Cultural needs then assume an independent importance and all members of the nation become concerned about the freedom of national self-determination. (Ibid., 43)

In such contexts both the intelligentsia and the working class can stop the national movement of the oppressed nation from becoming ethnocentric by stressing the people's struggle with universal and international ideals.

According to Borochov, when an oppressed people is liberated from foreign domination, it can begin the class struggle within its own society. In this manner Borochov highlights the interconnection between national aspirations for liberation and the class struggle. Orthodox Marxists, he argues, have failed to acknowledge how national differences affect class structures. In this light, he differentiates between various forms of nationalism and emphasizes that nationalism should be given the same consideration as other features of bourgeois society. *The National Question and the Class Struggle* therefore provides a general theory of the relationship between the nationalist and class struggles.

In the next year, Borochov developed this analysis in *Our Platform*, where he applies these observations to the Jewish problem. In Borochov's view, there are three different social units within the Jewish community:

1 the upper bourgeoisie;
2 the middle class and the intelligentsia; and
3 the working class.

The first group tends towards assimilation: this is most prevalent among Western Jews. In general the upper bourgeoisie attempts to solve its problems through social integration and economic success, and strives to integrate the Jewish masses into Western culture through philanthropic projects:

> In spite of themselves and despite their efforts to ignore the Jewish problem, the Jewish aristocrats must turn philanthropists. They must provide shelter for the Jewish emigrants and must make collections for pogrom-ridden Jews. Everywhere the Jewish upper bourgeoisie is engaged in the search for a Jewish solution to the Jewish problem and a means of being delivered of the Jewish masses. (in Hertzberg, 1969, 361)

Nonetheless the persistence of anti-Semitism poses a major threat to Jewish acceptance, even in the highest Jewish circles. It is thus unrealistic to assume that assimilation will help Jews successfully find their place in society.

Anti-Semitism is also a serious problem for the Jewish middle class and the intelligentsia. As society becomes increasingly democratic and capitalistic, the Jewish middle classes are capable of gaining respected positions in the professions such as medicine, law, journalism and business. Yet the more successful they become, the more they are disliked by non-Jews who regard them as interlopers. Such a situation creates strong feelings of ethnic and nationalist identity: 'Lacking any means of support in their struggle for a market, they tend to speak of an independent [Jewish existence] and of a Jewish state where they would play a leading political role (Ibid., 362). However, as long as this group retains its middle-class status, its centre of gravity lies in the diaspora – it does not feel the pressing need for a radical solution to the Jewish problem.

Neither this middle-class group nor the upper bourgeoisie, Borochov believes, is able to serve as the bearer of nationalist aspirations. Only the oppressed Jewish working class is able to do this, together with the persecuted Jewish lower middle class. These two entities form one social amalgam capable of demanding a revolutionary solution. In Borochov's opinion, emigration to a Jewish homeland will enable this body to establish a new body with a radically different infrastructure. The Jewish problem, Borochov states, calls for a territorial solution:

> The impossibility of penetrating into higher levels of production creates the need for concentrated immigration into an undeveloped country. Instead of being limited to the final levels of production, as is the case in all other countries, the Jews should in a short time assume a leading position in the economy of the new land. (Ibid., 364)

According to Borochov, only Palestine can serve as a feasible choice for such a Jewish settlement; there Jewry will be able to reconstruct a Jewish milieu with Jews at the base. Borochov stresses that the Jewish proletariat needs such a remedy more than any other class because of its sufferings. To liberate Jews from their dependence on non-Jewish economic structures, the Jewish proletariat must struggle for national independence. Such freedom, he believes, is an essential part of the universal struggle of the world proletariat. Hence by advocating nationhood, Borochov did not in fact abandon the universal vision for a better world order; instead, he maintained that only through the creation of a Jewish state with Jews controlling their destiny could the Jewish people be integrated into the universal evolutionary process.

References/Borochov's major writings

Ber Borochov, *The National Question and the Class Struggle*, Chicago, 1935
Ber Borochov, *Nationalism and the Class Struggle*, New York, 1937
A. Hertzberg (ed.), *The Zionist Idea: A Historical Analysis and Reader*, New York, 1969

Further reading

D. Katz, 'Ber Borochov, Pioneer of Yiddish Linguistics', *Jewish Frontier* 46, 1980
M. Mintz, *Ber Borochov, 1900–Purim 1906*, Jerusalem, 1968

MARTIN BUBER

Born in Vienna in 1878, Martin Buber grew up as a child in Lemberg (now Lwów, Poland) with his grandfather Solomon Buber, a noted authority on midrash (rabbinic Scriptural exegesis); later he attended a secondary school there. From 1896 he studied at the universities of Vienna, Leipzig, Zürich and Berlin; in 1898 he joined the Zionist movement, serving as a delegate to the Third Zionist Congress in 1899. Two years later he became editor of the weekly publication of the Zionist movement, *Die Welt*. At the age of 26 he began to study Hasidism, initially focusing on the aesthetic dimensions of the movement. From 1909 Buber was actively involved in public affairs, and with the outbreak of the First World War he helped found the Jewish National Committee in Berlin which worked on behalf of eastern European Jewry.

In the post-war period Buber became a spokesman for what he called 'Hebrew Humanism', advocating a policy of reconciliation with the Arab population of Palestine. In 1923 Buber published his most famous work, *I and Thou*, in which he outlines a religious philosophy of dialogue. Two years later the first volumes of his and Franz Rosenzweig's German translation of the Bible appeared. At this time Buber began to lecture on Jewish religion and ethics at the University of Frankfurt, and in 1930 he was appointed Associate Professor of Religion. However, with the rise of Nazism, he was forced to leave the university and in 1933 was appointed director of the Central Office for Jewish Adult Education and head of the *Jüdisches Lehrhaus* in Frankfurt. Five years later Buber settled in Palestine, becoming Professor of Social Philosophy at the Hebrew University where he taught until 1951. From 1960 to 1962 he served as first president of the Israel Academy of Sciences and Humanities. Buber died in 1965.

The central text for Buber's concept of dialogue was *I and Thou*; here he argues that there are two fundamental attitudes that a person can take up toward the world. The first, I–It, is based on a detachment of the self from others in which knowledge is objectified. But in the second type of relationship, I–Thou, there is an encounter between the subjects in which each stands over against the other. Such an attitude is characterized by total presentness: the I addresses the Thou spontaneously and intensely. In a relationship of I–It, however, there is predetermination and control. In presenting this thesis, Buber stresses that he can offer no description of the I–Thou posture; it can only be pointed to. The attitude of I–Thou is a basic dimension of human existence in the world and a key to the concept of 'relation'; it has the character of a dialogue and can only be properly understood through personal experience.

According to Buber, both modes of being are necessary: individuals must move back and forth between the two attitudes. From I–It comes a refinement of knowledge and understanding necessary for dealing with the world. Yet in modern society I–It is eclipsing the I–Thou encounter. This is tragic, Buber believes, since a fulfilled human life requires the experience of I–Thou. What is required in modern society is a restored balance between I–Thou and I–It. Buber links this discussion to God who is the 'Eternal Thou'. For Buber, God is the only Thou who can never become an It. He is the unifying ground for particular Thous which makes possible all relationships. And, conversely, it is through the encounter with all things that God is met:

> Every particular Thou is a glimpse through to the eternal Thou: by means of every particular Thou the primary word addresses the eternal Thou. Through this mediation of the Thou of all beings fulfil-ment, and non-fulfilment, of relations comes to them: the inborn Thou is realised in each relation and consummated in none. It is consummated only in the direct rela-tion with the Thou that by its nature cannot become It. (in Cohn-Sherbok, 1988, 177)

In his other writings, Buber applies this philosophy of dialogue to a wide variety of issues. In several biblical studies, for example, Buber contends that it is necessary to go beyond the scholarly approach to the biblical text; employing existentialist cate-gories, he seeks to penetrate to the original religious experience of the biblical writers. In Buber's view, Scripture contains the human response to the Divine. Hence Moses perceives in a natural event God's power and presence, leading him to serve as the Lord's representative. Again, at Sinai, the Israelite nation resolved to dedicate itself to the Lord who reveals Himself to His chosen people. According to Buber, the biblical covenant is not simply a legal contract – it is a bond of love similar to a marriage vow which links two partners in mutual trust. Similarly, in later Israelite history the prophets discovered the Divine in concrete historical situations, compelling them to speak in God's name against iniquity, transgression and sin.

In later Jewish history, this same process of religious immediacy was found in Hasidism. Applying an existentialist approach to the origins and development of this move-ment, Buber maintains that a new form of prophetic protest was manifest in Hasidism's emphasis on prayer and religious observance. For the *Hasid*, dedication and intention are of central importance. Further, Hasidism created pious communities of the faithful by translating *kabbalah* (Jewish mysticism) from esoteric knowledge to a living tradition.

> The Hasidic teaching is the consummation of Judaism. And this is its message to all: you yourself must begin. Existence will remain meaningless to you if you yourself do not penetrate into it with active love and if you do not in this way discover its meaning for yourself. Everything is waiting to be hallowed by you. (Buber, 1952, 44)

Another important dimension of Buber's writings is the relationship between Judaism and Christianity. As early as 1933 Buber engaged in a dialogue with the German Christian theologian Karl Ludwig Schmidt. In this encounter Buber emphasizes the diffi-culties involved in understanding the reli-gious views of another. Recognizing that one can only approach Christianity as an out-sider, Buber respects Christian religious con-victions – nonetheless he rejects the Christian claim that the world has been redeemed. Such a rejection was not based on hard-heartedness; rather it was grounded on Jewish experience. However, despite such an impasse, Buber believes that there can be positive discussion between Judaism and Christianity in which the participants do not reach any agreement but nevertheless respect each other for the sake of the one true God. This was Buber's point of depar-ture and hope for the future. He writes:

> What joins Jews and Christians together is their common knowledge about one uniqueness . . . . Every authentic sanctuary can acknowledge the mystery of every other authentic sanctuary. The mystery of the other one is internal to the latter and cannot be perceived from without. No one outside Israel can understand the mystery of Israel. And no one outside Christendom can understand the mental difference and

impart to each other with unreserved confidence our knowledge of the unity of this house, a unity which we hope will one day surround us without divisions. We will serve until the day when we may be united in common service. (Buber, 1936, 155)

Notwithstanding such reservations, in his later works Buber explores various aspects of Christianity. In his view, Christianity has created a dualism in nature; such a dichotomy, Buber believes, eventually resulted in a deep-seated pessimism which he firmly rejects. Judaism, on the other hand, extols all of creation and stresses the importance of human endeavour. Following this theme, Buber criticizes those periods of Christian history which were dominated by Pauline thought. In the modern world, he argues, the Pauline conception of faith should be replaced by the Jewish emphasis on human activity and enterprise. In spite of these criticisms, Buber expresses deep admiration for Jesus; Jews, he states, should attempt to accept him as a great religious figure in the history of Israel even though they cannot accept him as the Messiah.

Further, despite Buber's rejection of Pauline theology and its later development in Christendom, he believes that Jews and Christians should strive to find common ground between their two traditions:

It behooves both you [Christians] and us [Jews] to hold inviolably fast to our own true faith, that is to our deepest relationship to truth. It behooves both of us to show a religious respect for the true faith of others. This is not what is called 'tolerance'; our task is not to tolerate each other's waywardness but to acknowledge the real relationship in which both stand to the truth. Whenever we both, Christian and Jew, care more for God Himself than for our images of God, we are united in the feeling that our Father's house is differently constructed than our human models take it to be. (Buber, 1948, 40)

Here Buber urges that the adherents of both Judaism and Christianity continue along their separate paths, recognizing the ultimate mystery of faith; yet simultaneously he hoped to evoke a more sympathetic response from the Jewish community to the Christian faith. After twenty centuries of hatred and fear, he was convinced that opportunities exist for positive Jewish–Christian encounter in a new dialogical mode.

References/Buber's major writings

Martin Buber, *I and Thou*, New York, 1984
Martin Buber, *At the Turning*, New York, 1952
Martin Buber, *Die Stunde und die Erkenntnis*, Berlin, 1936
Martin Buber, *Israel and the World*, New York, 1948
D. Cohn-Sherbok, *The Jewish Heritage*, Oxford, 1988

See also in this book

Rosenweig

Further reading

M.A. Beele and J.S. Weiland, *Martin Buber, Personalist and Prophet*, Westminster, MD, 1968
A.S. Cohen, *Martin Buber*, London, 1957
M. Friedman, *Martin Buber: The Life of Dialogue*, London, 1955
M. Friedman, *Martin Buber's Life and Work*, New York, 1982–3
P.A. Schilpp and M. Friedman (eds), *The Philosophy of Martin Buber*, La Salle, IL, 1967

ARTHUR A. COHEN

Born in 1928, Arthur A. Cohen published a major theological study, *The Natural and the Supernatural Jew*; however it was not until the appearance of *Tremendum* in 1981, only five years before his death, that he faced the religious implications of the Holocaust. To distinguish the Holocaust from other events, Cohen refers to the destruction of European

A. COHEN

Jewry as the Tremendum. The use of this term is based on the German Protestant theologian Rudolf Otto's *The Idea of the Holy*; here the Holy is understood as a dimension of God's presence. According to Otto, God is near and present, yet no less terrifying and unfathomable. He is hence described as the Mysterium Tremendum, the utter mystery. The phenomenology of the Holy commences with the awareness of the terror–mystery of God which is modified by traditional modes of mercy, love and justice until His shattering presence becomes the still, small voice.

As Cohen writes, the counter to the Mysterium Tremendum is the human Tremendum:

> The enormity of an infinitized man, who no longer seems to fear death or, perhaps more to the point, fears it so completely, denies death so mightily, that the only patent of his refutation and denial is to build a mountain of corpses to the divinity of the dead, to placate death by the magic of endless murder. (Cohen, 1981, 18–19)

The death camps are the Tremendum; they are the monument of the orgiastic celebration of death. Arguably Jews are ideal victims because their survival is a celebration of the tenacity of life. Jewish converts who have adopted other faiths have maintained that Judaism has ceased to retain its vitality. The Jew is conceived as dead. Thus the living Jew must die so that the non-Jew can be saved. In this context Cohen refers to Martin Buber's contention that there is no caesura in the history of the Jewish nation. According to Buber, there is no gap to be filled by the Holy Spirit. Cohen agrees with this interpretation of Jewish history, yet he argues that it fails to take account of the underside of history: the corrupting caesura: 'For the Holy there may be no caesura, but the unholy its name is caesura' (Ibid., 20). In the epoch of the Tremendum, time and causality are interrupted. At this time the demonic tears the skein of events apart and human beings are forced to gaze into the abyss.

For Jewry this is not a novel experience. The destruction of the Temple and the destruction of the nation was also an abyss. There was a caesura:

> The abyss opened and the Jews closed the abyss by affirming their guilt, denying the abyss, and taking upon themselves responsiblity for the demonic. (Ibid., 21)

The expulsion of the Jews from Spain was a further caesura; again the abyss opened and Jews reaffirmed their guilt. They transformed this event into an end-time of history and the beginning of an unseen mystical realm. The third caesura of the demonic is the Holocaust. Yet it is no longer possible to respond as did those who survived the first caesura. Jews were not responsible for the destruction that befell them during the Nazi regime. Nor should modern Jews respond as did survivors of the second abyss. The kabbalistic interpretation of Spanish exile and the decimation of Sephardic Jewry has ceased to serve as a viable approach for modern Judaism. The third abyss should be confronted with neither guilt nor hope.

Cohen insists that the abyss of the death camps cannot be transcended: it must be inspected instead. A descent deep into its midst must be attempted. For Jews the death camps constitute the historically real; Jews are obliged to hear the winess as though they were witnesses themselves. They need to experience the Tremendum just as in each generation the Jewish community is obliged at Passover to consider that they themselves were redeemed from slavery in Egypt. It is not sufficient to make liturgy and midrash out of the Holocaust – rather Jews must create a new langauge. By separating the Tremendum from all things and entering the abyss, it should be possible to re-join this tragedy to the whole experience of humankind.

In Cohen's view, the Tremendum casts doubt on traditional Jewish ideas about the nature of God. It requires a response that takes account of the horrors of the extermination camps. Before the Holocaust the presuppositions of traditional Judaism had been under attack. Only by appealing to the concept of mystery could Jewish theologians reconcile the doctrine of a transcendent God with the biblical depiction of a loving, merciful and just redeemer. The Tremendum intensifies this perplexity: it is necessary today to provide an explanation for the death of six million Jews. In confronting this problem Cohen redefines the reality of God and His relation to the created order.

Cohen points out that the neo-Orthodox theologians of the past appealed to the notion of paradox to account for God's dealing with the world. Yet these formulations were limited by defining God as the pre-eminent object of wonder, and the existential situation of the believer as a person who faithfully eschews philosophical questioning. Such a view, however, is unsatisfactory since it situates the Tremendum as the counter of an absent or hidden God, enabling the immensity of the one to pass the mystery of the other in the dark night of this century without compelling them to their dreadful confrontation. According to Cohen, what is required instead is a constructive theology which has a number of important characteristics. First, the God who is affirmed must abide in a universe where history is scarred by evil. Second, the relation of God and creation must include demonic structures – unredeemable events must be understood as meaningful and valuable. Third, the reality of God cannot be seperated from God's involvement in history.

The Tremendum obligates Jews to accept the mystical Jewish belief that God was enlivened by the spark of non-being. The cosmogony of the *kabbalah* (Jewish mysticism) asserts that there are emissions of being which derive their nature and vitality from the Godhead – they emerge from the lowest to the highest, linked together by the complexity of their own structure to the Divine. They are imperfect in relation to their adhesion to the divine image. It is only through such kabbalistic ideas, Cohen stresses, that it is possible to make sense of

the Holocaust. The divine word is the origin of the creation out of the void. As the whole of the divine nature is enlarged by the presence of non-being, so creation is a necessity within God as is the freedom of the will in human beings. The divine overflows: what is absolute in God is seen by us under the aspect of His plenitude. New forms, beginnings and creations are already within God in the eternal Now. Their creative process is complemented by human beings whose essential character is freedom. God engenders possiblity, but men and women are free to act.

In previous ages Jews believed that God acts in human history. Hence they proclaim that he redeemed the chosen people from Egyptian slavery. For Cohen, however, 'God is not the strategist of our particularities or of our historical condition but rather the mystery of our futurity, always our *posse*, never our acts' (Ibid., 97). God, he continues, must not be seen as an interferer, but as the hope of our future. He is not the cause of historical events, nor indifferent to what takes place in the world. Rather the divine life is a filament within the historical. Nonetheless, historical occurrences are the domain of human freedom. The Tremendum thus means that human beings, not God, render the filament incandescent or burn it out: 'Man can obscure, eclipse, burn out the divine filament . . . it is this which is meant by the abyss of the historical, the demonic, the Tremendum' (Ibid., 98).

Previously Jews conceived of history as the arena for God's activity. Events were seen as means towards the fulfilment of God's eternal providential plan – history was the manifestation of God's will in which there would be the unfolding of the *eschaton*. The historical is in this view the scene for the manifestation of God's kingdom in which the Jewish people play a major role. But in the modern world the Jew is not the same as he was yesterday or at Sinai. The belief that God is the sole agent in the universe – its king, ruler and authority – is no longer feasible. It is an error to think that the only agency is the Divine.

Cohen therefore argues that the traditional conception of God's relation to the universe must be reformulated. Historical events should be understood as the result of human freedom rather than the effect of divine causality. In this light, the Tremendum is a human volcano which has scorched the earth. It is like a 'dead volcano, terrifying in its aspect but silent, monstrous in its gaping, raw in the entrails, a visible reminder of fire and magma, but now a quiet, immovable presence, yawning over the lives of man' (Ibid., 108–9). This destruction was a caesura in the life of the nation, and as such calls for a re-evaluation of the classical notion of an interruptive God who guides the course of history. For Cohen the Holocaust was a human creation rather than part of God's providential plan. It is ultimately human beings – not God-who should be held responsible for the tragedy that befell European Jewry.

References/Arthur Cohen's major writings

Arthur A. Cohen, *Tremendum*, New York, 1981

See also in this book

Buber

Further reading

S. Katz, *Post-Holocaust Dialogues: Cultural Studies in Modern Jewish Thought*, New York, 1983

HERMANN COHEN

Born in Coswig, Germany, in 1842, Hermann Cohen was the son of a cantor. After studying at the Jewish Theological Seminary in Breslau (now Wrocław, Poland), he decided not to become a rabbi. He then pursued philosophy at the universities of Breslau and Berlin, receiving a doctorate from the University of Halle in 1865. In 1873 he was appointed a lecturer in philosophy at the University of Marburg, becoming a professor three years later. The last years of his life were spent in Berlin where he taught at the *Hochschule für die Wissenschaft des Judentums*. He died in 1918.

Although an exponent of Kantian idealism, Cohen deviated from the Kantian system in several respects. First, Cohen conceived of the noumenal world, not as an unknowable realm, but as a symbol of the human quest to reformulate theories on the basis of rational analysis and empirical research. Abandoning the Kantian distinction between the receptivity of sense perception and the spontaneous activity of the understanding, Cohen envisaged human thought as a creative act of the mind (as opposed to an organizing process of that which is given in experience). Second, in the sphere of ethics, Cohen maintains that the concept of immortality is a compromise with intrinsic ethical values. In his view, the function of the idea of God is to guarantee the realization of ethical ideals in daily life – it is the only ground for the belief that moral obligation can be actualized.

Modeling his philosophical writing on Maimonides' *Guide of the Perplexed*, Cohen in his *Religion of Reason out of the Sources of Judaism* seeks to redefine the principles of the Jewish faith in the light of human reason. In this work, Cohen attempts to illustrate that the basic concepts of Judaism – God, creation, revelation, atonement, messiahship – are in fact central features of a scientific and ethical world view. Like the *Guide*, *Religion of Reason* has two central aims:

1 the foundation of a philosophical system; and
2 the interpretation of Jewish sources to demonstrate they are consonant with the religion of reason.

These two objectives are harmonized by Cohen's belief that there is an inherent connection between the principles of critical idealism and absolute monotheism.

According to Cohen, it in no way diminishes God to conceive of Him as an idea:

> What the idea as ethical reality means positively, and as such is able to achieve for actuality, becomes most clear in man's love for God, on the basis of God's love for man. The power of the idea to realize itself is nowhere so clear as in the love for the idea. How is it possible to love an idea? To which one should retort: how is it possible to love anything but an idea? Does one not love, even in the case of sensual love, only the idealized person, only the idea of the person? (Cohen, 1972, 160)

Cohen continues by stating that the central feature of the Jewish religion is God's uniqueness, rather than his oneness: the difference between God and the world is essentially qualitative. God is the source of the phenomenal world; hence the idea of God is the precondition for scientific activity. Further, since Cohen believes that the universe is eternal, the idea of creation involves constant renewal as expressed in the Jewish Prayer Book: 'God renewes daily the work of creation'. Similarly revelation, like creation, is not limited to particular historical events.

In Cohen's view, revelation means that human beings are the bearers of reason – such an interpretation is reflected in his understanding of the concept of holiness. The spirit of holiness, he argues, is the moral quality shared by God and humanity: God is holy in that He is the archetype of ethical action; holiness in human beings resides in their emulation of the Divine. For Cohen, it is vital that the Divine and human are brought into relationship without obscuring the distinction between them. Unlike Baruch Spinoza, Cohen rejects any form of pantheism which seeks to fuse God and the world. Such an approach, he contends, diminishes the gap between what is the case and what ought to be. The human quest resides

in bringing into existence that good which exists only in God.

To represent this reciprocity, Cohen uses the term 'correlate': ethical monotheism correlates man with God in three modes represented by the concept of the fellow-man, the individual and humanity. For Cohen, monotheism was the first religious ideology that disclosed the notion of fellow (*mitmensch*) in contrast to the idea of the other man (*nebenmensch*). The doctrine of fellow-man, he contends, implies an awareness of a common bond between the self and the other, combined with the moral duty of sympathy. Here the commandment 'Love your neighbour as yourself' means 'Love the fellow-man because he is like you'. Referring to the prophetic tradition, Cohen contends that the suffering of those who are oppressed and persecuted is guiltless suffering, evoking pity and requiring the improvement of everyday life. In this domain, religion is capable of achieving what philosophical ethics is unable to bring about: the concept of the God of social love. This is an archetype for human concern and mercy as well as a basis for social action.

Cohen further maintains that it is religion – rather than philosophy – that correlates the individual with God through the process of atonement. The notion of the intimate relationship of a person to God emerges in the confession of sinfulness and the process of repentance. Unlike the individual suffering of those who are exploited, the suffering of the penitent sinner has positive significance: the acknowledgement that one is worthy of suffering is the first step toward the transformation of self. For Cohen, the rituals associated with *Yom Kippur* (Day of Atonement) serve as a framework for self-purification, in preparation for God's forgiveness. Critical of the Church's contention that Christ is a mediator in the creation of a redeemed person, Cohen stresses that God does not collaborate in the process of moral self-perfection. Rather, His role is teleological: repentance provides the basis for human freedom with forgiveness as the goal.

Another correlation between the human and the Divine revolves around the prophetic idea of humanity. In Cohen's view, prophetic messianism transcends philosophical ethics by postulating a future in which war will disappear and all humankind will be united. Such an aim elevates human consciousness beyond past and present, postulating a glorious future. In this light, immortality should be stripped of its otherworldly connotations: it consists rather in the continuation of the individual in the historical continuity of the nation and humanity as a whole. The only reward for a good act is its contribution to the general welfare. In this context Cohen maintains that the Jewish people serve as a symbol for the ultimate unity of all human beings: citing Isaiah 53, he portrays Israel as God's suffering servant who is reconciled to his fate because of the consciousness of the people's historical mission to be a light to the nations.

Israel, Cohen contends, has been preserved for this messianic task through law and worship. Jewish law, he emphasizes, is inherently ethical: rituals and ceremonies serve as signs and memorials for spiritual perfection. The social isolation entailed by ritual observance strengthens the nation for such a mission. On this basis, Cohen rejects Zionism as a political and spiritual programme – Jews, he believes, must remain citizens of the countries where they reside because it is only through such association that they can serve as bearers of monotheistic ideals. Prayer is relevant in this regard because it makes the messianic future present in the assembly of Israel, reinforcing the religious values of the nation. According to Cohen, prayer fortifies the individual against the dangers of hypocrisy and self-delusion, enabling him to overcome despair.

Religion of Reason concludes with a discussion of the ways to morality: the virtues of truthfulness, modesty, justice, courage, faithfulness and peace. For Cohen, peace consists of the infinite perfection of the human race and the serenity of the soul that overcomes hatred:

Peace is the sign of eternity and also the watchword for human life, in its individual conduct as well as in the eternity of its historical calling. In this historical eternity the mission of messianic mankind is completed. (Ibid., 462)

Another dimension of Cohen's writing deals with the relationship between Judaism and Christianity. In a later work, *Jüdische Schriften*, he offers a critique of the Christian doctrines of the Trinity and the Incarnation as well as other aspects of Christian theology. Yet despite such criticisms, Cohen acknowledges Christianity's influence on the Jewish heritage. This is evident, he believes, in translations of the Hebrew Scriptures which unconsciously contain various Christian influences; it is also inherent in the manner in which the Christian tradition – based on Jewish teaching – has continued to animate Jewish consciousness. Christianity thus exerted an influence on Judaism through the ages, and in Cohen's vision of the future, he envisages Protestanism coming closer to its Jewish roots. This *rapprochement* has been prepared by the emergence of biblical criticism which has called into question the Church's reliance on traditional dogma.

Such an affinity between Protestantism and Judaism, however, does not signify that the distinction between these two traditions will be eliminated. On the contrary, Protestant Christianity will continue to remain a distinct faith. Nevertheless Cohen feels that Jews should encourage Protestants to promote the highest ideals. 'We neither await nor promote the abolition or dissolution of Christianity,' he writes, 'rather we wish and shall encourage all these profound endeavours which exert themselves to its idealization' (Cohen, 1924, vol. I, 64). In contemplating the future, Cohen pleads for a better relationship between the two faiths; in return he expects Christians to respect the Jewish heritage. Such mutual tolerance will result in the creation of a better world in which monotheism will be embraced by all people. In Cohen's view, by accomplishing this divinely appointed role of bringing knowledge of the one true God to all nations, the Jewish people can be aided by the purer forms of the Christian faith.

References/Hermann Cohen's major writings

Hermann Cohen, *Jüdische Schriften*, Berlin, 1924
Hermann Cohen, *Religion of Reason out of the Sources of Judaism* (trans. S. Kaplan), New York, 1972

See also in this book

Maimonides, Spinoza

Further reading

S.H. Bergmann in A. Altmann (ed.), *Between East and West*, London, 1958
S.H. Bergmann, *Faith and Reason*, New York, 1963
M. Kaplan, *The Purpose and Meaning of Jewish Existence*, Philadelphia, 1964
J. Melker, *Hermann Cohen's Philosophy of Judaism*, 1968
N. Rotenstreich, *Jewish Philosophy in Modern Times: From Mendelssohn to Rosenzweig*, New York, 1968

DOV BAER OF MEZHIRICH

Among the leaders of Hasidism, the eighteenth-century scholar Dov Baer of Mezhirich played a pivotal role in the growth of the movement. Born in 1710, as a youth he was educated at the *yeshivah* (rabbinical seminary) of Rabbi Jacob Joshua Falk; later he taught in Torchin, becoming a preacher in Korets and Rovno. Subsequently he settled in Mezhirich in Volhynia (now western Ukraine) which became the centre of the Hasidic movement. Near the end of his life he resided in Annopol. During his lifetime he was generally recognized as the successor to the Baal Shem Tov (Besht).

In addition to his study of talmudic law, Dov Baer was preoccupied with kabbalistic doctrines as propounded by Isaac Luria. Adopting an ascetic lifestyle, he subjected himself to a variety of mortifications which had an adverse effect on his health – he contracted a disease which affected his legs and caused him to become bedridden. According to tradition, he sought a cure from the Besht, and in consequence became an ardent disciple. After the death of the Baal Shem Tov in 1760, Dov Baer was widely recognized as the leader of the Hasidic movement although he was opposed by an older follower of the Besht, Jacob Joseph of Polonnoye. By 1766 Dov Baer's authority was recognized throughout the Hasidic world, yet unlike the Besht, Dov Baer was not a man of the people and his illness made it difficult for him to associate with the general populace – nonetheless he was an eloquent spokesman for the Hasidic way of life until his death in 1772.

In his autobiography the eighteenth-century Jewish philosopher, Solomon Maimon, provides a detailed account of his meeting with Dov Baer:

At last I arrived at Mezhirich, and after having rested from my journey, I went to the house of the Master [Dov Baer], under the impression that I would be introduced to him at once. I was told, however, that he could not speak to me at this time, but that I was invited to his table on the Sabbath .... Accordingly, on the Sabbath, I went to this solemn meal, and found there a large number of respectable men who had come from various districts. At length, the awe-inspiring Master appeared clothed in white satin .... He greeted every newcomer in turn. After the meal was over, he began to sing a melody awesome and inspiring. Then he placed his hand for some time upon his brow, and began to call upon such and such a person of such and such a place. Thus he called upon every newcomer by his own name and the name of his residence . . . . Each recited, as he was called, some verses of the Holy Scripture. Thereupon the Master began to deliver a sermon for which the verses recited served as a text, so that, although they were disconnected, verses taken from different parts of the Holy Scripture . . . they were combined with as much skill as if they had been formed as a single whole. What was still more extraordinary, every one of the newcomers believed that he discovered, in that part of the sermon which was founded on his verse, something that had special reference to the facts of his own spiritual life. (Maimon, 1954, 173–4)

Like Solomon Maimon, Dov Baer's disciples expressed similar great esteem for their Master. So overwhelming was his influence that one of his followers, Aryeh Leib Sarahs, was said to have visited Dov Baer to see how he put on his shoes and tied his shoelaces.

Endeavouring to popularize Hasidism among the masses, Dov Baer sent emmisaries to gain followers throughout Poland, which then extended far to the east of its present borders. Not only did such activity initiate the creation of an organized movement, but Dov Baer's leadership set the precedent for the institution of the *zaddik* (saintly leader). Under his direction, Hasidism spread to central Poland, through what is now the Ukraine and Lithuania, and as far west as Poznania. Outside the Hasidic community, Dov Baer was also widely respected as a talmudist and participated in communal affairs. Through his emissary Aaron of Karlin, he succeeded in obtaining an adjustment of tax regulations.

Nonetheless his methods of leadership and religious teaching evoked a hostile reaction from some quarters. In 1772 a ban on Hasidism was issued by the rabbinic leadership of Vilna (now Vilnius, Lithuania); a month after this decree was pronounced, a letter was circulated throughout all the communities of Lithuania and White Russia (Belarus) denouncing this new movement:

Our brethren in Israel, you are certainly already informed of the tiding whereof our fathers never dreamed, that a sect of the suspects has been formed . . . who meet together in separate groups and deviate in their prayers from the text valid for the whole people . . . . The study of the Torah is neglected by them entirely and they do not hesitate constantly to emphasize that one should devote oneself as little as possible to learning and not grieve too much over a sin committed . . . . When they pray according to falsified text, they raise such a din that the walls quake . . . and they turn over like wheels, with their head below and the legs above . . . . Do not believe them even if they raise their voices to implore you. (Cohen, 1943, 235–7)

According to legend, such denunciations of Hasidism affected Dov Baer's health and he died shortly afterwards.

The starting point of Dov Baer's mystical system is his conviction that God is present in all things. Explaining his teacher's theory, Dov Baer's disciple Shlomo of Lutsk writes:

In every movement God is present since it is impossible to make any move or utter a word without the might of God. This is the meaning of the verse, 'The whole earth is full of his glory' [Isaiah 6:3] . . . . There can be no thought except through the divine realm of thought. He is only like a *shofar* [ram's horn] that emits whatever sound is blown into it; if a person sounding it were to withdraw it would not bring forth any sound. Likewise, if God did not act in him he would not be able to speak or think. (in Cohn-Sherbok, 1995, 193)

According to Dov Baer, the divine emanation that is manifest throughout creation offers the basis for contact with God – the aim of human life is to reunite creation with the Creator. This is possible by focusing one's life and all worldly aspects on the divine dimension. This can be achieved by motivation that inspires action; all acts when motivated by the ultimate purpose of serving God become acts of unification:

> A person must not pray for his own concerns; rather he is to pray that the *Shekhinah* be redeemed from exile ... even if one performs a *mitzvah* (commandment) but does not direct it for the sake of God, that is, he acts for some ulterior motive, he thereby brings about estrangement .... For, as taught in the Zohar, the Torah and God are one, and if an individual performs a *mitzvah* properly, this *mitzvah* becomes one with God, one holy essence, constituted of one spiritual reality. On the other hand, if one performs it improperly he fashions an obstructing shell around the *mitzvah* so that it cannot unite itself with the holy essence of God. (Ibid.)

For Dov Baer, the process of attachment to God brings about the unification of all the worlds below and the Divine:

> When a person attachs himself to God, then all the worlds below him are united with God through him. In this way a person who is endowed with vitality through eating and wearing clothes, includes in himself the inanimate, vegetable, animal and rational life; they are all united with God through him. (Ibid. 194)

In presenting this theory Dov Baer maintains that the purpose of human existence is to return to *Ayin* (Nothingness) which precedes creation. In this quest the soul descends from the heavenly realm so as to raise up material existence through spiritual exaltation; by this means it is possible to restore cosmic harmony. In this process there is a mingling between the first *sefirah* (divine emanation), *Ayin* (Nothingness), and the second *sefirah*, *Hokhman* (Wisdom). In general Dov Baer did not differentiate between these two divine emanations; they were treated as related and he transposed them in order to demonstrate the true nature of the soul. Such a monistic approach stipulated that God is found everywhere: there is no place where

He is absent. Thus it is possible to worship Him through every action. Here the concept of divine immanence and the Lurianic concept of the lifting up of the sparks serve as the basis for the notion of worship through corporeality – the worship of God through *devekut* (cleaving to God) occurs even during the performance of physical activity.

Distinguishing himself from the Lurianic understanding of *tzimtzum* (divine contraction), Dov Baer returned to the ideological system of the sixteenth-century kabbalist Moses Cordovero who envisaged *tzimtzum* as an act of concealment from the aspect of Divine Essence, whereas from the standpoint of human beings it is a manifestation of God. Through his rejection of the Lurianic understanding, Dov Baer dissociated himself from the doctrine of the crisis in the relationship between God and himself as well as his relationship with the cosmos. For Dov Baer the breaking of the vessels is not catastrophic – rather its purpose is to illuminate the nature of existence. The *shevirah* (breaking of the vessels) is therefore depicted as an internal event in the life of human beings. According to Dov Baer, the role of the *zaddik* is to attain a life of complete holiness: he is called to supervise the scales of justice in the world and watch over its moral equilibrium. By virtue of his spiritual elevation, he can serve as an intercessor on behalf of his people.

References/Dov Baer's major teachings

Solomon Maimon, *Autobiography*, New York, 1954
Israel Cohen, *Vilna*, Philadelphia, 1943
Dan Cohn-Sherbok, *Jewish Mysticism: An Anthology*, Oxford, 1995

See also in this book

Baal Shem Tov, Luria, Maimon

Further reading

Martin Buber, *Tales of the Hasidim*, New York, 1947

Y. Dorfman, *The Maggid of Mezirich*, Southfield, MI, 1989

H.M. Rabinowicz, *The World of Hasidism*, London, 1970

H.M. Rabinowicz, *Hasidism: The Movement and Its Masters*, Northvale, NJ, 1988

J.I. Schochet, *The Great Maggid*, Brooklyn, NY, 1974

EMIL FACKENHEIM

Born in Halle, Germany in 1917, Emil Fackenheim graduated from the local *gymnasium* in 1935, subsequently attending the *Hochschule für die Wissenschaft des Judentums* in Berlin where he was ordained a Reform rabbi. During this period he attended the University of Halle, and then in 1938–9 he was detained in Sachsenhausen concentration camp. After his release he attended the University of Aberdeen and later the University of Toronto from which he received a doctorate in 1945. After serving as a rabbi in Hamilton, Ontario, he became Professor of Philosophy at the University of Toronto. In 1983 he moved to the Hebrew University of Jerusalem.

In his early work Fackenheim did not directly address the theological problems connected with the Holocaust, but in his later writings he argues that the events of the Nazi era raise the most central religious problems of the modern age. The turning point in his own thinking came when he discovered that Jews were committed to Jewish survival in the face of the tragedy of the death camps. As he explains:

Not until I found this scandal [of Auschwitz] did I make what to me was, and still is, a momentous discovery. Jews throughout the world – rich and poor, learned and ignorant, believer and unbeliever – were already responding to Auschwitz, and in some measure had been doing so all along. Faced with the radical threat of extinction, they were stubbornly defying it, committing themselves, if to nothing more, to the survival of themselves and their children as Jews. (in Cohn-Sherbok, 1989, 43)

In exploring the religious implications of the Holocaust, Fackenheim reflects on the meaning of the Holocaust for Jewish civilization: in a wide variety of writings he seeks to provide an authentic response to the horrors of the Nazi period. According to Fackenheim, the Holocaust was a unique event – even the term 'genocide' does not capture the most significant features of this catastrophe. There are, he believes, two central features of this tragedy which distinguish this event from other occurrences. First, six million Jews were killed not because of their religious beliefs, but because their grandparents perceived themselves within the Jewish covenant. Second, the process of murder was understood as an end in itself; unlike previous massacres, Jews did not face death so as to bear witness to the belief in God. The uniqueness of the Holocaust is therefore of central importance to Fackenheim because of the way in which the Nazis defined Jewishness so as to rid Europe of these 'unwanted aliens'. Killing Jews became a goal in itself; such an intention is an example of what Fackenheim refers to as 'radical' evil. This is what distinguishes the Holocaust from all other acts of genocide in which there was a rational aim. Even though contemporary Jews might wish to divorce the Holocaust from previous Jewish history, this is simply impossible – the destruction of millions of Jews is a terrifying reminder that the Jews cannot escape their own tragedy.

For Fackenheim, God's presence was manifest in the death camps just as he disclosed himself in ancient times. As the root experience of God's presence on Mount Sinai resulted in a series of divine ordinances as recorded in Scripture, so in the death camps God revealed a further commandment. This 614th commandment, added to the 613 commandments contained in the Five

Books of Moses, is directed to a post-Holocaust community. In *God's Presence in History* Fackenheim gives a full explanation of this decree:

> Jews are forbidden to hand Hitler posthumous victories. They are commanded to survive as Jews, lest the Jewish people perish. They are commanded to remember the victims of Auschwitz lest their memory perish. They are forbidden to despair of man and his world, and to escape into either cynicism or other-worldliness, lest they co-operate in delivering the world over to the forces of Auschwitz. Finally, they are forbidden to despair of the God of Israel, lest Judaism perish . . . . A Jew may not respond to Hitler's attempt to destroy Judaism, by himself co-operating in its destruction. In ancient times, the unthinkable Jewish sin was idolatry. Today, it is to respond to Hitler by doing his work. (Ibid., 45–6)

In Fackenheim's view, it is a sacred duty to remember the events of the Holocaust. The desire of the Nazis was to eliminate all Jews – no survivor was to be left to recount the horrors that took place in the camps. Their intention was to wipe out every trace of memory. Millions would thus become as though they had never existed. The Commanding Voice of Auschwitz, however, demands that those who perished must never be forgotten. It is a holy duty to remember what occurred and to give an account of this tragedy; such an obligation is not negotiable. Furthermore, Fackenheim insists that the Commanding Voice of Auschwitz bids Jews not to abandon the world to the forces of darkness. Rather, they must continue to work to establish a better world. They must not despair of society because of the events of the Nazi period; nor should they abandon the age-old identification with the downtrodden. It is because of the uniqueness of Auschwitz and their role as Jews that the Jewish community must identify with all humanity.

In a subsequent work, *To Mend the World*, Fackenheim argues that the Nazis were intent on making individuals into *Muselmänner* (people who are dead while alive). Yet despite this aim, some of those who were deported to the camps resisted. For Fackenheim such acts of resistance embody the religious response to the Holocaust and the beginning of *tikkun* (cosmic repair). Fackenheim emhasizes that rebellion in the death camps took various forms. Some victims consciously refused to become *Muselmänner*; pregnant women were unwilling to abort their pregnancies in order that their children would survive; Jewish partisans fled to the woods to fight against the Nazis; Hasidic Jews prayed although forbidden to do so. Such gestures were infrequent – but they demonstrate that there were some individuals who resisted the Nazi onslaught. Their heroism illustrates the fact that the logic of destruction can be overcome.

Fackenheim maintains that the Holocaust must continue to be resisted in modern society. Civilization now includes the realities of death camps and *Muselmänner* – those who understand what occurred during the Second World War cannot overlook the rationally organized, systematic assault on the Jewish people of the Nazi era. As a result, resistance to the Holocaust and the quest to bring about cosmic repair are neverending imperatives. Further, Fackenheim contends that only because of the act of resistance can resistance in thought become effective. In the case of those who had the courage to act against inhumanity, thought and action were unified. Just as the Holocaust constitutes a *novum* in history, so this resistance was also a *novum*; it was a way of being and a way of thought.

In this regard, Fackenheim cites the example of Pelagia Lewinska, a Polish Catholic, who represents such a combination of thought and deed:

> At the outset the living places, the ditches, the mud, the piles of excrement behind the blocks, had appalled me with their horrific filth . . . and then I saw the light! I saw that

it was not a question of disorder or lack of organization but that, on the contrary, a very thoroughly considered, conscious idea was in the back of the camp's existence. They had condemned us to die in our own filth, to drown in mud, in our own excrement. They wished to abase us, to destroy our human dignity, to efface every vestige of humanity . . . to fill us with horror and contempt towards ourselves and our fellows . . . . From the instant when I grasped the motivating principle . . . it was as if I had been awakened from a dream . . . . I felt under orders to live . . . . And if I did die in Auschwitz, it would be as a human being, I would hold on to my dignity. I was not going to become the contemptible, disgusting brute my enemy wished me to be . . . . And a terrible struggle began which went on day and night. (Ibid., 49–50)

In Fackenheim's view, such dedication is of fundamental significance. As a Catholic, Lewinska felt under an obligation to resist the Nazi terror; her experience, Fackenheim believes, is evidence of God's Commanding Voice in the death camps. Fackenheim asserts that the rupture brought about by the Holocaust must be mended by similar acts of repair. Previously Jewish mysticism depicted the disasters that beset the Jewish community as catastrophes within the Godhead; such rupture separated God from Himself.

According to Fackenheim, reconciliation in both the earthly and heavenly spheres can only take place through prayer and ritual practice. In contemporary society, however, acts of resistance must take the place of religious observance. Hence, the most important reaction to the Holocaust is the establishment of a Jewish state for the survivors of the camps. In the Jewish homeland, Jewry is able to find a refuge against any future catastrophes. Fackenheim argues that the post-Holocaust *tikkun* involves both religious and non-religious Jews who share a common ancestry. Together they can ensure

Jewish survival in a war-torn and desecrated world.

References/Fackenheim's major writings

Dan Cohn-Sherbok, *Holocaust Theology*, London, 1989

Emil Fackenheim, *God's Presence in History: Jewish Affirmations and Philosophical Reflections*, New York, 1972

Emil Fackenheim, *Encounters between Judaism and Modern Philosophy*, New York, 1973

Emil Fackenheim, *To Mend the World: Foundations of Future Jewish Thought*, New York, 1982

Further reading

S. Katz, *Post-Holocaust Dialogues: Critical Studies in Modern Jewish Thought*, New York, 1983

M. Meyer, 'Judaism after Auschwitz: The Religious Thought of Emil L. Fackenheim', *Commentary*, 1972

Michael L. Morgan, *The Jewish Thought of Emil Fackenheim*, Detroit, MI, 1987

SOLOMON FORMSTECHER

Born in 1808 in Offenbach, Solomon Formstecher studied philosophy, philology and theology at the University of Giessen, later serving as a rabbi at Offenbach until his death in 1889. An active member of the Reform movement, he edited the periodicals *Der Freitagabend* and *Die Israelitische Wochenschrift*. His major work, *Die Religion des Geistes* (Religion of the Spirit) was influenced by the writings of the German philosophers Friedrich Wilhelm Joseph von Schelling and Georg Wilhelm Friedrich Hegel.

In this study Formstecher maintains that ultimate reality is the Divine World Soul, a cosmic unity which manifests itself in nature and in spirit. For Formstecher nature is an organic hierarchy of events and forces which attains self-awareness in Spirit. As knowledge of nature, Spirit takes the form of logic; as knowledge of the ideal to be realized by natural objects, Spirit takes the form of aesthetics. Hence it is through physics, logic and aesthetics that Spirit becomes active in nature and achieves awareness of human existence by means of ethical ideals. As the highest form of consciousness, human beings are capable of apprehending the Divine World in these various manifestations of Spirit. Nonetheless, Formstecher states that such knowledge is only symbolic – it neither depicts nor describes its essence. According to Formstecher, the Divine World Soul in itself is a mystery.

In presenting this metaphysical scheme, Formstecher distinguishes between two types of religion: the religion of nature and the religion of Spirit. The religion of nature, he argues, consists of pagan cults which defy natural forces. Paganism, he continues, culminates in 'physical monotheism' in which nature is perceived as a single divine being. Thus physical monotheism is in essence a pantheistic conception of the world and everything it contains; within such a religious system the goal of human beings is to return to God. The religion of the Spirit, however, identifies God with nature and the ethical ideal, thereby placing the individual above the natural world. In such a religious framework humans are encouraged to become Godlike by choosing the moral good.

In Formstecher's view, Judaism was the first religion of the Spirit, yet even within the history of the faith there has been an evolution of ideas. Because its development takes place within the context of a religion of the Spirit, it continually remains opposed to paganism in its quest for perfection. 'Judaism', he writes, 'attains the stage of perfection only when its ideal is realized in the life of the individual' (Formstecher, 1841, 70). Pagan religions, on the other hand, develop within the limits of their relationship to the objects of nature. Within history these two types of religion are in constant conflict:

Paganism and Judaism must continue throughout history to develop as opponents, and they must move on until each religion has recognized and attained the ideal set for it; when paganism has reached the culmination of its development, it will be convinced that in deifying the forces of nature it has only grasped one manifestation of God. (Ibid., 71)

In Formstecher's opinion Judaism is the ultimate form of the religious life. In time all peoples will come to acknowledge this truth, and in the unfolding of true consciousness Christianity and Islam play an important role:

Christianity and Islam are the northern and southern missions of Judaism to the pagan world; they are the means used by providence to overthrow the deification of nature and to lead the generations of man to the apex of perfection. Both are an amalgamation of Judaism within paganism, and both consider themselves to possess the absolute truth and find their mission in the tasks of advancing this truth till it is the common property of all mankind. (Ibid, 411)

According to Formstecher, Judaism cannot grant equality to these other monotheistic faiths because they embody only a few of the truths of Judaism as a means of preparing humanity for the full realization of God's providential plan. 'In essence,' he writes, 'their mission is a movement of Judaism, which leads itself through paganism and then back to itself' (Ibid., 365).

For Formstecher, Judaism is at the summit of the religious life. In its early stages, the Jewish tradition influenced the pagan world indirectly through Christianity and Islam. As far as Christianity is concerned, its missionary role was limited and transitory:

Christianity recognizes salvation as its task and atonement as the goal for which it aspires . . . . The living symbol of this salvation and atonement is found in Christianity in the death of Jesus. (Ibid., 369)

Yet despite such a positive evaluation, Formstecher is critical of the Christian faith. In the elaboration of its ethical ideals, Christianity surrounded Jewish ethics with the metaphysics of paganism; further, it stripped away the ceremonies and practices particular to Judaism, replacing them with universal principles.

It is these pagan elements of the Christian heritage which constitute its major weakness. Christianity, Formstecher argues, was initially forced to adopt pagan beliefs and observances. However, when the Church gained power, it strove to abandon these influences, but such a struggle was exceedingly difficult because paganism has become an important feature of the Christian faith:

> The heathen–Jewish element, which was tolerated in Judaism and which was always considered of secondary importance, became the living substratum of Christianity; it appeared as the primary Christian element, first with predominantly Jewish and then with predominately pagan characteristics; finally it will lead back to the realm of Judaism. (Ibid., 389)

In discussing the pagan features in Christianity, Formstecher points to a variety of doctrines which, he believes, are essentially pagan in character: transubstantiation, the cult of relics, prayer for the dead, and the elevation of sainthood.

Formstecher's writing is thus a blend of Jewish exclusivism and inclusivism. In his view, the monotheistic religions have an important role in the unfolding of God's eschatological plan for all people – in this providential scheme both Christianity and Islam play significant, though secondary, roles in combating paganism. In all its manifestations paganism is both misguided and harmful, and therefore must be overcome by these three religious traditions. Judaism, however, is the superior faith and the ultimate fulfilment of God's disclosure to humanity. Formstecher's vision of Judaism as the universal ethical religion is hence exclusivist in its rejection of paganism, but inclusivist in its endorsement of both the Christian and Muslim faiths.

References/Formstecher's major writings

Solomon Formstecher, *Die Religion des Geistes*, Frankfurt, 1841

Further reading

B. Bamberger, 'Formstecher's History of Judaism', *Hebrew Union College Annual*, Cincinnati, OH, 1950–1

I. Maybaum, 'Samuel Formstecher: A Contribution to the History of Jewish Religious Philosophy in the 19th Century', *Monatsschrift für Geschichte und Wissenschaft des Judentums*, 1872

N. Rotenstreich, *Jewish Philosophy in Modern Times*, New York, 1968

ABRAHAM GEIGER

Born in 1810 into a distinguished Jewish family in Frankfurt, Abraham Geiger received a traditional Jewish education; his primary teacher was his elder brother, Solomon Geiger. From 1829 he embarked on the study of oriental languages, first at the University of Heidelberg, and then at the University of Bonn where he came into contact with Samson Raphael Hirsch, who later became the founder of Neo-Orthodoxy. In 1832 he served as rabbi in Wiesbaden where he introduced various reforms to the liturgy and began publishing the *Scientific Journal for Jewish Theology*. Five years later he convened the first meeting of Reform rabbis at Wiesbaden. In the following year Geiger was elected *dayyan* (rabbinic judge) and assistant rabbi in Breslau (now Wrocław, Poland).

Opposing Geiger's suitability for this post, the head rabbi of Breslau, Solomon Tiktin, maintained that Geiger was critical of

Orthodox Judaism and that he advocated religious reforms to the faith in his journal. Owing to such criticism, Geiger was prevented from occupying this position until 1840. Two years later Tiktin issued a pamphlet stressing the abiding importance of the laws contained in the *Shulhan Arukh* (Code of Jewish Law) and the integrity of the rabbinic tradition. Geiger's supporters responded by issuing a tract entitled *Rabbinic Responses on the Compatibility of Free Investigation with the Exercise of Rabbinic Functions*. The bitterness evoked by this controversy was reflected in the writing of one of Geiger's supporters, the chief rabbi of Trier, Joseph Kahn, who wrote: 'We must publicly express our contempt for those who, like Tiktin and company, blindly damn and ban, and in just indignation we must brand them as men who "some day will have to account for their deeds", so that "they should hear and fear and do not sin any more"' (Plaut, 1963, 70).

During this period Geiger was an active participant in Reform synods in Frankfurt (1845) and Breslau (1846); in addition, he helped to establish the *Jüdisch-Theologisches Seminar* (Jewish Theological Seminary) in Breslau in 1854. From 1863 Geiger served as a Reform rabbi in Frankfurt, later becoming rabbi of the Berlin Reform congregation. In 1872, the *Hochschule für die Wissenschaft des Judentums* (Academy for the Scientific Study of Judaism) was founded in Berlin, with Geiger at its head until his death in 1874.

Although Geiger did not write a systematic Jewish theology, his works constitute a coherent approach to the Jewish religion. Familiar with contemporary German idealist philosophy and the critique of religious origins advanced by radical Christian thinkers, Geiger desired to reformulate Judaism so as to achieve theological clarity in accord with the scientific spirit of the age. In Geiger's view, Samson Raphael Hirsch's espousal of a Neo-Orthodox approach to the tradition was in essence a return to the past

– what was needed instead was a radical vision for the future. In line with the spirit of Romanticism, Geiger viewed the eighteenth-century Enlightenment as lacking in spiritual depth. Religion, he believed, was based on the recognition of human finitude, and the quest for the Infinite. Religion is more than a rational philosophy, he argues – it is an inborn longing of the whole person who desires to act morally. In a letter written in 1836, Geiger states that he conceives of Judaism as:

> a faith founded on the trust in One who guides the universe and on the task imposed upon us to practise justice and mercy, a faith that becomes manifest in acts that fulfil this demand and that is clothed in uplifting ritual forms designed to awaken such sentiments. (Wiener, 1962, 84)

Of fundamental importance in Geiger's conception of religion is his notion of human nature. Adapting the nineteenth-century theme of Hebraism versus Hellenism, Geiger maintains that ancient Greek civilization embraced the view that fate controls the destiny of the gods and human beings. The Hebrew Bible, however, contains a constant striving for higher purity. Ancient Judaism was based on the conviction that humans struggle against sensuality to attain the good – this is a striving that ennobles and elevates humanity.

According to Geiger, the spiritual core of Judaism which reached its culmination in the teaching of the biblical prophets should be distinguished from the shell of faith which is shaped by external circumstances and can be subsequently discarded. Animal sacrifice, for example, was an essential feature of biblical Judaism but was later eliminated when the Temple was destroyed; its disappearance did not in any way diminish the tradition. Likewise Geiger believes that the concept of nationhood which was an important element of Judaism in previous times was no longer required at a later stage. In this regard, he writes that if a people can continue when 'the fetters which national life had put upon it have been broken – if it continues to live when those who are its standard-bearers no longer exist as a political unit – then this religion has passed a great trial on the way to demonstrating its reliability and its truth'. (Geiger, 1911, 25)

In Geiger's view, the development of Jewish history is divided into four stages. First, in the age of revelation, the concept of Judaism was perceived as essentially moral and spiritual, capable of continual development. In the second stage – the age of tradition – the Bible was continually reshaped and reinterpreted so that the idea of Judaism would continually be relevant. During the third period, the age of legalism, the Babylonian Talmud served as the fulcrum of Jewish existence. The fourth period – the era of critical study – marks a significant break from the past: during this epoch the constraints of the legalistic heritage have been overcome through critical reflection and historical research. Yet, though *halakhah* (Jewish law) has not been considered as binding in this fourth stage, this does not imply that Judaism is cut off from its roots. On the contrary, historical studies can revitalize the traditon. Those aspects of the Jewish past which are to be discarded should be viewed as medieval abnormalities resulting from various restraints: they are not inextricably connected to the core of the faith.

In propounding this interpretation of Jewish history, Geiger was concerned to understand the Jewish background of Christianity and thereby combat the anti-Jewish features of eighteenth-century New Testament scholarship. In Geiger's view, Jesus 'was a Jew, a Pharisee Jew with some Galilean colorations; he was an individual who shared the hopes of his time and believed that this hope had been fulfilled in him. He uttered no new thoughts nor did he break through the boundaries of nationalism' (Geiger, 1910, 118). According to Geiger, Jesus fitted into the religious context of first-century Palestine. Even though he viewed himself as the Messiah, such a claim was in no sense heretical; his life and thought are thus authentically Jewish. Given such a conception of Jesus, Geiger concludes:

> We cannot deny him a deep introspective nature, but there is no trace of a decisive stand that promised lasting results ... there was no great work of reform nor any new thoughts that left the usual paths. He did oppose abuses, perhaps occasionally more forcefully than the Pharisees, yet on the whole it was done in their manner. (Geiger, 1875, vol. II, 113)

In Geiger's view, Jesus believed that a new world of history had been initiated in his lifetime, and his followers awaited this new age. Concerning Paul, Geiger argues that he was profoundly influenced by Hellenistic Judaism and Philo's conception of the *logos*; in his teaching Paul transformed the original messianic sect in which Jesus was understood as the intermediary between God and humanity. Jesus, as well as early Christianity, he continues, was also influenced by the Sadducees. 'The High Priesthood of Jesus', Geiger writes, 'his death as a sacrifice, the participation in the eucharist with his blood and body became a new priesthood endowed with the sacredness and holiness of the old' (Geiger, 1874, 715). In Geiger's estimation, the Judaeo-Christian sect eventually began to spread its message to gentiles. The first stage of this development was essentially Jewish – this period is marked by the original version of the Gospel of Mark. A later stage contained the expression 'Son of God' which was subsequently used by other Gospel writers. For Geiger, Christianity's final break with its Jewish past was initiated by Paul, who had been influenced by Hellenistic Jewish thought with its emphasis on the Messiah and the *logos*. This initiative gained impetus with the destruction of the Jerusalem Temple and the defeat of bar Kokhba.

In his *Introduction to Jewish Theology*, Geiger explores the impact of Christianity on civilization. The strength of the Christian tradition, he argues, consists in its struggle against human nature and its quest to unite all people. Yet such a strength is also its greatest weakness: in its quest to draw non-Christians to Christ, Christianity has destroyed the civilizations of the ancient world. In addition, the Church has been overly preoccupied with preserving its influence, and has frequently attempted to subdue human reason. Judaism, on the other hand, has never been burdened by such concerns. For this reason it is the superior faith:

> Judaism is self-sufficient, developed out of its own resources and may abandon the outer garb of a particular period without surrendering anything of its essence; Christianity on the other hand, rests upon the configuration of the Judaism of a particular period and must eternally cling to what appeared at that particular time in the historical flow of life; for it these elements must remain eternally complete. (Jacob, 1974, 47)

In Geiger's view, Christianity is an inferior religion since the doctrine of the Incarnation compromises the original purity of the Jewish concept of God. Further, Geiger assumes that the concept of original sin undermines the biblical view that human beings are capable of moral advancement. Geiger also points out that the validity of Judaism does not rest on a historical figure like Jesus, nor does the Jewish faith denigrate earthly life as does Christianity. Finally Geiger emphasizes that Judaism does not contain fixed dogmas which constrain free inquiry. For these reasons Geiger believes that Judaism rather than the Christian faith is the ideal religious system for the modern age. Within this framework, emancipation is of vital consequence since it is only in an age of scientific investigation that Judaism can discover its true nature. Historical knowledge can provide a basis for determining what is anachronistic in the tradition and should be discarded, and which features of the faith are eternally valid.

References/Geiger's major writings

Abraham Geiger, 'Enstelehung des Christentums', *Jüdische Zeitschrift für Wissenschaft und Leben* 11, Breslau, 1874

Abraham Geiger, 'Einleitung in das Stadium der jüdische Theologie in Ludwig Geigen (ed.), *Nachgelassene Schriften*, Berlin, 1875

Abraham Geiger, *Das Judentum und seine Geschichte*, Breslau, 1910.

Abraham Geiger, *Judaism and Its History*, New York, 1911

Walter Jacob, *Christianity through Jewish Eyes*, Cincinnati, OH, 1974

G. Plaut, *The Rise of Reform Judaism*, Cincinnati, OH, 1963/1975

Max Wiener (ed.), *Abraham Geiger and Liberal Judaism*, Philadelphia, 1962

Further reading

M. Kaplan, *Greater Judaism in the Making*, New York, 1960

D. Philipson, *The Reform Movement in Judaism*, New York, 1967

G. Plaut, *The Rise of Reform Judaism*, Cincinnati, OH, 1971

S. Schechter, *Studies in Judaism 3*, Philadelphia, 1924

M. Wiener (ed.), *Abraham Geiger and Liberal Judaism*, Philadelphia, 1962

GERSONIDES

Born in 1288, Levi ben Gershom (Gersonides) resided in Bagnols-sur-Cèze in Languedoc, and later in Avignon and Orange. Like Maimonides, he was a philosopher, halakhist and man of science. Of his scientific works, the *Treatise of Astronomy* is the most important – in this study he criticizes various aspects of Ptolemy's astronomical theories: relying on his own astronomical observations, he refers to ten eclipses of the sun and moon as well as nearly a hundred other astronomical occurrences which he witnessed. In addition, he deals with the method of constructing and using the Baculus Jacob which enables one to measure the angular distance between stars or planets.

Between 1325 and 1338 Gersonides composed biblical commentaries in which different methods are deployed according to the nature of the books being treated. Added to these commentaries, Gersonides wrote philosophical studies on Averroes' *Short Commentaries* and *Middle Commentaries* as well as poems, a confession, a parody for the *Purim* Festival, two responsa, and a commentary on the talmudic treatise *Berakhot*. Gersonides' most famous philosophical work, *Wars of the Lord*, took twelve years to complete and was finished in 1329. In the introduction Gersonides outlines the topics to be treated in this investigation:

1 whether a person that has only partly achieved perfection can enter into the afterlife;
2 whether a person can know the future either through dreams, divination, or prophecy;
3 whether God knows existing things;
4 whether there is divine providence for existing things;
5 how the movers of the spheres operate; and
6 whether the world is eternal or created.

Concerning the doctrine of God, Gersonides rejects the view of Aristotelian philosophers that it is possible to derive the existence of a Prime Mover from the motions that exist in the universe. Instead, Gersonides offers a proof of God's existence based on the orderly processes that take place in the world. According to this proof – the argument by design – the regularity of the processes of generation in the sublunar world implies that they are caused by an intelligence, the Active Intellect, which rules over this domain. The Active Intellect endows matter with its different forms and is conscious of the order it generates; its activites are mediated by natural heat which is found in the seeds of plants and the sperm of animals. In turn this natural heat is produced by the motions of the celestial spheres. Because these motions contribute to the perfection of the earthly realm, they must also be produced by intelligences which are the cause of them, namely the intelligences of the celestial spheres. Hence, the celestial and terrestrial worlds constitute an ordered whole requiring the existence of a supreme being which knows this order.

Critical of Maimonides' notion of the negative attributes, Gersonides argues that it is possible to ascribe positive attributes to God; these attributes, he believes, do not undermine God's unity. Accepting that multiplicity exists when objects are composed of form and matter, he maintains that all those attributes which are predicated of a non-material being are derived from the subject: these predicates are simply an explanation of its nature. In Gersonides' view, human beings are capable of attaining a positive knowledge of God based on His action of which the essential activity is thought. All the attributes which human beings recognize in themselves are just so many attributes of God, and – since the attributes which are shared by human beings and God have the nature of cause and effect – it is a mistake to regard them as homonyms (terms which are different except for their names).

According to Gersonides, God eternally perceives the general laws of the universe, namely those laws which order the movements of heavenly bodies and through them sublunar beings. Thus God is aware of what awaits all persons as members of collectivities, yet as specific individuals each person is able to exercise freedom of the will. When such free choice is made, human beings are able to liberate themselves from the constraints of determinism. They cease to be subject to the universal laws known by God, and their acts are therefore totally undetermined and unknown to the Deity. In presenting this explanation of divine knowledge and human freedom, Gersonides contends that God's knowledge does not undergo any modification; it remains true regardless of individual choices since each agent is no longer included in the necessary and universal propositions which are thought by God. For Gersonides, God's knowledge embraces all events of this world with the exception of freely chosen actions that cannot be foreseen. By means of this theory Gersonides believes he is able to resolve the seeming contradiction between omniscience and freedom of the will.

As far as providence is concerned, Gersonides argues that this manifestation of divine direction increases in relation to a person's moral and intellectual perfection. Through the activities of the stars which are predetermined, God ensures a maximum of good to human beings. Hence premonitions, dreams and prophecies – as well as the exercise of free will – rescue individuals from the harmful effects of determinism. Yet, it is impossible to deny the existence of evil since the righteous occasionally do suffer; nonetheless Gersonides maintains that the true human good is the immortality of the soul which is bestowed in preportion to an individual's moral excellence and intellectual perfection.

In contrast with Maimonides, who held that creation cannot be demonstrated philosophically, Gersonides attempts to prove that the world came into being. Thus he maintains that everything which is produced by a final cause, ordained for a certain end, and serving as a substratum for accidents, cannot exist eternally. Because the universe fulfils all these conditions, it follows that it must have a beginning in time. In his opinion, many of Aristotle's arguments used to prove the eternity of the world actually beg the question: they are based on the presupposition that the physical laws operating in the world can be applied to its beginning. This assumption, however, is without substance; even though there are some similarities between the events taking place in the world and creation, the origin of the universe is unique. Terrestrial motions take place in time, whereas creation occurred in an instant. Yet, since nothing can be created out of nothing,

the world has a formless substratum – it does not have existence in the technical sense since existence is derived from form.

Regarding Gersonides' conception of human nature, God arranged the universe in such a way that human beings are the most perfect of all creatures in the sublunar world. Hence revelations of various types protect them from danger: through their imaginations – which are under celestial influences – they are able to envisage the problems that can befall them. Possessing a practical intellect, man is able to learn the means of self-preservation; through the speculative intellect, he is able to perceive truth and attain immortality. The material or potential intellect is not a substance, but a disposition whose substratum is the imagination. On the basis of sensations, the human intellect is able to form abstract concepts, yet true knowledge should be conceived as the comprehension of intelligibles. Having understood what is intelligible and eternal, the human intellect becomes immortal.

Gersonides' philosophical system also deals with the concept of Israel's chosenness. Providence, he argues, extends particularly to the Jewish people. In his view, prophecy should be conceived as a form of revelation which is superior to all other types of divine disclosure. The prophet must necessarily be a distinguished philosopher who is able to comprehend the general laws governing the sublunar world as they are manifest in the agent intellect. Through his imagination, he is able to apply this knowledge to individual or communal events; such knowledge enables him to proclaim whatever is to befall both individuals and groups as a result of the operation of the laws of nature.

Further, the prophet is capable of foreseeing a miraculous occurrence which violates the laws of nature. According to Gersonides, a miracle takes place at a specific time and place when the agent intellect suspends natural laws. Though such extraordinary occurrences are not consonant with natural law, they nonetheless follow patterns of their own. However, since miracles are produced by the agent intellect which can only act in the sublunar realm, no miracles take place in the translunar world. Commenting on Moses' prophetic role, Gersonides maintains that through his intermediacy, God gave Israel the Torah which enables the Jewish people to attain moral and intellectual perfection: in this way they are able to attain immortality.

Finally, Gersonides outlines an eschatological unfolding of human history in which two Messiahs – the Messiah ben Joseph and the Messiah ben David – play a fundamental role. As Gersonides explains, the Messiah ben David will be greater than Moses since he is able to accomplish a greater miracle than Moses was able to achieve – the resurrection of the dead, an event which will result in the transformation of earthly existence. In propounding this view, Gersonides predicted that the Messiah would arrive in 1358. Gersonides had died in 1344.

Gersonides' major writings

Gersonides, *The Wars of the Lord*, Book IV in J.D. Bleich, *Providence in the Philosophy of Gersonides*, New York, 1973
Gersonides, *The Wars of the Lord*, Book III in N.M. Samuelson, *Gersonides on God's Knowledge*, Toronto, 1977
Gersonides, *The Wars of the Lord*, Book VI, part 2, chapter 1 in J.J. Staub, *The Creation of the World according to Gersonides*, Chico, CA, 1982

See also in this book

Maimonides

Further reading

N.H. Adlerblum, *A Study of Gersonides in His Proper Perspective*, New York, 1967
D.D. Bleich, *Providence in the Philosophy of Gersonides*, New York, 1973
R. Eisen, *Gersonides on Providence, Covenant and the Chosen People*, Albany, New York, 1995
B.R. Goldstein, *The Astronomical Tables of Levi ben Gerson*, New Haven, CN, 1974

J.J. Staub, *The Creation of the World according to Gersonides*, Chico, CA, 1982
H.A. Wolfson, 'Maimonides and Gersonides on Divine Attributes as Ambiguous Terms', in H.A. Wolfson (ed.), *Studies in the History of Philosophy and Religion*, vol. II, Cambridge, 1977

AHARON DAVID GORDON

Born in a village in the province of Podolia (now southern Ukraine) in 1856, Aharon David Gordon grew up on an estate which his father managed for the family of Baron Horace Günzburg. After his marriage, he was an official on a tract of land leased by the Günzburgs. Later, at the age of 47, he settled in Palestine where he worked in the vineyards and wineries of Petah Tikva. Subsequently he worked in Galilee; his last days were spent in Deganyah, one of the earliest kibbutzim, where he died in 1922. In his writings, Gordon offered a solution to the problem of Jewish regeneration in the Holy Land.

In Gordon's view, manual labour is fundamental to personal and national salvation. In his essay, 'Some Observations', published in 1910, he sketches the alternatives facing the Jewish community in the Holy Land. The first is the practical way of the worldly-wise: the continuation of exile life, with all its shortsighted practical wisdom. For Gordon exile is not simply a geographical desolation; rather it brings about psychological and existential alienation, combining dependence on others with an estrangement from creative life. The second alternative calls for the rebirth of Jewish life – the way of manual labour. This latter option, he argues, will renew the energies of the nation:

We have as yet no national assets because our people have not paid the price for them. A people can acquire a land only by its own effort, by realizing the potentialities of its body and soul, by unfolding and revealing its inner self. This is a two-sided transaction, but the people comes first – the people comes before the land. But a parasitical people is not a living people. Our people can be brought to life only if each one of us recreates himself through labour and a life close to nature. (in Hertzberg, 1969, 376)

Gordon's conception of Jewish life in the diaspora is related to his theories of anthropology and psychology. According to Gordon, an individual can become fully human only through contact with nature. Hence physical labour is essential for spiritual growth and fulfilment. In this light, Jewish existence outside Israel is a distorted mode of living, not only because the Jewish people has lost its homeland, but also because it lacks the land where Jews can realize their full human potential through physical work. For Gordon, a Jewish national renaissance can only take place through a return to the self by cultivating the land. Thus a fundamental distinction must be drawn between a transference of exiles to the Holy Land, and a radical reconstruction of Jewish life through agricultural activity.

Such a radical analysis calls for the total transformation of Jewish existence. The way of national rebirth, he writes,

embraces every detail of our individual lives. Every one of us is required to refashion himself so that the *Galut* [diaspora] Jew within him becomes a truly emancipated Jew; so that the unnatural, defective, splintered person within him may be changed into a natural, wholesome human being who is true to himself; so that his *Galut* life, which has been fashioned by alien and extraneous influences, hampering his natural growth and self-realization, may give way to one that allows him to develop freely, to his fullest stature in all dimensions. (Ibid.)

Such a process of rehabilitation must occur if Jewish exile is to cease, even if Palestine becomes populated with Jewish emigrants.

In Gordon's opinion, traditional Jewish life in the diaspora was richer than modern existence in a post-Emancipation world. Prior to the Enlightenment, Jews sought to improve their position in society without abandoning the Torah. Yet in the modern world material prosperity has overshadowed all other concerns. To counteract this corrosive attitude, the 'religion of nature' needs to become the dominant ideology. In an essay entitled 'Labour', Gordon maintains that the Jewish people is inextricably linked to its homeland; if it becomes divorced from agricultural labour, it becomes disfigured. According to Gordon, modern Zionist writers in their advocacy of a Jewish state have overlooked the fundamental requirements for a vibrant national life:

A people that was completely divorced from nature, that during two thousand years was imprisoned within walls, that became inured to all forms of life except to a life of labour, cannot become once again a living natural, working people without bending all its willpower toward that end. We lack the fundamental element: we lack labour (not labour done because of necessity, but labour to which man is organically and naturally linked), labour by which a people becomes rooted in its soil and its culture. (in Avineri, 1981, 155)

The absence of physical labour, he believes, is a central defect in the Jewish character. This condition was a product of exile, and its continuation has contributed to the perpetuation of the diaspora; paradoxically the denigration of physical work enabled Jews to accommodate themselves to a diaspora existence. However, if the Jewish people had been more involved with land, they would have been more inclined to return to their ancient homeland. Now that the Jews have a country of their own, Gordon is fearful of the resurgence of such contempt for natural labour:

Now let us assume that somewhere we already have settled a goodly number of Jews. Will this attitude of ours change there of itself? Will a transformation of our soul take place without a radical cure? Will not our Jewish people at all times prefer trading, speculation, especially business in which others will labour while they will manage the enterprise? (Ibid.)

In Gordon's view, what is now required is a cultural revolution: the Holy Land must be cultivated, buildings constructed, and roads built:

Each piece of work, each deed, each act is an element of culture. Herein is the foundation of culture, the stuff of which it is made. Arrangement, method, shape, the way in which a thing is done – these are forms of culture. What a man does, what he feels, thinks, lives, while he is at work, and while he is not working, the conditions arising from these relations – these mould themselves into the spirit of culture. From these, higher culture draws nourishment – science, art, beliefs, opinions, poetry, ethics, religion. (Ibid., 156)

Authentic Zionism must bring to Palestine the foundations of manual labour which can serve as the basis for a higher culture. The main task of Zionism is therefore to encourage dedication to ordinary toil:

[We have] to work with our very own hands at all things which make up life [in Palestine], to labour with our own hands at all kinds of works, at all kinds of crafts and trades from the most skilled, the cleanliest and the easiest to the coarsest, the most despised, the most difficult. We must feel all that the worker feels, think what he thinks, live the life he lives, in ways that are our ways. Then we can consider that we have our own culture, for then we shall have life. (Ibid.)

What is missing in contemporary Zionism, Gordon asserts, is a recognition of the funda-

mental link between man and nature. This is the cosmic aspect of national identity. Jews who have been uprooted must learn about the soil and prepare it for the transplantation of the Jewish nation. It is necessary to learn about climatic conditions and everything required to grow agricultural produce: 'We who have been torn away from nature, who have lost the savour of natural living – if we desire life, we must establish a new relationship with nature, we must open a new account with it' (Ibid., 157). Such a quest to bring about a radical transformation in Jewish consciousness was motivated by a utopian conception of Jewish life in the Holy Land. Although Gordon's thinking lacked the religious dimensions of Orthodox Jewish Zionists, it has spiritual connotations reminiscent of previous writers who longed for the redemption of the Jewish people.

References

Shlomo Avineri, *The Making of Modern Zionism: The Intellectual Origins of the Jewish State*, New York, 1981
Arthur Hertzberg, *The Zionist Idea: A Historical Analysis and Reader*, New York, 1969

Gordon's major writings

A. Hertzberg, *The Zionist Idea: A Historical Analysis and Reader*, New York, 1969

Further reading

S.H. Bergman, *Faith and Reason*, New York, 1963
M. Buber, *Israel and Palestine: The History of an Idea*, London, 1952
D. Cohn-Sherbok, *Israel: The History of an Idea*, London, 1992
H.H. Rose, *The Life and Thought of A.D. Gordon*, New York, 1964

HEINRICH GRAETZ

Born in Xions (now Książ) near Poznań, in 1817, Heinrich Graetz was the son of a butcher. Initially he pursued rabbinic studies at Wolstein (now Wolsztyn, Poland) where he also immersed himself in secular studies. After undergoing a spiritual crisis, he regained his faith after reading Samson Raphael Hirsch's *Nineteen Letters on Judaism*. He subsequently accepted Hirsch's invitation to continue his studies under his guidance. Eventually, Graetz distanced himself from his teacher and left Oldenburg, working as a private tutor in Ostrów (not far from Xions). In 1842 he obtained permission to study at the University of Breslau (now Wrocław, Poland); however since no Jew was allowed to obtain a doctorate from the university, Graetz presented his thesis to the University of Jena. This dissertation was published as *Gnosticism and Judaism* in 1846. By this time Graetz had come under the influence of Zechariah Frankel, contributing to his scholarly journal.

Because of his lack of ability as an orator, Graetz failed to obtain a post as rabbi and preacher. On acquiring a teaching diploma, he served as head teacher of the orthodox religious school of the Breslau community, and later at the Jewish school of Lundenburg, Moravia. In 1852 he left Lundenburg for Berlin where he lectured on Jewish history to theology students; at this time he completed the fourth volume of his *History of the Jews*. In 1853 he was appointed lecturer in Jewish history and Bible at the Jewish Theological Seminary of Breslau; sixteen years later he became honorary professor at the University of Breslau. At Breslau, Graetz published his eleven-volume *History of the Jews*, and also became actively engaged in the struggle against German anti-Semitism. Near the end of his life an abridged version of the *History of the Jews* appeared in three volumes. He died in 1891.

Graetz's understanding of the significance of Judaism was first formulated in an essay 'The Construction of Jewish History' which appeared in 1846. Here his aim is to illustrate that the essence of Judaism is not simply a theoretical idea: rather, it comprises those features of the heritage which reformers sought to discard because they were perceived as no longer relevant in modern society. Influenced by Hegelian thought, Graetz believed that all aspects of the Jewish tradition constitute an unfolding of a unique system of belief and practice. Like Abraham Geiger, Graetz viewed this process not simply as a logical outcome, but as a historical development which emerged as the Jewish religion responded to various challenges throughout its development. The result is that which Graetz refers to as 'a conceptual construction of Jewish history' which seeks to illustrate how the laws and doctrines of Judaism – inherent in the original concept of the faith – manifested themselves over time.

According to Graetz, all attempts made by philosophers to reduce Judaism to an abstract single definition have failed; they are unsuccessful because the totality of the Jewish heritage is only discernible in its history. The root of Judaism, he argues, is a principle more fundamental than monotheism: the belief that God is not to be identified with nature. Hence Judaism was originally totally opposed to paganistic religions which asserted that nature is an omnipotent and immanent intermingling of forces. In such belief systems the pagan gods are in essence nature idealized, subject to necessity and fate. In line with Solomon Ludwig Steinheim, Graetz maintains that only the biblical notion, of a spiritual Deity who created the material world out of nothing, can provide a basis for ethical freedom and the moral life. For Graetz, Jewish history constitutes a test of the genuineness and truth of this root idea. Judaism, he asserts, is not an abstraction – it must transcend the dormant state of ideal into the changing flux of reality, disproving paganism and opposing its deleterious effects on communal life.

In Graetz's view, Jewish history should be divided into three major periods. The first begins with the entrance of the Israelites into

Canaan and ends with the destruction of the First Temple in 587 BCE. This epoch is dominated by communal life: the emphasis is on the well-being of the community rather than individual salvation. Yet even though biblical Judaism was preoccupied with political concerns, in the course of its struggle with paganism a more purified form of the religion emerged. The second period begins with the Babylonian exile, continuing until the destruction of the Temple in 70 CE. At this stage the religious dimensions of the faith overshadowed socio-economic factors, resulting in the development of Judaism as a religious tradition rather than the continuation of a political entity. The overriding issue during this second stage of Jewish history was the struggle against Greek paganism – this led to the rise of the Pharisees who introduced the concept of an afterlife into the religious system. Even though there appears to be a discontinuity between these two epochs of Jewish history, biblical and post-biblical Judaism retained political as well as religious features; hence when the Jewish nation no longer existed, the idea of a Jewish commonwealth continued to animate Jewish life as a messianic expectation for the future.

The third cycle of Jewish history – the diaspora period – was dominated by Judaism's quest to achieve intellectual self-perception as well as to transform the Jewish religion into rational truths. This was possible in the diaspora world, Graetz believes, because the Jewish faith was found wherever old truths were transmuted into eternal verities and new truths emerged. In this process Judaism was able to discover through comparison and contrast the full depths of its own content. Simultaneously, there had to be an internal force which could prevent the complete disintegration of the tradition: this was the talmudic system which served as a portable homeland and a fence around the Jewish heritage. Talmudic law, Graetz asserts, is a logical consequence of Judaism's basic ideals; its function is to strengthen the

distinctive lifestyle of the Jewish people. Protected in this way, Judaism increasingly came to self-consciousness.

Philosophical *aggadah* (rabbinic interpretation) which was influenced by Platonism originally speculated on the allegorical meaning of Scripture and later on its mystical significance. Subsequently medieval Jewish philosophy sought to discover the metaphysical principles of the faith. Finally, from the time of Moses Mendelssohn, Judaism began to penetrate the inner signficance of Jewish observance. Owing to modern philosophy, Graetz writes:

Men now discover eternal truths not only in the ideas of the spirit but also in the far higher realm of the actions of the spirit, not only in the formalism of logic, in the abstractions of metaphysics and the externalism of nature, but especially in the concrete forms of art, science, religion, in the composite of all these factors, in the formation of the state, and particularly in the developments of history. Thus Judaism must merely appropriate this point of view, and its philosophical justification will be a simple matter. (Graetz, 1975, 122)

In conclusion, Graetz asserts that is now Judaism's task to found a religious state which is conscious of its activity, purpose, and connection with the world.

The ideas contained in this early essay underlie the presentation of Graetz's view of Jewish civilization in his eleven-volume *History of the Jews*. Published between 1853 and 1876, this work presents an overview of the evolution of the Jewish people. In Graetz's view, it is not only in the pre-Christian era, but later in the diaspora that Jewry continued to remain true to itself despite changing circumstances. Its external history in the diaspora was a unique catalogue of suffering; its internal history, on the other hand, was marked by a unique literary development. Even so, the Jewish nation never became a religious association; instead, it was always a folk community:

Though scattered over the civilized portion of the earth and attached to the lands of their hosts, the members of the Jewish race did not cease to feel themselves a single people in their religious conviction, historical memory, customs and hopes. (in Meyer, 1974, 230)

Further, Jews became a messianic people, bearing a burden of responsiblity for all peoples in anticipation of the coming of a Messiah who would transform earthly life.

Unlike Geiger, who viewed the national form of Jewish life as a means for the development of the religious idea of Judaism, Graetz perceived Jewish nationhood as fundamental: it was an intrinsic and essential characteristic of the faith. World history, he believed, not only needed the idea of Judaism – it required the physical presence of Jews. In espousing such an interpretation, Graetz distanced himself from those reformers who wished to reshape Judaism into a religion like any other. The Jewish tradition, he maintained, is not simply a theory; it is a theory turned into practice. Paradoxically it has universal significance because it is national in character.

Yet despite such reservations about religious reform, Geiger was committed to emancipation. Although critical of Judaism's elaborate system of ritual which he regarded as a fungoid growth, he maintained that once stripped of such excesses, Jewish law could enable individuals to resist the corrupting influence of paganism. The Jewish mission, he believed, was destined to spread Judaism's ideas among the nations: sanctity of life, justice for the poor, and sexual self-control. Above all, Jewry must survive because of its role as defender of monotheism among the nations of the earth.

References/Graetz's major writings

Heinrich Graetz, *History of the Jews*, Philadelphia, 1967
Heinrich Graetz, *The Structure of Jewish History and Other Essays*, New York, 1975

M. Meyer (ed.), *Ideas of Jewish History*, New York, 1974

See also in this book

Geiger, S.R. Hirsch, Steinheim

Further reading

S. Avineri, *The Making of Modern Zionism*, New York, 1981
S. Baron, *History and Jewish Historians*, Philadelphia, 1964

HASDAI CRESCAS

Born in 1340, Hasdai Crescas was a Spanish theologian and statesman from Barcelona, where he was a merchant and communal leader. In 1367 he was imprisoned along with his teacher, Nissim Gerondi, and Isaac ben Sheshet for desecrating the Host but was later released. In 1370 he participated in a competition with the Hebrew poets of Barcelona and Gerona. Subsequently he served as a delegate of the Catalonian Jewish community who sought for a renewal and extension of Jewish privileges with the King of Aragon. In 1387 with the accession of King John I, Crescas became associated with the court of Aragon and was accorded the title of *familiaris, de casa del senyor rey* (member of the royal household). In this same year he was empowered by royal decree to exercise judicial powers to issue an edict of excommunication in accordance with Jewish law.

Subsequently Crescas moved to Saragossa where he served as a rabbi in the place of Isaac ben Sheshet who had settled in Valencia. In 1390 John I allowed Crescas to prosecute informers against Jews and enact punishments on them. Later the queen appointed Crescas as judge of all cases dealing with informers in the Jewish communities throughout the kingdom of Aragon. During this period one of Crescas' sons died in Barcelona in the anti-Jewish riots of 1391. In Saragossa, which was the seat of the royal court, Crescas himself was safe from such attack, and he collected funds from the Aragon Jewish community to pay for their protection. In a letter of this period, he described the nature of such massacres of the Jewish community. In 1393 Crescas together with two representatives of the Saragossa and Calatayud communities was authorized by the crown to choose Jews from the communities of the kingdom to resettle in Barcelona and Valencia; in addition he was given authority to raise contributions for the reconstruction of the Jewish quarters in these cities. In 1401 Crescas spent several weeks in Pamplona, possibly to discuss with King Charles III problems regarding the Jewish population.

Given such a busy existence right up to his death in 1412, Crescas had little time to engage in Jewish scholarship. Nonetheless as part of his quest to combat Christian propagandizing literature, he wrote his 'Refutation of the Principles of the Christians' in the Catalan language in 1397–8. In addition, he composed another Catalan work opposing Christianity and he influenced Profiat Duran to write his polemic against the Christian faith. His own refutation consists of a critique of the central tenets of Christianity: original sin, redemption, the Trinity, the incarnation, the virgin birth, transubstantiation, baptism, Jesus' messiahship, the New Testament and demonology. Crescas' most important literary work is the *Or Adonai* (Light of the Lord), an anti-Aristotelian tract.

In this work Crescas attempts to refute Aristotelianism by criticizing a number of doctrines found in the writings of Aristotle and Maimonides. In opposition to these thinkers Crescas argues that there is an infinite void outside the universe – hence there may be many worlds. By positing the existence of the infinite, Crescas also calls into question the Aristotelian concept of an unmoved mover which was based upon the impossiblity of a regression to infinity. Similarly, Crescas argues that Maimonides'

proofs of the existence, unity and incorporeality of God are invalid because they are based on the concept of finitude. In addition, Crescas disagrees with Maimonides' opinion that no positive attributes can be applied to God. According to Crescas we cannot avoid making a comparison with human beings when we apply the terms 'cause' and 'attribute of action' to God. Maimonides was simply mistaken in thinking that such ascriptions do not imply a relationship between God and humans.

Regarding divine providence, Crescas holds that God acts either directly or through intermediate agents such as angels and prophets. Providence itself is essentially of two types: general providence which governs the order of nature, and special providence which is concerned with the Jewish nation as well as the lives of individuals. In this respect Crescas rejects the intellectualism of Jewish philosophers such as Maimonides. Intellectual perfection, he insists, is not the criterion of divine providence nor the basis for reward and punishment. In his discussion of prophecy, Crescas also adopts an anti-intellectual position. Unlike Maimonides, Crescas accepts the traditional understanding of the prophet as a person chosen by God because of his moral virtues rather than intellectual attainment. In advocating such views, Crescas was anxious to present a rational defence of the Jewish faith on non-Aristotelian grounds. Throughout his treatment of the central beliefs of the Jewish tradition, Crescas presents a view of Judaism based on the spiritual and emotional sides of man's nature rather than his intellectual and speculative capacities. In this respect he shares the same view as Judah Halevi who was equally critical of a rational presentation of the faith.

Another feature of Crescas' theology concerns the fundamental principles of the Jewish faith. In the *Commentary on the Mishnah*, Maimonides outlines what he believes to be the thirteen central principles of Judaism:

1 belief in the existence of God;
2 belief in God's unity;
3 belief in God's incorporeality;
4 belief in God's eternity;
5 belief that God alone is to be worshipped;
6 belief in prophecy;
7 belief in Moses as the greatest of the prophets;
8 belief that the Torah was given by God to Moses;
9 belief that the Torah is immutable;
10 belief that God knows the thoughts and deeds of human beings;
11 belief that God rewards and punishes;
12 belief in the advent of the Messiah;
13 belief in the resurrection of the dead.

In Maimonides' view, it is necessary for every Jew to accept these beliefs; otherwise he is a transgressor in Israel:

> When ... a man breaks away from any of these fundamental principles of belief, then of him it is said that 'he has gone out of the general body of Israel', and 'he denies the root truth of Judaism'. And he is then termed 'heretic' and 'unbeliever'. (in Jacobs, 1988, 15)

Critical of this formulation, Crescas proposed an alternative system in *Or Adonai*. According to Crescas, the central belief of Judaism – that God exists, is One and incorporeal – is in a separate category from other beliefs. In addition to this fundamental principle of Judaism there are three categories of beliefs, namely

1 Fundamentals without which the Jewish religion is unimaginable:
  1 God's knowledge of his creatures;
  2 God's providence;
  3 God's power;
  4 prophecy;
  5 human freewill; and
  6 the belief that the Torah leads to man's true hope and ultimate bliss.
2 True opinions independent of precept and belief:
  1 creation;

  2 the immortality of the soul;
  3 reward and punishment;
  4 resurrection;
  5 the immutability of the Torah;
  6 Moses' God-given authority;
  7 the belief that the High Priest had the oracle of Urim and Thummim; and
  8 the Messiah.
3 True opinions dependent on precept and belief:
  1 beliefs implied in prayer and the blessings of the priests;
  2 beliefs implied in repentance; and
  3 beliefs implied in *Yom Kippur* (the Day of Atonement) and other Jewish festivals.

In Crescas' view, anyone who denies any of the fundamental beliefs or any of the true opinions is an unbeliever, yet the only difference between these two categories is that the Jewish faith is inconceivable without the fundamental beliefs whereas it is imaginable with the true opinions. These two categories are further supplemented by probablities; these are opinions which are based on Jewish teaching which Crescas deduces as being valid. Yet, because these conclusions are neither obvious nor simple, they are not mandatory for Jewish believers. Many of these probabilities are expressed as questions:

1 Is the world eternal?
2 Are there many worlds?
3 Are the spheres living creatures?
4 Have the stars an influence over human destiny?
5 Is there any efficacy to charms and amulets?
6 Do demons exist?
7 Is the doctrine of metempsychosis true?
8 Is the soul of an infant immortal?
9 Paradise and Hell.
10 Are the mystical doctrines of *Maaseh Bereshit* (work of creation), and *Maaseh Merkavah* (work of the heavenly chariot) to be identified with physics and metaphysics?

11 The nature of comprehension.
12 The First Cause.
13 Can the true nature of God be understood?

All of these topics are discussed in traditional Jewish sources, but Crescas is aware that they remain open questions; thus, one who does not accept the views of the sages as expressed in rabbinic literature is not to be regarded as an unbeliever.

After the time of Crescas the philosophical approach to religion lost its appeal for most Jewish thinkers in Spain. Though some writers were still attracted to the Maimonidean system, Aristotelianism ceased to be the dominant philosophy in the Jewish world. Instead of philosophizing about Judaism, a number of subsequent Jewish writers directed their attention to defining the basic doctrines of the Jewish faith. Such Spanish thinkers as Simeon ben Zemah Duran, Joseph Albo, and Isaac Arama devoted their writings to critiques of Maimonides' formulation of the thirteen principles of the Jewish religion.

References

L. Jacobs, *Principles of the Jewish Faith*, Northvale, NJ, 1988

Crescas' major writings

H. Crescas, 'The Light of God' in H. Wolfson, *Crescas' Critique of Aristotle*, Cambridge, 1929

See also in this book

Albo, Judah Halevi, Maimonides

Further reading

S. Feldman, 'A Debate Concerning Determinism in Late Medieval Jewish Philosophy, *Proceedings of the American Academy of Jewish Research* 51, 1984
M. Nehorai, 'Crescas Polemics with Gersonides', *Bar-Ilan* 22/23, 1988
S. Pines, *Scholasticism after Thomas Aquinas and the Teachings of Hasdai Crescas and his Predecessors*, Jerusalem, 1967
C. Toutai, 'La Providence divine chez Hasday Crescas', *Daat* 10, 1983
H.A. Wolfson, *Crescas' Critique of Aristotle*, Cambridge, 1929
H.A. Wolfson, 'Crescas on the Problem of Divine Attributes' in H.A. Wolfson (ed.), *Studies in the History of Philosophy and Religion*, vol. II, Cambridge, 1977

THEODOR HERZL

Born in Budapest in 1860, Theodor Herzl as a child used to attend the Liberal Temple with his father. Although he may have been aware of Zionist ideas in his youth, his mother sought to educate him in the spirit of the Jewish Enlightenment. In 1866 Herzl enrolled at the Jewish elementary school in Pest; subsequently he attended the municipal *Realschule*, and in 1878 graduated from the classical evangelical high school. After the death of his sister, the family moved to Vienna where Herzl began legal studies at the university. In 1881 he joined a German student's society, but left in 1883 in protest against anti-Semitic attitudes expressed by some of its members. In 1884 he received a doctorate in law and worked in the law courts in Vienna and Salzburg. Soon, however, he decided to devote himself to writing, and in 1885 he published a series of *feuilletons* and philosophical stories. During this period he also wrote plays which appeared on the Austrian and German stage, and travelled extensively throughout Europe. In 1881 he married, becoming the father of three children.

From 1891 to 1895 Herzl served as the Paris correspondent of the *Vienna Neue Freie Presse* and witnessed the Dreyfus Affair. Convinced that the Jewish problem could only be solved by the creation of a homeland for the Jewish people, he requested an interview with Baron Maurice de Hirsch to consider this project. When Herzl failed to persuade the baron of the urgency of this plan, he wrote a sixty-five page proposal explaining his views which he sent to the Rothschilds – this work was an outline of *The Jewish State* which appeared in February 1896. This work was followed by a utopian study, *Alteneuland* (Old–New Land), published in 1902. Herzl's discussion of modern Jewish life was not original; many of his ideas were preceded in the works of early Zionist thinkers such as Moses Hess and Leon Pinsker. Yet what was novel about Herzl's advocacy of a Jewish state was his success in stimulating interest and debate in the highest diplomatic and political circles.

Convinced of the importance of his scheme, Herzl pointed out that the creation of a Jewish homeland would transform Jewish existence. The first entry in his diary of 1895 reflects the intensity of his convictions:

> I have been occupied for some time past with a work which is of immeasurable greatness. I cannot tell today whether I shall bring it to a close. It has the appearance of a gigantic dream . . . . What it will lead to, it is impossible to surmise as yet. But my experience tells me that it is something marvellous even as a dream, and that I should write it down – if not as a memorial for mankind, then for my own delight or meditation in later years. And perhaps for something between these possibilities: for the enrichment of literature. If the romance does not become a fact, at least the fact can become a romance. Title: The Promised Land! (in Hertzberg, 1969, 204)

In the preface to *The Jewish State*, Herzl argues that his campaign to find a Jewish homeland is not simply a utopian theory; rather, this enterprise is a realistic proposal arising out of the terrible conditions of Jewish oppression and persecution. The programme, he contends, would be impractical if only a single individual were to undertake it. But if many Jews agreed about its significance, then its implementation would be entirely plausible. Like Pinsker, Herzl believes that the Jewish question can be solved only if Jewry reconstitutes itself as a single people:

> We have sincerely tried everywhere to merge with the national communities in which we live, seeking only to preserve the faith of our fathers. It is not permitted us. In vain are we loyal patriots, sometimes superloyal; in vain do we make the same sacrifices of life and property as our fellow citizens; in vain do we strive to enhance the fame of our native lands in the arts and sciences, or her wealth by trade and commerce. In our native lands where we have lived for centuries we are still decried as aliens . . . . The majority decide who the 'alien' is; this, and all else in the relations between peoples, is a matter of power. (Ibid., 209)

Old prejudices against the Jewish nation are ingrained in Western society – assimilation will not provide a cure of the ills that beset the Jewish population. There is only one remedy for the sickness of anti-Semitism: the creation of a Jewish commonwealth. In *The Jewish State*, Herzl sketches the nature of such a political and social entity. The project, he contends, should be carried out by two bodies: the Society of Jews and the Jewish Company. The scientific programme and political policies should be put into practice by the Jewish Company. This body would be the liquidating agent for the business interests of Jews who emigrate, and would organize trade and commerce in the new country of settlement. Given this framework, the immigration of Jews would proceed gradually. Initially the poorest would settle in the Jewish state; they would construct roads, bridges, railways and telegraph installations. In addition, they would regulate rivers and provide themselves with homesteads. Through such labour, trade would be created, and in its wake markets would be established. Such economic activity would attract new settlers, resulting in an increase in population.

Those individuals who agree with the creation of a Jewish state should support the Society of Jews and encourage its endeavours. In this way they would provide it with authority in the eyes of other nations, and eventually ensure that the state would be recognized through international law. If other countries were willing to grant Jews sovereignty over their own land, then the Society would be able to enter into negotiations to acquire it. In response to the question where such a Jewish homeland should be located, Herzl proposed two options: Palestine or Argentina. Argentina, Herzl points out, is one of the most fertile countries in the world, extending over a vast area with a small population. On the other hand, Palestine is the Jews' historic homeland. If the sultan could be persuaded to allow the Jews to have this land, the Jewish community could in return undertake the complete management of the finances of Turkey. In this way the Jewish people could form part of a wall of defence for Europe and Asia, and the holy places of Christianity could be placed under some type of international extraterritoriality. Both of these proposals have certain advantages, and Herzl maintains that the Society should accept whatever it is given and whatever the Jewish community as a whole favours.

In the conclusion of this work, Herzl passionately expresses the longing of the entire nation for the establishment of a refuge from centuries of persecution:

What glory awaits the selfless fighters for the cause! Therefore I believe that a wondrous breed of Jews will spring up from the earth. The Maccabees will rise again. Let me repeat once more my opening words: The Jews who will it shall achieve their state. We shall live at last as free men on our own soil, and in our own homes peacefully die. The world will be liberated by our freedom, enriched by our wealth, magnified by our greatness. And whatever we attempt there for our own benefit will rebound mightily and beneficially to the good of all mankind. (Ibid., 225–6)

In his novel, *Alteneuland*, Herzl discusses the social and economic structure of such a Jewish state in Palestine. The foundations of the economy, he states, should be co-operative. Here he envisages the New Israel as realizing the vision of nineteenth-century European utopian socialism. Further, Herzl argues that universal suffrage as well as the full participation of women should be a crucial feature of such a society. In Herzl's view, schooling should be free and universal from kindergarten to university. Both men and women, he continues, should give two years' service to the community through such institutions as hospitals, infirmaries, orphanages, vacation camps and homes for the aged. Urban planning is also described in the novel: new towns are to be planned so as to eliminate urban sprawl. There would also be a system of mass transport and the creation of hydro-electric plants to provide cheap electricity. Herzl also suggests that the biblical principle of the jubilee year should be integrated into the landowning patterns of society.

These two works – one a plea for the building of a Jewish country, and the other a novelistic proposal for Jewish life in Palestine – strengthened the case for secular Zionism. In 1903 the British government offered Herzl a tract of land in Uganda; in the Zionist Congress of that year, Herzl pressed that this offer be accepted as a temporary solution. Although a resolution was passed to investigate this proposal, the Russian Zionist faction rebelled. Exhausted by his labours, Herzl died on 3 July 1904. Nearly fifty years later – on 17 August 1949 – his remains were flown on an aeroplane bearing the flag of the State of Israel which he had longed to create.

References

A. Hertzberg (ed.), *The Zionist Idea: A Historical Analysis and Reader*, New York, 1969

Herzl's major writings

Theodor Herzl, *A Jewish State* (trans. H. Zohn), New York, 1970
Theodor Herzl, *Zionist Writings*, New York, 1973–5

See also in this book

Hess, Pinsker

Further reading

J. Adler, *Herzl Paradox, Social and Economic Theories of a Realist*, New York, 1962
A. Bein, *Theodor Herzl*, Cleveland, OH, 1962
A. Chouraqui, *A Man Alone*, Jerusalem, 1970
J. De Haas, *Theodor Herzl*, New York, 1927
A. Elon, *Herzl*, New York, 1975
B. Halpern, *Idea of the Jewish State*, Cambridge, MA and London, 1961

ABRAHAM JOSHUA HESCHEL

Born in 1907, Abraham Joshua Heschel was descended on his father's side from Dov Baer of Mezhirich and Abraham Joshua Heschel of Apt, and from Levi Isaac of Berdichev on his mother's side. After studying Talmud and *kabbalah* (Jewish mysticism), he enrolled at the University of Berlin where he obtained a doctorate, and also taught at the *Hochschule für die Wissenschaft des Judentums*. In 1937 he was appointed Martin Buber's successor at the central organization for Jewish adult education and at the *Jüdisches Lehrhaus* at Frankfurt-am-Main. After being deported by the Nazis in 1938 to Poland, he taught at the Warsaw Institute of Jewish Studies. He then emigrated to England where he established the Institute for Jewish Learning in London. From 1940 he taught philosophy and rabbinics at the Hebrew Union College in Cincinnati, Ohio, but later transferred to the Jewish Theological Seminary of America where he became professor of Jewish ethics and mysticism. He died in 1972.

In a variety of writings, Heschel was concerned with faith and its antecedents: the experiences, insights, emotions, attitudes and acts out of which faith arises. According to Heschel, certain experiences and acts that are generally viewed as aspects of faith are also antecedents of faith. Wonder before the sublime mystery of nature, for example, is not in itself an aspect of the Jewish faith. Such wonder may occur prior to the emergence of faith – it can ignite the flame of religious fervour. Realities through which God is revealed – like nature and tradition – may be considered sources of faith even prior to the perception of God's presence, insofar as they occasion the perception of, and response to, God. Such wonder then can be understood as an antecedent of the Jewish faith. When faith in God emerges, what were the antecedents of faith become aspects of the life of faith.

Again, other expressions which Heschel claims give rise to faith, such as indebtedness, praise and *mitzvah* (commandment) might at first be considered aspects rather than antecedents of faith. Unlike wonder, which is a response to nature, indebtedness is a response to God. For Heschel, indebtedness is an antecedent of faith in that it prepares us to see the source of our ultimate indebtedness. After faith itself emerges, the sense of indebtedness continues. In this fashion what was an antecedent of faith becomes one of its central features. Regarding praise, Heschel asserts that the praise which precedes faith is a moment of responding to God; it is an experience of faith that precedes the loyalty of faith. In this respect praise is both an antecedent and an aspect of faith. But this does not imply that there is no form of prayer that might precede the initial act of faith. The prayer of empathy which attempts to feel the meaning of ritual words may be a prayer for the ability to praise and believe in God. Thus, by empathizing with the words, we can arrive at the kind of prayer that is a form of faith. Such prayers involve the remembrance of sacred events which can inspire faith. Once faith emerges, the ritual prayer continues to nourish the life of faith. In this sense, ritual prayer – like other *mitzvot* – functions as both the antecedent and aspect of faith. It is the beginning of faith that leads to religious fidelity.

Utilizing this framework, Heschel argues that the basic intuition of reality occurs on what he calls a 'preconceptual level'. The great achievements of human civilization take place in moments when the individual senses more than he is able to express. For modern man, the quest to capture a personal awareness of the Divine is difficult; yet Heschel states that it is possible:

> Wonder goes beyond knowledge. We do not doubt that we doubt, but we are amazed at our ability to wonder .... We are amazed not only at particular values and things, but at the unexpectedness of being as such, at the fact that there is being at all. (Heschel, 1956, 12)

In Heschel's opinion, the individual confronts the ineffable – that which cannot be expressed in human language. The ineffable, he insists, is not a psychological state, but an encounter with mystery. The Divine is within, since the self is transcendent. Further, the Divine is beyond, because it is

> a message that discloses unity where we see diversity, that discloses peace where we are involved in discord .... God means: No one is ever alone; the essence of the temporal is the eternal; the moment is an image of eternity in an infinite mosaic. God means: Togetherness of all beings in holy otherness. (Heschel, 1951, 109)

Here Heschel is espousing a form of panentheism in which God is perceived as including and permeating the universe.

Another experience that awakes the individual to God's presence is a pervasive anxiety that he refers to as 'the need to be needed'. For Heschel, religion entails the certitude that something is demanded of human beings. When persons feel the chal-lenge of a power which is not the product of their will, that deprives them of self-sufficiency – then God's concern for his creatures is understood:

> Unless history is a vagary of nonsense, there must be a counterpart to the immense power of man to destroy, there must be a voice that says NO to man, a voice not vague, faint, and inward, like qualms of conscience, but equal in spiritual might to man's power to destroy. (Heschel, 1959, 75)

Heschel stresses that it is the Hebrew Scriptures that offer a primary model for the authentic spiritual life. In his view, biblical revelation is not a mystical act, but an awareness of being confronted by God. The prophets bear witness to God's reaching out. It is not truths about God or norms and values that are being transmitted, but the divine pathos. Heschel argues that this consists of God's outraged resonse to human sinfulness as well as His response to suffering and anguish. Distancing himself from the Aristotelian concept of an 'Unmoved Mover', Heschel contends that through divine pathos, God is able to express His dynamic attentiveness to human beings. God, he maintains, is moved and affected by human action.

Alongside this conception of prophetic consciousness, Heschel adds a third way of apprehending God's presence. Through a life of holiness, the believer is able to gain an awareness of the Divine. This can be attained, he argues, by following the *halakhah* (Jewish law): a Jew is asked to take a leap of action rather than a leap of thought. He is asked to do more than he understands so as to understand more than he does. In Heschel's view, the concept of ceremony denotes what we think, whereas the term *mitzvah* expresses what God wills. In his view, a Jew is required to adhere to law which is obtainable solely through reason. The commandments are disclosed to us from on high as points of eternity in the flux of temporality. Hence Jewish law expresses how human beings are divinely ordained to act. Here both intention and action are crucial – it is not enough simply to carry out the law in a mechanistic fashion.

According to Heschel, Jewish survival is a spiritual act. God's preoccupation with His chosen people is expressed through the notion of the covenant which binds God and the Jewish people together. In this context, chosenness means responsibility, rather than indicating the superiority of the Jewish nation. The significance of the term 'chosen people' is genuine in relation to Jewry; it signifies, not a quality inherent in the community, but a relationship between Jews and God. It is a 'kinship with ultimate reality', requiring self-transcendence of both the community and the individual: 'There is a price to be paid by the Jew. He has to be exalted in order to be normal. In order to be a man, he has to be more than a man. To be a people, the Jews have to be more than a people' (Heschel, 1966, 64).

Hence, unlike other Jewish theologians of the modern age, Heschel emphasizes the limitations of human reason in grasping the nature of Ultimate Reality. His writings are devotional and mystical, emphasizing the dependence of humanity on God's will. Heschel himself described his approach as 'depth theology', an attempt to rediscover those questions for which religion is the answer. Critical of the liberal assumption that human beings are capable of perfecting themselves without an appeal to forces greater than themselves, Heschel sought to recover the biblical tradition as an inward dynamic process. In his writings, traditional Hasidic piety found a modern exponent.

References/Heschel's major writings

Abraham Heschel, *Man is Not Alone*, Philadelphia, 1951
Abraham Heschel, *God in Search of Man*, Philadelphia, 1956

Abraham Heschel, *Between God and Man: An Interpretation of Judaism*, New York, 1959
Abraham Heschel, *The Earth is the Lord's and The Sabbath*, New York, 1966

See also in this book

Buber, Dov Baer

Further reading

J.C. Merkle (ed.), *Abraham Joshua Heschel: Exploring His Life and Thought*, New York, 1985
F.A. Rothschild (ed.), *Between God and Man: An Interpretation of Judaism from the Writings of Abraham J. Heschel*, New York, 1951

MOSES HESS

With the writings of Moses Hess, modern secular Zionism began to take a hold on Jewish consciousness. Born in Bonn, Germany in 1812, he published his first work, *The Holy History of Mankind,* 'by a young Spinozist', in 1837. By 1840 Hess had moved to Paris where he was attracted to socialism. In 1842–3 he worked as the Paris correspondent of the *Rheinische Zeitung*, which was edited by Karl Marx. In 1862 he published his major work, *Rome and Jerusalem*, in which he encouraged fellow Jews to press for the creation of a Jewish homeland. In his work he explains that, after years of estrangement, he returned to the faith of his ancestors:

Once again I am sharing in its festivals of joy and days of sorrow, in its hopes and memories. I am taking part in the spiritual and intellectual struggles of our day, both within the house of Israel and between our people and the gentile world. The Jews have lived and laboured among the nations for almost two thousand years, but nonetheless they cannot become rooted organically within them. A sentiment which I believed I had suppressed beyond recall is alive once again. It is the thought of my nationality, which is inseparably connected with my ancestral heritage, with the Holy Land and the eternal city, the birthplace of the belief in the divine unity of life and of the hope for the ultimate brotherhood of all men. (in Hertzberg, 1969, 119)

According to Hess, anti-Jewish attitudes are unavoidable. Reform Jews believe they can escape from hostility by rejecting any form of national expression. Yet hatred of the Jewish nation is inescapable. No alteration of the faith is radical enough to avoid such antipathy; even conversion to Christianity cannot rid the Jew of this disability. 'Jewish noses', he writes, 'cannot be reformed, and the black, wavy hair of the Jews will not be changed into blond by conversion or straightened out by constant combing' (Ibid., 121). Jews will always remain aliens among the nations and nothing can be done to alter this state of affairs. The only solution to the Jewish problem is for Jews to come to terms with their national identity.

For Hess, the restoration of Jewish nationalism will not deprive humankind of the benefits championed by Jewish reformers, who desire to dissociate themselves from the particularistic aspects of the faith. On the contrary, the values of universalism will be extolled by various elements of Judaism's national character. Judaism, he maintains, is the source of the modern universalist view of life. Until the French Revolution, the Jewish people was the only nation whose religion was national and universalist. Hence it is through Judaism that the history of humankind can become sacred – this is a unified development that has its origin in the love of the family. This process can be completed only when members of the human race are bound together by the Holy Spirit.

This conception of history is based on the Jewish messianic vision of God's Kingdom on Earth. From the beginning of their history, the Jews have been bearers of the faith in the eschatological unfolding of history leading to messianic redemption. This conviction is symbolically conveyed by Sabbath celebrations:

The biblical story of the creation is told only for the sake of the Sabbath ideal. It tells us, in symbolic language, that when the creation of the world of nature was completed, with the calling into life of the highest organic being of the earth – man – the Creator celebrated his natural Sabbath, after the completion of the tasks of world history, by ushering in the messianic epoch. (Ibid., 131)

Biblical Sabbath observances therefore inspire Jews with a feeling of certainty that a divine law governs the world of nature and history. This belief, which is rooted in the spiritual life of the nation, points to a universal salvation of the world.

What is now required, Hess argues, is for Jewry to regenerate the Jewish nation and keep alive the hope for the political renaissance of the Jewish people. In support of this endeavour, Hess quotes from the work of the contemporary French writer, Ernst Laharanne, *The New Eastern Question*, which argues for the existence of a Jewish homeland:

No member of the Jewish race can renounce the incontestable and fundamental right of his people to its ancestral land without thereby denying his past and his ancestors. Such an act is especially unseemly at a time when political conditions in Europe not only do not obstruct the restoration of a Jewish state but will rather facilitate its realization. What European power would today oppose the plan that the Jews, united through a Congress, should buy back their ancient fatherland? Who would object if the Jews flung a handful of gold to decrepit old Turkey and said to her: 'Give me back my home and use this money to consolidate the other parts of your tottering empire?'

... You will come to the land of your fathers decorated with the crown of age-long martyrdom, and there, finally, you will be completely healed from all your ills. Your capital will again bring the wide stretches of barren land under cultivation; your labour and industry will once more turn the ancient soil into fruitful valleys, reclaiming it from the encroaching sands of the desert, and the world will again pay its homage to the oldest of peoples. (Ibid., 133–4)

On the basis of such observations, Hess asserts that a Jewish renaissance is possible once national life reasserts itself in the Holy Land. In the past the creative energies of the Jewish nation deserted Israel when Jewry became ashamed of its national heritage. But the Holy Spirit, he contends, will again animate the Jewish population once the nation awakens to a new life. The only question which remains is how it might be possible to encourage the patriotic senti-ments of modern Jewry as well as liberate the Jewish masses by means of this restored national loyalty. This is a serious challenge, yet Hess contends that it must be met. Although Hess acknowledges that there could not be a total emigration of world Jewry to Palestine because of the size of the Jewish nation, he stresses that the existence of a Jewish state will function as a spiritual centre for the Jewish people and all humanity. It is, he writes, the duty of all of us to carry 'the yoke of the Kingdom of Heaven' until the very end. Hess himself died in 1875.

References

Arthur Hertzberg, *The Zionist Idea: A Historical Analysis and Reader*, New York, 1969

Hess's major writings

Moses Hess, *Rome and Jerusalem* (trans. M. Waxman), New York, 1943

Further reading

I. Berlin, *Life and Opinions of Moses Hess*, Cambridge, 1959
I. Cohen, *Moses Hess, Rebel and Prophet*, New York, 1951
M. Schulman, *Moses Hess, Prophet of Zionism*, New York and London, 1963
E. Silberner, *Moses Hess: An Annotated Bibliography*, New York, 1951
J. Weiss, *Moses Hess, Utopian Socialist*, Detroit, MI, 1960

SAMSON RAPHAEL HIRSCH

Born in Hamburg in 1808, Samson Raphael Hirsch studied Talmud with his grandfather Mendel Frankfurter; subsequently his educa-tion was influenced by Rabbi Jacob Ettlinger and Isaac Bernays as well as his father. Athough Hirsch's father was an opponent of Reform Judaism, he endorsed Bernays' encouragement of secular studies in the local *talmud torah* (Jewish school). Later Hirsch attended the University of Bonn where he pursued classical languages, history and philosophy; there he befriended Abraham Geiger and together they organized a society of Jewish students.

In 1830 Hirsch became *Landrabbiner* of Oldenburg where during his eleven years of office he wrote *Nineteen Letters on Judaism* as well as a collection of essays called *Horeb – Essays on Israel's Duties in the Diaspora*. These two works were designed to encourage young Jewish men and women to remain faithful to the tradition. In 1841 Hirsch moved to Emden where he served as a rabbi of Aurich and Osnabrück in Hanover. Five years later he moved to Nikolsburg (now Mikulov in the Czech Republic) where he became *Landrabbiner* of Moravia. Here Hirsch participated in the struggle to obtain emancipation for Austrian and Moravian Jews during the revolution of 1848 – in that year he was elected chairman of the Committee for the Civil and Political Rights of the Jews in Moravia.

In Nikolsburg Hirsch was active in reorganizing the internal structure of Moravian Jewry, drafting a constitution for the central religious authority of the country. Despite such involvement in Jewish affairs, the extreme wing of Orthodox Jewry was critical of his liberal attitudes as well as some of his practices, such as wearing a robe during services. In 1851 he became rabbi of the Orthodox congregation *Adass Jeschurun* in Frankfurt-am-Main where he officiated until his death in 1888. Here Hirsch attracted a circle of loyal friends who shared his views.

In the *Nineteen Letters on Judaism*, Hirsch provided a defence of traditional Judaism in the form of essays allegedly written by a young rabbi to a Jewish friend who questions the importance of remaining a Jew. At the beginning of this work, the friend offers a variety of criticisms of the faith: 'While the rest of mankind climbed to the summit of culture, prosperity and wealth, the Jewish people remained poor in everything that makes human beings great and noble, and that beautifies and dignifies our lives' (Hirsch, 1960, 24). Furthermore, he argues, Judaism restricts the attainment of both happiness and perfection, separates Jews from their neighbours, evokes suspicion and contempt, and through the teaching of *halakhah* fills the mind with trivial and confusing information.

In response, the young rabbi asks whether happiness and perfection constitute the goal of human life. Before it is possible to answer this question, he argues, it is necessary to see what the Torah teaches about the meaning of life. As Hirsch explains, the Torah declares that everything was created for a divine purpose and that everything is united in love. Only human beings, he continues, have the duty to serve God through free choice; this means that at times it is necessary to learn how to obey God's decree. According to the biblical narrative, initially human beings engaged in idolatrous practices, believing that nature is controlled by many gods; further, they envisaged pleasure and wealth as ends in themselves rather than means to something higher.

Given such iniquity and ignorance, it became necessary to form a single people who would be able to demonstrate that true happiness is found only by serving the Creator who made all things:

> This mission required for its execution a nation, poor in everything upon which the rest of mankind reared the edifice of its greatness and power, externally subordinate to the nations armed with proud self-sufficiency, but fortified inwardly by direct reliance upon God, so that, by the suppression of every enemy force, God might reveal Himself directly as the sole Creator, Judge, and Master of nature and history. (Ibid., 54)

According to Hirsch, the ancient Israelites received the land of Canaan so that they could carry out the precepts of the Covenant. Subsequently, Israel went into exile so that it would be able to become the bearer of divine truth to all the nations of the world by remaining faithful to God's decrees. As God's suffering servant, Israel has been able teach universal love despite centuries of persecution and oppression.

In propounding this conception of the role of the Jewish people through history, Hirsch outlines the various categories of Israel's duties to God. In his view, there are six types of commandments:

1 commandments that convey truths about God, the world and Israel's mission;
2 laws dealing with social justice;
3 duties dealing with justice toward both the animate and inanimate world;
4 commandments to love all living things;
5 festivals and ceremonies that teach fundamental truths; and
6 laws related to worship.

For Hirsch the Jewish legal code is designed to subordinate the desire for pleasure and happiness to the quest to live a spiritual life. In his view, any economic disadvantages that result from not working on the Sabbath and holy days, as well as from restricting contact with Christians, are of little consequence in comparison with the messianic ideal of the unity of all humankind.

Drawing on secular notions, Hirsch argues that just as science posits theories to explain natural events, the true science of Judaism must envisage revealed law as the given. The Torah is an organic unity whose meaning is disclosed through its inner principles. In presenting his interpretation of the tradition, Hirsch rejects the modernizing tendencies of Reform Judaism: in his view, the most serious error of Reform is its desire to alter the Code of Jewish Law. What is required instead is the reform of Jews, rather than Judaism.

Regarding emancipation, Hirsch welcomes the improvement of Jewish life, yet he maintains that it would be a mistake to regard such changed circumstances as a primary goal. In Hirsch's view, the changes to Judaism required by the granting of full citizenship rights are peripheral; Jews are united only by a spiritual duty to observe God's commandments. This condition will apply until the time when God will bring about the reunification of world Jewry in the Holy Land – this is the messianic goal as foreseen by seers of old, and it would be a usurpation of God's rule to attempt to hasten such deliverance. But as long as Jewry continues to remain faithful to the covenant, it is permissible to engage in secular affairs.

Such a traditionalist stance was based on a fundamentalistic understanding of Scripture. For Hirsch the Torah was revealed by God to Moses on Mount Sinai, an event witnessed by over two million people. Hence the Five Books of Moses are authoritative and its precepts are eternally binding on the Jewish nation:

The whole question is simply this. Is the statement 'And God spoke to Moses saying', with which all the laws of the Jewish Bible commence, true or not true? Do we really and truly believe that God,

the Omnipotent and Holy, spoke thus to Moses? Do we speak the truth when in front of our brethren we lay our hand on the scroll containing these words and say that God has given us this Torah, that His Torah, the Torah of truth and with it of eternal life, is planted in our midst. If this is to be no more than lip-service, no mere rhetorical flourish, then we must keep and carry out this Torah without omission and and without carping, in all circumstances and at all times. (Ibid., 65)

The Torah therefore is outside time: it is unchanging and inerrant, serving as the blueprint for Jewish living despite the altered political circumstances of Jewry in the modern world.

Thus, for Hirsch, it is possible to integrate Judaism into modern life as long as the community remains loyal to the Torah. Such a Neo-Orthodox perspective, however, did not gain favour with those individuals who sought to assimilate into Western European society. These proponents of Jewish acculturation aspired to a greater degree of integration than was permitted by Hirsch's traditionalism. Yet Hirsch's concept of *Torah im derekh eretz* (Torah with a practical livelihood) has gained widespread acceptance in subsequent years, becoming the credo of modern Orthodoxy. Such an ideology provides a basis for harmonizing the beliefs and practices of the tradition with contemporary culture and secular life.

References/S.R. Hirch's major writings

Samson Raphael Hirsch, *The Nineteen Letters of Judaism*, New York, 1960
Samson Raphael Hirsch, *Horeb: A Philosophy of Jewish Laws and Observances* (vols. 1–2), London, 1962

Further reading

M. Breuer, *The 'Torah-im-derekh-eretz' of Samson Raphael Hirsch*, Jerusalem, 1970

I. Grunfeld, *Three Generations: The Influence of S.R. Hirsch on Jewish Life and Thought*, London, 1958
J. Rosenheim, *Samson Raphael Hirsch's Cultural Ideal and Our Times*, London, 1951

SAMUEL HIRSCH

Born in Thalfang, Prussia, in 1815, Samuel Hirsch served as a rabbi in Dessau from 1839 to 1841, becoming chief rabbi of Luxemburg from 1843 to 1866. During this whole period he opposed attempts by various lay Reform groups to introduce radical reforms to the Jewish tradition. As a leading participant at the Reform rabbinical conferences at Brunswick, Frankfurt and Breslau in 1844–6, he supported the rite of circumcision and the use of Hebrew in worship; nonetheless, he was the first rabbi to support the idea of transferring the Sabbath to Sunday. In the latter part of his life he served as the rabbi of *Keneset Israel* in Philadelphia. As a leading Reform rabbi in the United States, he became the president of the first Conference of American Reform Rabbis which took place in Philadelphia in 1869. Subsequently he played a central role in formulating the Pittsburgh Platform of the movement in 1885. He died in 1889.

In his major work, *Die Religions Philosophie der Juden* (The Religious Philosophy of Judaism) Hirsch views Judaism as an evolving religious system. In the spirit of contemporary speculative idealism Hirsch argues that human beings come to perceive the freedom of the will by which they are capable of transcending the determinism of the natural world. Such freedom is given, implying a transcendent source which he refers to as God.

Influenced by Hegelianism, Hirsch maintains that individuals become aware of such freedom by seeing themselves as distinct persons over and against the world. Yet in one important respect Hirsch departs from Hegel's view. For Hegel, primary, abstract freedom leads to actual, concrete liberty when human beings realize that they are finite creatures rooted in nature but destined for reason. For Hegel this is the philosophical meaning of the awareness of sin: sin can be vanquished only when this dialectically necessary contradiction is resolved through rational self-determination. Hirsch, however, maintains that sin is a moral rather than intellectual state. In his view, sin is inherent in the capacity to choose between alternatives, and can only be overcome through moral action. Hence Hirsch concludes that the essential content of religion is not the self-realization of God, but the actualization of human moral freedom. As a divine gift, such liberty gives rise to the task of subordinating natural sensuality to ethical responsibility.

According to Hirsch, there are two fundamental types of religion: passive and active religion. In passive religion freedom is renounced and human beings are dominated by sensual desire; in such cases nature becomes an all-consuming force. Such paganism, Hirsch writes, is not even partially valid because, in the course of history, pagan consciousness will inevitably come to recognize its futility. In active religions, on the other hand, human beings are able to rise to the level of self-chosen liberty in realizing that this is God's desire. Judaism, Hirsch affirms, possessed the insight of active religion from the time of Abraham, Isaac and Jacob. Moreover, the miracles as well as prophecies in Scripture were historically necessary so as to eliminate a residue of paganism among the Jewish population. However, the need for miracles has now ceased – the only permanent miracle in the history of the nation is the survival of the Jewish people itself.

On the basis of this interpretation, Hirsch was critical of Hegel's contention that Judaism is only a passive tradition which has been superseded by the religious consciousness of Protestant Christianity. In the Jewish faith, he stresses, there is no evolution of religious truth; development consists solely in the ethical instruction of Jewry. The purpose of such teaching is to ensure that each Jew embodies intensive religiosity by choosing virtue rather than immorality. Further, the Jewish people has the task of drawing humanity closer to divine truth by acting as God's suffering servant. Christianity also has a role in the unfolding of God's plan for humanity: it is the task of the Church to bring true religious consciousness to pagans.

In explaining the nature of this mission, Hirsch discusses the gospel witness. Like other nineteenth-century scholars, he draws a distinction between Jesus as presented in the Synoptic Gospels, and the depiction of Christ found in the Fourth Gospel. Although Christians have favoured the abstract Christ as presented in the Gospel of John, Hirsch contends that modern Christianity should emphasize the historical Jesus as portrayed in the Gospels of Mark, Matthew and Luke. In this way, Jesus can be seen as a real flesh-and-blood figure rather than an abstract ideal. Such an historical personage, he believes, is of significance to both the Jewish nation and all humanity:

Every Jew, for that matter every man, should be what Jesus was: that was the summons of every prophet. Every Jew and every man will become so; that is the promise of the Messianic hope. (Hirsch, 1842, 728)

Hirsch believes Jesus' major contribution to have been the renewal of the prophetic voice: at the time of Jesus' appearance, Judaism had forgotten the source of its truth – the voices of living prophets had faded away. Jesus therefore directed his message to fellow Jews because he wished to make the goal of all Israel meaningful for each person. Instead of intending to create a new religion, he sought to realize the total content of the old.

The evolution of Christianity into a new religion did not take place through Jesus' influence. Rather, Hirsch insists that Jesus stood firmly within the Jewish tradition:

All that he taught, as he himself admitted, had already been given by Moses and the prophets. He did not die for an idea; nor did he leave his disciples a legacy independent of his person. The unusual attainment of Jesus lay in something that was far more than an idea, it lay in his personality. He understood, realized, and fulfilled the idea of Judaism in its deepest truth – that was the greatness of Jesus. (Ibid., 688)

Instead, it was John and Paul who brought about this alteration of the faith.

For Hirsch the Gospel of John transformed Jesus into an abstraction as opposed to an historical figure; moreover, the Fourth Gospel ignores his Jewish background. But it is in Paul's epistles that the Church found its roots. In the first eleven chapters of the Epistle to the Romans, Paul expounds ideals that were to become the foundation of the Church: eventually such beliefs as original sin, divine grace and the divinity of Jesus came to separate the two faiths and were responsible for Christianity's polemical stance against the Jewish tradition. In explaining Paul's influence, Hirsch emphasizes that Paul had failed to comprehend the true nature of Judaism since he was attacking something he did not understand. His erroneous evaluation of the law and other Jewish doctrines was based on a misapprehension of the Jewish heritage:

Paul carried on a sharp and violent polemic against Judaism . . . unfortunately the Judaism he attacked was and is only the Judaism of Paul and his followers; it is not the Judaism of the Jews. (Ibid., 726)

According to Hirsch, Paul's distorted views paved the way for the development of later Christian doctrine.

Although Hirsch found little of worth in Pauline Christianity, he believes that the Christian faith has played a dominant role in history by bringing ethical monotheism to the pagan world. As he writes in *Die Humanität als Religion*:

The heathens shall arrive at these thoughts, and for this reason the Pauline form of Christianity was a necessity.... Therefore, the two supporting pillars (Original Sin and divine Grace) were necessary in order to bring the consciousness of the truth to the pagan world; that is the mission of the Catholic Church. (Hirsch, 1854, 243)

When paganism has been conquered, he continues, a religion of tolerance and love will be created: this, he believes, will be a purified form of Judaism as represented by Jesus himself. In this messianic project, Christianity has an instrumental role, but for Hirsch Judaism is the only possible hope for the religious future of humanity.

References/Samuel Hirsch's major writings

Samuel Hirsch, *Die Religions Philosophie der Juden*, Leipzig, 1842
Samuel Hirsch, *Die Humanität als Religion*, Trier, 1854

Further reading

M. Kaplan, *Greater Judaism in the Making*, New York, 1960
D. Philipson, *The Reform Movement in Judaism*, New York, 1967
N. Rotenstreich, *Jewish Philosophy in Modern Times*, New York, 1968

VLADIMIR JABOTINSKY

Among the major figures of modern secular Zionism, Vladimir Jabotinsky was one of the most controversial; his writings and political activity inspired a wide circle of followers as well as opponents. Born in Odessa in 1880 to a middle-class family, he was educated in Russian schools. Before his bar mitzvah he took Hebrew lessons but, according to Jabotinsky's own account, he had little contact with the Jewish tradition. In 1898 he went to Berne and Rome, where he studied law and served as a foreign correspondent of two Odessa dailies. Initially he embraced socialist ideals, although he rejected Marxism as a political philosophy; later, however, he radically revised his attitude toward socialism.

Returning to Odessa, Jabotinsky joined the editorial staff of *Odesskiya Novosti* in 1901. Two years later when a pogrom against the Jewish population appeared imminent he joined a Jewish self-defence unit. After the pogrom in Kishinev (then in Bessarabia, now in Moldova) the same year, he became increasingly involved in Zionist activities. As a delegate to the Sixth Zionist Congress, he was deeply impressed by Theodor Herzl, but nonetheless voted against Herzl's Uganda project. As a member of the editorial board of the Zionist journal *Razsvet*, he contributed to the development of Zionism in Russia, and was an advocate of the Helsingfors Programme of 'synthetic' Zionism which pressed for a Jewish settlement in the Holy Land alongside political and educational activity in the diaspora. In 1909 the World Zionist Organization appointed him editor of a series of publications in Constantinople and entrusted him with political activity in Ottoman circles, although a disagreement with David Wolffsohn – the president of the World Zionist Organization – led to his resignation.

After the outbreak of the First World War, Jabotinsky served as a correspondent for a liberal Moscow daily in northern and western Europe. Once Turkey joined on the side of Germany, he became convinced that the future of Jewish interests in Palestine rested with the allies. In opposition to the Zionist leadership which advocated neutrality, Jabotinsky persuaded the British government to form three Jewish battalions; however, after the war Jabotinsky became increasingly sceptical of British support of Jewish interests and during the riots of 1920 he organized a self-defence corps in

Jerusalem. He was subsequently imprisoned by the British military administration and sentenced to fifteen years' imprisonment for illegally possessing arms, but was eventually pardoned. In 1921 Jabotinsky was elected to the Zionist Executive, but was bitterly opposed to the views of Chaim Weizmann. In 1925 he organized the Revisionist Party; several years later this group left the Zionist movement and created the New Zionist Organization. Under Jabotinsky, illegal immigration to Palestine took place and the underground military organization, the Irgun, engaged in a struggle with the British.

In his autobiography, Jabotinsky notes that he first became interested in Zionism as a young man in Berne when he heard a lecture by Nachman Syrkin. At that gathering, he writes:

I spoke Russian, in the following vein: I do not know if I am a socialist, since I have not yet acquainted myself with this doctrine; but I have no doubt that I am a Zionist, because the Jewish people is a very nasty people, and its neighbours hate it, and they are right; its end in the diaspora will be a general Bartholomew Night, and the only rescue is general immigration to Palestine. (in Avineri, 1981, 162)

Later, in Italy, he was influenced by the national movement and became convinced that liberalism is irrelevant in modern society. In an essay written in 1910, 'Man is a Wolf to Man', he argues that it is an error to rely on liberal ideals to bring about political change:

It is a wise philosopher who said, 'Man is a wolf to man'; worse than the wolf is man to man, and this will not change for many days to come. Stupid is the person who believes in his neighbour, good and loving as the neighbour may be; stupid is the person who relies on justice. Justice exists only for those whose fists and stubbornness make it possible for them to realize it . . . . Do not believe anyone, be always on

guard, carry your stick always with you – this is the only way of surviving in this wolfish battle of all against all. (Ibid., 164)

Such beliefs were fundamental to Jabotinsky's insistence on Jewish self-defence and self-determination.

Jabotinsky's commitment to Jewish nationalism was expressed in a variety of articles dealing with national unity and discipline. In his view, the essential element of the nation consists in its racial characteristics. It is not land, religion or language that constitutes the substance of nationhood; instead its essential character is determined by its racial composition. In an essay 'On Race', he argues that 'a nation's substance, the alpha and omega of the uniqueness of its character – this is embodied in its specific physical quality, in the component of its racial composition' (Ibid., 167). In this regard Jabotinsky maintains that the Jews are a superior race. In a dialogue between an imaginary Russian and a Jew published in reaction to an anti-Semitic tract, the Jewish disputant declares:

But if we are going to make comparisons, everything depends on the criteria to be used, and then, you should know, I will insist on my own criterion: he who is steadfast in spirit – he is superior . . . . He who will never give up his internal independence, even when under a foreign yoke – he is superior . . . . We are [a] race that will never be harnessed.' (Ibid., 169)

For Jabotinsky the Jewish people as an emerging nation needs founders and builders who will be able to bring out its latent potential.

We need a generation ready for all kinds of adventures and experiences, a generation that can find its way in the most dense forest. We need young people who can ride horses and climb trees and swim in the water and use their fists and shoot a gun; we need a people with a healthy imagination and a strong will, striving to express themselves in the struggle for life. (Ibid., 170)

In addition, Jabotinsky asserts that it is vital that the Jewish populace is disciplined in its dedication to nationhood. In an article describing the organizational structure around which he built the youth movement of the Revisionists, Betar, he writes:

Betar is structured around the principle of discipline. Its aim is to turn Betar into such a world organism that would be able, at a command from the centre, to carry out at the same moment, through the scores of its limbs, the same action in every city and every state. The opponents of Betar maintain that this does not accord with the dignity of free men and it entails becoming a machine. [We are] not to be ashamed and to respond with pride: Yes, a machine. (Ibid., 172)

In his writings Jabotinsky encourages the reorganization of social and economic life along the lines of a corporate state. Alongside a Representative Assembly of Jews living in Palestine, he advocates the creation of a Trades' Parliament. Every person, he insists, should elect his representative to this Upper Chamber according to his corporation or guild:

One has to create in the Yishuv [the Jewish community in Palestine] the idea of professional corporations, corporations in which will be associated all those who take part in one of the branches of Jewish economic life in industry, commerce, agriculture, banking and finance, trade, transportation, professional occupations, clerking, etc . . .
After such an overall organization has materialized, each corporation will elect its representative to a new National Committee – this will be the Trades' Parliament. Its role will be, first of all, to control all economic life . . . secondly, this Trades Parliament will establish the Arbitration System from the top downwards, and this system will regulate all the relations between the various economic groups. (Ibid., 177)

Concerning the Arab population, Jabotinsky stresses that the Jewish people in returning to the Holy Land is not returning to oriental culture. Thus, in 'The Arabesque Fashion', he maintains that the Jews are a European people. The Muslims, however, are backward, and the Western powers have nothing to fear from the Arab nations if they support Zionist policies. In 1937 Jabotinsky gave evidence before the Royal Commission on Palestine, arguing for the creation of a Jewish state covering all of the original Palestine Mandate, including Transjordan. Aware that this would turn the Arabs into a minority in such a state, he alleges that this would not be detrimental to the Arab population:

I have also shown to you already that, in our submission, there is no question of ousting the Arabs. On the contrary, the idea is that Palestine on both sides of the Jordan should hold the Arabs, their progeny, and many millions of Jews. What I do not deny is that in the process the Arabs of Palestine will necessarily become a minority in the country of Palestine. What I do deny is that it is a hardship. It is not a hardship on any race, any nation, possessing so many national states now and so many more national states in the future. One fraction, one branch of that race, and not a big one, will have to live in someone else's state. Well, that is the case with all the mightiest nations of the world. (Ibid., 181)

Jabotinsky's legacy to modern Zionism was his acknowledgment of the importance of power in determining the fate of the Jewish people. According to Jabotinsky, it is not moral values but power which is of supreme importance in world affairs. In the subsequent history of the Jewish state, this principle has become a central element of Israel's defence policy. Yet Jabotinsky's unwillingness to recognize the national aspirations of the Arabs was a failure of insight – the bloody history of Arab–Jewish relations in the years following Jabotinsky's death in

1940 illustrates his lack of perception about Arab intentions in the Holy Land.

References

Shlomo Avineri, *The Making of Modern Zionism: The Intellectual Origins of the Jewish State*, New York, 1981

Jabotinsky's major writings

A. Hertzberg (ed.), *The Zionist Idea: A Historical Analysis and Reader*, New York, 1969

See also in this book

Herzl

Further reading

O.K. Rabinowicz, *Vladimir Jabotinsky's Conception of a Nation*, New York, 1946
J.B. Schechtman, *Vladimir Jabotinsky Story* (2 vols), New York, 1956–61

JUDAH HALEVI

Born in Tudela in *c.* 1075 Judah Halevi received an Arabic and Hebrew education. While a young man, he travelled to Granada where he won a poetry contest. During this period he came into contact with Moses ibn Ezra as well as other great poets of Granada, Seville and Saragossa. However, with the conquest of Andalusia by the Almoravides after 1090, he settled in Granada. During the next two decades he travelled from town to town in Christian Spain, eventually settling at Toledo and practising medicine there until his benefactor, Solomon ibn Ferrizuel, was murdered. On his return to Muslim Spain, he went to Cordoba, Granada and Almeria. In addition, he made a journey with Abraham ibn Ezra to North Africa. After deciding to go to the Holy Land, he travelled to Alexandria in 1140; four months later he sailed to Palestine where he died several weeks later, in 1141.

In addition to a variety of poetic works written in Hebrew, Halevi composed his best known work, the *Kuzari*. According to the author, this tract was written in order to combat the heretical views of the Jewish Karaite movement. The work itself describes the conversion to rabbinic Judaism of the King of the Khazars. Although a literary fiction, the *Kuzari* is based on historical fact – in the tenth century Hasdai ibn Shaprut engaged in correspondence with the King of the Khazars, who converted to the Jewish faith.

Book I of the *Kuzari* opens with an exposition of different ideologies: philosophical, Christian, Muslim and Jewish. Questioned by the king, the rabbi who represents the Jewish tradition states:

I believe in the God of Abraham, Isaac and Israel, who brought the children of Israel out of Egypt by means of signs and miracles, took care of them in the wilderness, and gave them the land of Canaan after crossing the sea and the Jordan by means of miracles. He sent Moses with his religious law by means of promises to whoever observed it and threats to whoever transgressed it. (Halevi, 1946, I, 11)

Here the rabbi proclaims his faith in the Creator who chose Israel as His special people who watches over their destiny. In response, the king argues that the rabbi believes in a national God because of the suffering of the Jewish people: owing to historical circumstances, he is unable to envisage the Deity as the Lord of all creation. Undeterred by this criticism, the rabbi points out that the God of Judaism is not the God of the philosophers, but the God of faith. In his view, the way of the prophets is superior to that of philosophical reflection; in making this observation, Halevi is implicitly critical of Aristotelian metaphysics, which he regards as misguided.

Continuing his presentation, the rabbi explains why he began his discourse by emphasizing God's role in the history of the

Jewish people. This is because God's existence and providential care of the Jewish nation is proven: it is authenticated by Israel and the Egyptians who witnessed His intervention in the life of the nation. The king then states that, if this is so, then Jewry has received an exclusive revelation from God. Agreeing with the king, the rabbi states that those who have converted to Judaism are not equal to born Jews in that they are incapable of receiving prophecy.

After discussing the pre-eminence of the prophets over ordinary humankind, the rabbi goes on to explain that all human beings accept a number of truths based on the insights of these gifted individuals. After a discussion of the concept of nature, the rabbi proceeds to explain how the Jewish people originated. Israel was not founded by a small community of like-minded individuals, but through God's intervention: God selected Moses to free the Israelites from bondage, and to forge them into a unified people. The miracles he performed on their behalf were crowned by the giving of the Law on Mount Sinai.

This historical narrative is interrupted by the king's observation that the nation was guilty of making a Golden Calf, and he asks: How can one maintain that the Jewish people is superior to others given such disobedience? In defence, the rabbi stresses that this idolatrous act was undertaken by only a small segment of the community. And he adds that those elders who had a hand in its creation acted so as to distinguish the rebellious from believers so that those who worshipped the calf would be eliminated.

Persuaded by the sage's arguments, the king is ready to convert to the Jewish faith. Yet, the rabbi proceeds to deal with two further questions: why did God choose only one people rather than all human beings? and are reward and punishment reserved for the soul after the death of the body? From this point the dialogue between the king and the rabbi becomes a vehicle for the rabbi to enunciate his views. As the rabbi explains,

God revealed Himself by choosing a people, land and language. These acts constitute the only real proof of His existence. Hierarchically structured, the order of the universe consists of the prophets, Adam and his sons, Noah, and the people of Israel – this is superimposed on the mineral, vegetative, animal and rational realms. Such a scheme follows the general pattern of Aristotlian teaching.

In Halevi's opinion, the progression from union with the Intellect to union with the prophetic faculty is not a gradual and natural process. While it is possible to ascend to the Intellect through the study of philosophy, to reach the level of the prophets, it is necessary to advance through the Torah. This path has been reserved for God's chosen people. Parallelling the selection of Israel is God's choice of the Holy Land as the place for prophecy to occur. In a similar vein, the Hebrew language occupies a central role in Halevi's thought:

Hebrew in its essence is more noble [than other languages] both traditionally and rationally. Traditionally, it is the language in which revelation was made to Adam and Eve and by means of it they spoke . . . . Its superiority [may be shown] rationally by considering the people who utilized it insofar as they needed it for addressing one another, especially for prophecy, which was widespread among them, and the need for preaching, songs, and praises. (Halevi, 1946, ii, 68))

Further, Halevi asserts that the divine commandments – expressed through God's revelation to Moses – can be perfectly observed only in Israel: it is the means God uses to ensure Israel's survival. Hence the king observes:

I have reflected about the situation and I have seen that God has a secret means of giving you permanence. Indeed, He has certainly made the sabbaths and the festivals become one of the strongest reasons for making permanent your esteem and splendour. The nations [of the world] would have divided you [among themselves], would have taken you as servants on account of your intelligence and your quickness, and they would certainly have made you soldiers also were it not for [the observance of these] times which you are so mindful of because they are from God. (Halevi, 1946, iii, 10)

The *Kuzari* ends with the Jewish sage's decision to leave the land of the Khazars in order to travel to Jerusalem. Such dedication to the Holy Land is reflected in Halevi's other works where he glorifies Zion. In one of his poems, he extols Jerusalem in the most glowing terms – these sentiments help to explain Halevi's own determination to go to *Eretz Israel* (the land of Israel) near the end of his life:

If only I could roam through those places where God was revealed to your prophets and heralds! Who will give me wings, so that I may wander far away? I would carry the pieces of my broken heart over the rugged mountains. I would bow down, my face on your ground; I would love your stones; your dust would move me to pity. I would weep, as I stood by my ancestors' graves, I would grieve, in Hebron, over the choicest of burial places! I would walk in your forests and meadows, stop in Gilead, marvel at Mount Abarim .... The air of your land is the very life of the soul, the grains of your dust are flowing myrrh, your rivers are honey from the comb. It would delight my heart to walk naked and barefoot among the desolate ruins where your shrines once stood; where your Ark was hidden away. (in Carmi, 1981, 348–9)

Such lyricism highlights the rhapsodic character of Halevi's spirituality. Unlike other thinkers of the medieval period, he rejects the philosophical approach of those thinkers who attempted to reconcile Greek patterns of thought with the Torah. In place of such speculation, he encourages his fellow Jews to rediscover the God of the patriarchs. It is through such dedication to the faith, he contends, that Jewry will be able to reclaim the past splendour of Jewish history and rekindle hope for the coming of the Messiah.

References

T. Carmi (ed.), *The Penguin Book of Hebrew Verse*, Harmondsworth, Middlesex, 1981
Judah Halevi, *Book of Kuzari* (trans. H. Hirschfeld), New York, 1946

Halevi's major writings

Judah Halevi, *Book of Kuzari* (trans. H. Hirschfeld), New York, 1946
I. Heinemann, *Three Jewish Philosophers*, New York, 1969

Further reading

H. Davidson, 'The Active Intellect in the Cuzari and Hallevi's Theory of Causality', *Revue des études juives* 131, 1972
A.L. Motzkin, 'On Halevi's Kazari as a Platonic Dialogue', *Interpretation* 9.1, 1980
S. Pines, 'Shi'ite Terms and Conceptions in Judah Halevi's Kuzari', *Jerusalem Studies in Arabic and Islam* 2, 1980
L. Strauss, 'The Law of Reason', *Proceedings of the American Academy of Jewish Research* 3, 1943
M. Winner, 'Judah Halevi's Concept of Religion and a Modern Counterpart', *Hebrew Union College Annual*, Cincinnati, OH 23, 1951

ZEVI HIRSCH KALISCHER

Within nineteenth-century Orthodoxy there emerged a new approach to Jewish messianism. Rather than adopting a passive attitude towards the coming of the Messiah, a number of thinkers argued that the Jewish community must create a homeland in anticipation of messianic redemption. Pre-eminent among such figures was Zevi Hirsch Kalischer; like his contemporary, Yehuda hai

Alkalai, he was a pioneer of religious Zionism.

Born in 1795 in Lissa, Posen district (now Leszno, Poland), Kalischer studied under Jacob of Lissa and Akiva Eger. Later he lived in Thorn (Toruń) where he served as an underpaid rabbi surviving on the small income from his wife's business. There he published books on Jewish law and religious philosophy and also contributed to the Hebrew press. His major concern, however, was to promote the idea of the creation of a Jewish presence in Palestine. In his view, the Torah prescribes faith in messianic redemption and dedication to the Holy Land. In 1836 he expressed his commitment to the creation of a Jewish settlement in the Holy Land in a letter to the head of the Berlin Rothschild family. 'The beginning of redemption', he writes, 'will come through natural causes by human effort and by the view of the governments to gather the scattered of Israel into the Holy Land' (in Hertzberg, 1969, 109–10).

Initially Kalischer believed that the observance of the *mitzvot* (commandments) connected with *Eretz Israel* (including those of sacrifice) would lead to a future redemption, yet at a later stage he abandoned this notion. Following Alkalai, he based his theory on the talmudic saying in Sanhedrin 97b: 'It [the coming of the Messiah] depends solely on the return to God'; here he interprets the word 'return' as a return to Zion. Hence he introduced an active element into the concept of divine deliverance, in opposition to the opinion of most Orthodox rabbis of the day.

Such a commitment did not motivate Kalischer to act until 1860 when Hayyim Lorje established a society in Frankfurt-am-der-Oder to stimulate Jewish settlement in Palestine. Although this society did not last long, it did publish Kalischer's Zionist tract, *Derishat Zion*, in which he presses for the return of Jews to their native soil. The redemption could only take place, he argues, after human effort; it is not a miraculous event independent of Jewish activity:

The Almighty blessed be His Name, will not suddenly descend from on high and command his people to go forth. Neither will he send the Messiah from Heaven in a twinkling of an eye, to sound the great trumpet for the scattered of Israel and gather them into Jerusalem. He will not surround the holy city with a wall of fire or cause the holy Temple to descend from Heaven. (in Avineri, 1981, 53)

Rather the deliverance of the Jewish people will occur slowly, through arousing support from philanthropists and obtaining permission from other countries for the ingathering of the Jewish people into the Holy Land. Such a vision of redemption, Kalischer maintains, is rooted in Scripture. As the prophet Isaiah proclaimed:

In the days to come Jacob shall take root, Israel shall blossom and put forth shoots, and fill the whole world with fruit . . . . In that day from the River Euphrates to the Brook of Egypt the Lord will thresh out the grain, and you will be gathered one by one, O people of Israel. And in that day a great trumpet will be blown, and those who were lost in the land of Assyria and those who were driven out of the land of Egypt will come and worship the Lord on the holy mountain at Jerusalem. (Isaiah 27:6, 12–13).

For Kalischer this passage implies that the return from exile will take place in stages as Isaiah predicted in Isaiah 11:10: 'In that day the root of Jesse shall stand as an ensign to the peoples: him shall the nations seek, and his dwellings shall be glorious.' In this verse, he insists, both a first and second ingathering are implied – the first ingathering will toil on the land; this will be followed by the flowering of the nation.

According to Kalischer, the advent of the messianic age will therefore be preceded by the establishment of a homeland in *Eretz Israel*. It is not sufficient to wait for miraculous events to occur; rather the Jewish people must act. Quoting from a medieval devotional work, he asserts:

> When many Jews, pious and learned in the Torah, will volunteer to go to the Land of Israel and settle in Jerusalem, motivated by a desire to serve, by purity of spirit, and by love of holiness; when they will come, by ones and twos, from all four corners of the world; and when many will settle there and their prayers will increase at the holy mountain in Jerusalem, the Creator will then heed them and hasten the day of redemption. (in Hertzberg, 1969, 112–13)

Aware that there were many Jews unwilling to support the poor in the Holy Land, he argues that such resistance is an argument put forward by Satan since those resident in Palestine had risked their lives to become pioneers:

> In this country, which is strange to them, how could they go about finding a business or occupation, when they had never in their lives done anything of this kind? Their eyes can only turn to their philanthropic brethren, of whom they ask only enough to keep body and soul together, so that they can dwell in that land which is God's portion on earth. (Ibid., 113)

What is now needed is the creation of an organization which would stimulate emigration as well as purchase and cultivate farms and vineyards. This project would be a ray of deliverance to those who currently languish in the Holy Land owing to poverty and famine. Such a situation would be entirely altered if those capable of contributing to this effort were inspired by the vision of a Jewish refuge. One advantage of this scheme would be to bring to fruition those religious obligations that relate to the working of the soil in the Holy Land. Even those individuals who supervise labourers would be aiding in the working of the land – they would thereby have the same status as if they had personally fulfilled these commandments. Yet beyond all this, Kalischer was persuaded that Jewish

farming could serve as a spur to messianic deliverance. The programme of active participation in the cultivation of the soil would not divert the Jewish people from the task of divine service; instead, it would add dignity to God's law. By working the land, Jewry would be dedicating themselves to bringing about the messianic age.

Such a policy, Kalischer believes, will raise the dignity of the Jewish people since other nations will say that Jews possess the will to redeem the land of their ancestors. Thus he declares:

> Let us take to heart the examples of the Italians, Poles and Hungarians, who laid down their lives and possessions in the struggle for national independence, while we, the children of Israel, who have the most glorious and the holiest of lands as our inheritance, are spiritless and silent. We should be ashamed of ourselves! All the other peoples have striven only for the sake of their own national honour; much more should we exert ourselves, for our duty is to labour not only for the glory of our ancestors but for the glory of God who chose Zion. (Ibid., 114)

Because Kalischer was financially independent, he was able to undertake a wide range of activities directed at bringing about the fulfilment of this plan. In 1866 he played an important role in persuading a group of individuals to purchase land on the outskirts of Jaffa for colonization. Subsequently, he influenced the *Alliance Israélite Universelle*, (an organization created in France in 1860 to protect Jewish rights throughout the world) to establish an agricultural school in Jaffa. Nevertheless, Orthodox critics denounced his efforts, believing them to be a departure from the faith. Even in Jerusalem pious Jews who benefited from the collection of alms for the poor in the Holy Land attacked his stance. In the view of these zealots, the creation of agricultural settlements where Jews were engaged in tilling the soil would inevitably lead the people away from the study of Torah, and also provoke heretical opinions contrary to the Jewish faith. Yet despite such criticism, Kalischer was able to see a small beginning of his ideal near the end of his life – in 1870 an agricultural settlement was founded at Mikveh Israel, and he even considered moving there to supervise the observance of the *mitzvot* connected with the Holy Land. After Kalischer's death in 1874, his son Zeev Wolf continued his father's activities, and a tract of land was purchased near Rachel's tomb from funds in Kalischer's estate.

References

Shlomo Avineri, *The Making of Modern Zionism: The Intellectual Origins of the Jewish State*, New York, 1981
Arthur Hertzberg, *The Zionist Idea: A Historical Analysis and Reader*, New York, 1969

Kalischer's major writings

Arthur Hertzberg, *The Zionist Idea: A Historical Analysis and Reader*, New York, 1969

Further reading

Shlomo Avineri, *The Making of Modern Zionism: The Intellectual Origins of the Jewish State*, New York, 1981
A.I. Bromberg, *Ha Rav Z. H. Kalischer*, 1960
J. Katz, 'Zevi Hirsch Kalischer' in L. Jung, *Guardians of Our Heritage 1724–1953*, New York, 1958
J.E. Myers, 'Zevi Hirsch Kalischer and the Origins of Religious Zionism' in F. Malino and D. Sorkin (eds), *From East and West: Jews in a Changing Europe*, Oxford, 1989
N. Sokolow, *Hibbath Zion*, Jerusalem, 1934

MORDECAI KAPLAN

Born in Svencionys, Lithuania, in 1881, Mordecai Kaplan had a traditional education in Vilna (now Vilnius) and emigrated to New York City with his family in 1889. Although reared as an Orthodox Jew he became increasingly attracted to unorthodox approaches to Judaism. After graduating from the City College of New York, he was ordained at the Jewish Theological Seminary. Subsequently he obtained a master's degree from Columbia University. He then served as an associate minister of Rabbi Moses S. Margolis at New York's Orthodox congregation, *Kehillath Jeshurun*. Although formally observant, Kaplan became disenchanted with traditional Jewish theology. In 1909 he was invited to head the Teachers' Institute of the Jewish Theological Seminary; in the following year he was appointed Professor of Homiletics at the Seminary's rabbinical school where he also taught philosophy of religion.

During the 1910s and 1920s Kaplan engaged in a wide range of activities. At this time he, along with several former *Kehillath Jeshurun* members, organized the New York Jewish Centre where he experimented with the concept of Judaism as a civilization. Two years later the first stage of a synagogue–centre was constructed on West 86th Street where Kaplan served as a rabbi. In addition to overseeing Jewish worship, he introduced a programme of activities including study, drama, dance, song, basketball and callisthenics. During this period, Kaplan endorsed a number of controversial policies and challenged traditional Jewish beliefs. Eventually, however, Kaplan resigned and founded the Society for the Advancement of Judaism which he led for the next twenty years.

In 1935 Kaplan published his major work, *Judaism as a Civilization*, which provided the foundation for the creation of Reconstructionism as a movement. In this work, Kaplan begins by assessing the main religious groupings of American Jewry. In his view, all of these movements – from Orthodox to Reform Judaism – are incapable of accommodating the Jewish heritage to the modern age; what is needed, Kaplan argues, is a definition of Judaism as an evolving religious civilization.

In the light of this new conception of Judaism, Kaplan called for the re-establishment of a network of organic Jewish communities that would ensure the continuation of the Jewish tradition. Membership of this new movement, he maintains, should be voluntary: leaders should be elected democratically and private religious opinions respected. Further, Kaplan proposed the formation of a world-wide Jewish assembly which would adopt a covenant defining the Jews as a transnational people. For Kaplan, a religion constitutes the concretization of the collective self-consciousness of a group which is manifest in spiritual symbols. Such *sancta* inspire feelings of reverence, commemorate what the group believes to be important, provide historical continuity, and strengthen the collective consciousness of the nation.

According to Kaplan, what is now required is a reconstruction of the religious foundations in the light of this conception of religious civilization. For Kaplan, Judaism is something far more comprehensive than the Jewish faith – it includes the nexus of history, literature, language, social organization, folk sanctions, ethics, social and spiritual ideas, and aesthetic interests. Given this understanding of the nature of Jewish existence, Kaplan maintains that only in Israel is it possible to live a fully Jewish life; nevertheless, it is possible to sustain a Jewish form of life in the diaspora. The programme of Reconstructionist Judaism places Israel at the hub of Jewish history from which all dynamic forms of Judaism radiate.

The philosophy of such an Israel-centred movement is based on ten fundamental tenets:

1 Judaism as an evolving religious civilization: Judaism, or that which has united successive generations of Jews into one people, is not only a religion; it is an evolving religious civilization. In the course of its evolution, Judaism has passed through three distinct stages, each reflecting the conditions under which it functioned.

2 What the present state calls for: During those stages the Jews constituted a people apart. Now the Jewish people, like every other, must learn to live in both its own historic civilization and the civilization of its environment. That will usher in the democratic stage of Judaism during which the reconstitution of the Jewish people, the revitalization of its religion, and the replenishment of its culture will be achieved.

3 Unity in diversity: Jewish unity should transcend the diversity among Jews, which is the result of geographical dispersion and of differences in cultural background and in world outlook.

4 The renewal of the ancient covenant: Jews the world over should renew their historic covenant binding themselves into one transnational people, with the Jewish community in Israel, henceforth to be known as 'Zion', as its core.

5 *Eretz Israel* [the land of Israel] as the spiritual home of World Jewry: *Eretz Israel* should be recognized as the home of the historic Jewish civilization.

6 Outside Israel, the foundation of organic communities: elsewhere, Jewish peoplehood should lead to the establishment of organic communities. All activities and institutions conducted by Jews for Jews should be interactive and should give primacy to the fostering of Jewish peoplehood, religion and culture.

7 Prequisites to the revitalization of religion: The revitalization of religion can best be achieved through the study of it in the spirit of free inquiry and through the separation of church and state.

8 How the belief in God is to be interpreted: The revitalization of the Jewish people requires that the belief in God be interpreted in terms of universally human, as well as specifically Jewish, experience.

9 What gives continuity to a religion: The continuity of a religion through different stages, and its identity amid diversity of

belief and practice, are sustained by its *sancta*. These are the heroes, events, texts, places and seasons, which that religion signalizes as furthering the fulfilment of human destiny.

10 Torah as synonymous with ongoing Jewish culture: The traditional concept of Torah should be understood as synonymous with Jewish religious civilization and should, therefore, embrace all the ongoing ethical, cultural and spiritual experiences of the Jewish people.

In propounding his theory about the nature of Judaism, Kaplan advanced a radical theology consonant with a scientific understanding of the universe. For Kaplan, God should not be understood as a supernatural being, but as the power that makes for salvation. 'God', he writes, 'is the sum of all the animating organizing forces and relationships which are forever making a cosmos out of chaos' (Kaplan, 1962, 76). In his opinion, the idea of God must be understood fundamentally in terms of its effect:

We learn more about God when we say that love is divine than when we say that God is love. A veritable transformation takes place .... Divinity becomes relevant to authentic experience and therefore takes on a definiteness which is accompanied by an awareness of authenticity. (Kaplan, 1970, 73)

For Kaplan God is a 'trans-natural', 'suprafactual' and 'super-experiential' transcendence which does not infringe the laws of nature. Such a conception is far removed from the biblical and rabbinic notion of God as the creator and sustainer of the universe who chose the Jewish people and guides humanity to its ultimate destiny. Such an interpretation of the nature of God calls for a reformulation of the spiritual dimension of the faith. Hence Kaplan argues that salvation must be understood in humanistic terms:

When religion speaks of salvation it means in essence the experience of the worth-whileness of life. When we analyse our personal experience of life's worthwhileness we find that it is invariably based on specific ethical experiences – moral responsibility, honesty, loyalty, love, service. If carefully pursued, this analysis reveals that the source of our ethical experience is found in our willingness and ability to achieve self-fulfilment through reciprocity with others. This reciprocity in turn is an expression of a larger principle that operates in the cosmos in response to the demands of a cosmic force, the force that makes for creativity and interdependence in all things. (Ibid., 70)

Given this naturalistic conception of religion, what is the role of prayer? For Kaplan, religious worship is necessary for subjective reasons – it is as essential as the release of emotions. Through prayer, human beings are able to become aware of the force that operates in one's inner consciousness, human relationships and the environment. Further, through worship one is able to focus on the spiritual goals of a religious community. The petitioner, for example, can gain spiritual nourishment in times of crisis as well as consolation for bereavement. Worship thus offers considerable psychological benefits and is able to shape an individual's ideals. Many of the ideas found in *Judaism as a Civilization* and Kaplan's other writings were reflected in the religious literature that appeared during the early period of the development of Reconstructionism.

The New Haggadah, edited by Kaplan, Eugene Kohn and Ira Eisenstein, for example, applied Kaplan's theology to liturgical texts, subordinating miracles and plagues in the traditional *Haggadah* to the narrative of Israel's redemption from Egypt and its contemporary significance. Again, the *Sabbath Prayer Book* was designed for those who were dissatisfied with synagogue worship; its aim was to arouse emotion by eliminating theologically unacceptable passages and adding inspirational material drawn from the tradition. This new prayer-book deleted all references to the revelation of the Torah on Mount Sinai, the Jews as God's chosen people, and the doctrine of a personal Messiah. Not suprisingly, such a departure from the tradition was bitterly opposed by the Orthodox establishment and Kaplan was excommunicated for expressing atheism, heresy and disbelief. Nonetheless, Kaplan's thought has had a profound effect on many Jews who seek to live as modern Jews in a secularized world, in which Kaplan survived until 1983.

References/Kaplan's major writings

Mordecai Kaplan, *Judaism Without Super-naturalism*, New York, 1958
Mordecai Kaplan, *The Meaning of God in Modern Jewish Religion*, New York, 1962
Mordecai Kaplan, *Judaism as a Civilization*, New York, 1967
Mordecai Kaplan, 'The Meaning of God for the Contemporary Jew' in A. Jospe (ed.), *Tradition and Contemporary Experience*, New York, 1970

Further reading

M. Davis (ed.), *Mordecai Kaplan Jubilee Volume*, New York, 1953

ABRAHAM ISAAC KOOK

Following in the footsteps of such religious Zionists as Yehuda hai Alkalai and Zevi Hirsch Kalischer, Abraham Isaac Kook formulated the conception of messianic redemption which embraced the creation of a Jewish homeland in Palestine. Such a vision was influenced by the thinking of the religious wing of the *Hovevei Zion* (Lovers of Zion) movement which emerged at the end of the nineteenth century: leading thinkers such as Samuel Mohilewer, Yitzhak Yaakov Reines and Jehiel Michael Pines paved the way for Kook's endorsement of Jewish nationalism. In his writings there is the first

systematic attempt to combine the centrality of *Eretz Israel* with the Jewish religious quest to resettle the Jewish people in their ancient homeland.

Born in Greiva, Latvia, in 1865, Kook received a traditional Orthodox education. Yet, at a very early age, he was anxious to supplement his talmudic studies with a knowledge of the Bible, Hebrew language, Jewish and secular philosophy, and mysticism. In 1888 he became rabbi of Zaumel, and seven years later rabbi of Bausk. In 1904 he moved to Palestine where he was the rabbi of Jaffa. During this period he wrote a variety of works, becoming an important figure in the Jewish community. In 1914 Kook travelled to Europe, but was stranded in Switzerland at the outbreak of the First World War. From 1916 to 1919 he served as a rabbi in London, eventually returning to Palestine where he became chief rabbi of the Ashkenazi Jews in Jerusalem. In 1921 he was elected Ashkenazi head of the new rabbinic court of appeals – a position which in effect made him Ashkenazi chief rabbi of Palestine. He served in this post until his death in 1935.

Unlike secular Zionists, who encouraged practical activity to secure a Jewish state, Kook engaged in the task of reinterpreting the religious tradition so as to transform religious messianic anticipation into the basis for collaboration with the aspirations of modern Zionism. In Kook's view, Israel is fundamental to the Jewish faith and a crucial element in Jewish religious consciousness. Nonetheless, throughout Jewish history the belief in messianic deliverance has not been accompanied by an active policy of resettlement. The disparity between religious expectations for the return from exile and the desire of most Jews to live in the diaspora illustrates the confusion in Jewish thinking about the place of Israel in Jewish life. Hence there is a serious contradiction between the messianic belief in a return to the Holy Land and the accommodating attitude to exile of most Jews throughout history.

According to Kook, this conflict at the heart of Jewish existence must be faced and resolved. The land of Israel, he maintains, 'is not something apart from the soul of the Jewish people; it is no mere national possession, serving as a means . . . of survival. *Eretz Israel* is part of the very essence of nationhood' (in Hertzberg, 1969, 419). The fact that Jews have been separated from their ancestral home is a central difficulty. Kook states that Jews in the diaspora are capable of observing all the *mitzvot* (commandments) and live as pious Jews. But because they reside outside *Eretz Israel*, a major dimension of Jewishness is absent from their lives.

Residing in the diaspora involves one in unholiness, whereas by settling in Palestine it is possible to live a spiritually unalloyed life. The return to Zion is mandatory for an authentic Jewish existence:

A Jew cannot be as devoted and true to his own ideas, sentiments and imagination in the diaspora as he can in *Eretz Israel*. Revelations of the Holy, of whatever degree, are relatively pure in *Eretz Israel*; outside it, they are mixed with dross and much impurity . . . . In the Holy Land, man's imagination is lucid and clear, clean and pure, capable of receiving the revelations of divine truth and of expressing in life the sublime meaning of the ideal of prophecy and to be illuminated by the radiance of the Holy Spirit. In gentile lands the imagination is dim, clouded with darkness and shadowed with unholiness, and it cannot serve as the vessel for the outpouring of the divine light. (Ibid., 420–1)

If such a belief had animated religious Jews in the diaspora, the history of the Jewish people would have been utterly different – accommodation to exile would have been regarded as a betrayal of religious principles. Now that Zionism has become an active force in Jewish life, however, it is possible to reconsider the nature of Jewish identity. For Kook, peoplehood, the Torah and the land are inextricably linked. It is an error to argue, as did nineteenth-century proponents of religious reform, that Judaism can be separated from the Holy Land. Rather, the return to Zion is a fundamental feature of the faith. What is of significance is not an idealized notion of a heavenly Jerusalem distant from everyday concerns, but the manifestation of Jewish existence on earth. For this reason Kook stresses that 'a valid strengthening of Judaism in the diaspora can come only from a deepened attachment to *Eretz Israel*. The hope for the return to the Holy Land is the continuing source of the distinctive nature of Judaism' (Ibid., 419).

Kook argues that this attachment to the Holy Land must become the fulcrum of Jewish life in the modern world. Even though the secular pioneers who came to Palestine were motivated by ideological commitments alien to traditional Judaism, their actions are absorbed into the unfolding of God's providential scheme for his chosen people. The pioneers have thus unintentionally contributed to the coming of the Messiah – without consciously recognizing the significance of their work, they served God's purposes. As Kook writes:

Many of the adherents of the present national revival maintain that they are secularists. If a Jewish secular nationalism were really imaginable, then we would, indeed, be in danger of falling so low as to be beyond redemption. But Jewish nationalism is a form of self-delusion: the spirit of Israel is so closely linked to the spirit of God that a Jewish nationalist, no matter how secularist his intention may be, must, despite himself, affirm the divine. An individual can sever the tie that binds him to life eternal, but the house of Israel as a whole cannot. All of its most cherished national possessions – its land, language, history and customs – are vessels of the spirit of the Lord. (Ibid., 430)

These observations led Kook to the view that a divine spark is apparent in the efforts of secular zionists who sacrificed themselves to create a Jewish settlement in Palestine. Such pioneers were not godless heretics, but God's servants. Unaware of their divine mission, they participated in bringing about God's Kingdom. Religious Zionism, Kook believes, must grasp the underlying significance of these efforts to redeem the land, and educate secularists about the real nature of their labours:

> Our quarrel with them must be directed only to the specific task of demonstrating their error and of proving to them that all their efforts to fragmentize the higher unity of Israel are foredoomed to failure. Once this truth is established, our opponents will ultimately have to realize that they were wasting their efforts. The values they attempted to banish were nonetheless present, if only in an attentuated and distorted form. (Ibid. 426)

For Kook, the redemption of Israel is part of a universal process involving all humanity. The salvation of the Jewish people is not simply an event of relative importance; instead, it provides the basis for the restoration of the entire world (*tikkun olam*). Through the rebirth of the Jewish nation in their previous homeland, all human beings will be redeemed. This is the true significance of the creation of Israel:

> All the civilizations of the world will be renewed by the renascence of our spirit. All quarrels will be resolved, and our revival will cause all life to be luminous with the joy of fresh birth. All religious Jews will don new and precious raiment, casting off whatever is soiled, abominable and unclean; they will unite in imbibing of the dew of the holy lights, that were made ready for all mankind at the beginning of time in the well of Israel. The active power of Abraham's blessing to all the peoples of the world will become manifest and it will serve as the basis of our renewed creativity in *Eretz Israel*. (Ibid., 423)

Such a vision of global transformation is directly related to the aspirations of earlier Jewish writers who awaited messianic deliverance to bring about the end of human history. For Kook, however, the rebuilding of the Jewish state – even by those who rejected Judaism – is an essential ingredient for this process of universal salvation.

References/Kook's major writings

Arthur Hertzberg, *The Zionist Idea: A Historical Analysis and Reader*, New York, 1969

Further reading

S.H. Bergman, *Faith and Reason*, New York, 1963
I. Epstein, *Abraham Yitzhak Kook: His Life and Times*, 1951
L. Jung (ed.), *Guardians of Our Heritage, 1724–1953*, New York, 1958
N. Rotenstreich, *Jewish Philosophy in Modern Times*, New York, 1968

ISAAC LURIA

Isaac Luria's father, a member of the Ashkenazi family of Luria of Germany and Poland, emigrated to Jerusalem where he married into the Sephardi Frances family. Isaac Luria was born in Jerusalem in 1534, but his father died when Isaac was still a child, and his mother took him to Egypt; there he grew up in the home of her brother Mordecai Frances. In Egypt Luria studied under David ben Solomon ibn Abi Zimra and his successor, Bezalel Ashkenazi. During this period he collaborated with his teacher Ashkenazi in writing a number of legal works; in addition Luria engaged in various commercial activities. While still in Egypt, Luria began his study of *kabbalah* (Jewish mysticism), retiring to a life of seclusion on the island of Jazirat al-Rawda, on the Nile near Cairo, which was owned by his father-in-law. In his mystical study Luria concentrated on the works of early Jewish mystics, the Zohar, and the writings of Moses Cordovero. It appears that at this time Luria wrote a commentary on the *Book of Concealment*, a short section of the Zohar. In 1569 Luria moved to Safed in Israel with his family where he embarked on the study of *kabbalah* with Moses Cordovero. Luria died in 1572.

In Safed, Luria gathered around himself a group of disciples to whom he imparted his teachings about theoretical *kabbalah* and the way to attain communion with the souls of the righteous – this was achieved by unifying the *sefirot* (divine emanations) and by meditating on the divine names. Of primary importance in Luria's system is the mystery of creation. In the literature of early mystics creation was conceived as a positive event: the will to create was awakened within the Godhead, resulting in a long process of emanation. According to Luria, however, creation was a negative act – the *Ayn Sof* (Infinite) had to bring into being an empty space in which creation could take place since divine light was everywhere leaving no room for creation to occur. This was accomplished by the process of *tzimtzum* – the contraction of the Godhead into itself. Hence the first act was not positive, but one that demanded divine withdrawal. God had to go into exile from the *tehiru* (empty space) so that the process of creation could be initiated. *Tzimtzum* therefore postulates divine exile as a first stage of creation.

After this stage of withdrawal, a line of light flowed from the Godhead into the empty space and took the shape of *sefirot* (divine emanations) in the form of *Adam Kadmon* (Primal Man). From the ears, nostrils and mouth of Primal Man rays of divine light issued forth. In this process divine lights created the vessels – the eternal shapes of the *sefirot* – which gave specific characteristics to each emanation. Nonetheless these vessels were not strong enough to contain such pure light and they shattered; this breaking of the vessels (*Shevirat ha-Kelim*) resulted in the upheaval of the emerging

emanations. The lower vessels broke down and fell – the three highest emanations were damaged, and the empty space was divided into two parts. The first consisted of the broken vessels with many sparks clinging to them. The second part was the upper realm where pure divine light escaped to preserve its purity.

In explaining the purpose of such divine contraction, Luria stressed that the *Ayn Sof* before creation was not entirely unified; there were elements in it that were potentially different from the rest of the Godhead. The *tzimtzum* separated these elements from one another. After this event, a residue was left behind like water clinging to a bucket after being emptied. This residue included various elements that were part of the Godhead, and after the withdrawal they were poured into the empty space. Thus the separation of different elements from the Godhead was achieved. The reason for the emanation of the divine powers and the formation of Primal Man was the quest to integrate those now separate elements into the scheme of creation and thereby transform them into co-operative forces. Their task was to form the vessels of the *sefirot* into which divine lights would flow. But the shattering of the vessels constituted a rebellion of these elements, a refusal to be involved in the process of creation. By this act, they were able to attain a realm in the lower part of the empty space; after the breaking of the vessels, these elements expressed themselves as the power of evil.

According to Luria, the cosmos was split into two parts after the shattering of the vessels: the kingdom of evil in the lower part and the realm of divine light in the upper part. For Luria evil is opposed to existence and therefore it was not able to exist by its own power. Rather it had to derive spiritual force from divine light. This was achieved by keeping captive the sparks of the divine light that descended with them when the vessels were broken and subsequently gave sustenance to the satanic domain. Divine attempts to bring unity to all things now had to focus on the struggle to vanquish the evil forces. This was accomplished by a continuing process of divine emanation which at first created the *sefirot*, the sky, the earth, the Garden of Eden and human beings.

Humanity was designed to serve as the battleground for this conflict between good and evil. In this regard Adam reflected symbolically the dualism in the cosmos – he possessed a sacred soul while his body represented the evil forces. God's intention was that Adam defeat the evil within himself and bring about Satan's downfall. But when Adam failed, a catastrophe occurred parallel to the breaking of the vessels; instead of divine sparks being saved and uplifted, many new lights fell and evil became stronger. Rather than relying on the action of one person, God then chose the people of Israel to vanquish evil and raise up the captive sparks. The Torah was given to symbolize the Jews' acceptance of this allotted task. When the ancient Israelites undertook to keep the law, redemption seemed imminent. Yet the people of Israel then created the golden calf, a sin parallel to Adam's disobedience. Again divine sparks fell and the forces of evil were renewed. For Luria, history is a record of attempts by the powers of good to rescue these sparks and unite the divine and earthly spheres. Luria and his disciples believed they were living in the final stages of this last attempt to overcome evil in which the coming of the Messiah would signify the end of the struggle.

Related to this eschatological scheme was Luria's understanding of *tikkun* (cosmic repair). This concept refers to the mending of what was broken during the shattering of the vessels. After the catastrophe in the divine realm, the process of restoration began and every disaster was seen as a setback in this process. In this battle, keeping God's commandments was understood as contributing to repair – the divine sparks which fell can be redeemed by ethical and religious deeds. According to Luria, a spark is attached to all prayers and moral actions;

if a Jew keeps the ethical and religious law these sparks are redeemed and lifted up. When the process is complete, evil will disappear. But every time a Jew sins a spark is captured and plunges into the satanic abyss. Every deed or misdeed thus has cosmic significance in the mystical system of Lurianic *kabbalah*.

Pre-eminent among Safed mystics who recorded Isaac Luria's teachings was Hayyim Vital, who was born in Safed and studied the *kabbalah* according to the system of Moses Cordovero. After Luria's arrival in Safed, Vital became his most dedicated disciple and studied with him until Luria died in 1572. Later he organized Luria's teachings, putting them into written form; in addition, he formulated his own interpretation of kabbalistic themes. In 1575 twelve of Luria's disciples signed a pledge to study Luria's theories only from Vital; however this group ceased to exist when Vital settled in Jerusalem, where he served as the head of a *yeshivah* (rabbinical academy) from 1577 to 1585. There he composed his presentation of Lurianic *kabbalah*, returning to Safed in 1586. In the centuries following Luria's death, his teachings were widely disseminated and had a profound influence on the history of Jewish mystical thought. In the various systems of *kabbalah* formulated since the early modern period, Luria's conception of the contraction of God, the shattering of the vessels, the exiled sparks, and cosmic repair have played a major role.

See also in this book

Vital

Further reading

S. Dreznits, *Tales in Praise of the Ari* (trans. A. Klein and J. Machlowitz Klein), Philadelphia, 1970

L. Jacobs, *Jewish Mystical Testimonies*, New York, 1978

A. Kaplan, *Meditation and Kabbalah*, Northvale, NJ, 1995

G. Scholem, *Major Trends in Jewish Mysticism*, New York, 1995

MOSES HAYYIM LUZZATTO

Born in Padua in 1707, into a distinguished Jewish family, Moses Hayyim Luzzatto engaged in the study of the Bible, Talmud, midrash, halakhic sources and classical languages as well as secular literature. As a result of his vast knowledge, he became the leader of a group of young scholars there. At the age of twenty, while immersed in mystical speculation, he heard a voice which he believed to be that of a *maggid* (divine messenger). Subsequently Luzzatto received further messages from this same source which he wrote down. In his teaching he passed on these divine communications to the members of a kabbalistic circle who were preoccupied by messianic speculation.

One of the members of this group, Jekuthiel Gordon, depicted the activities of this circle in a series of letters. In one, written to Mordecai Yoffe of Vienna, he gave an account of this *maggid*:

> There is here a holy man, my master and teacher, the holy lamp, the lamp of God, his honour Rabbi Moses Hayyim Luzzatto. For these past two and a half years a *maggid* has been revealed to him, a holy and tremendous angel who reveals wondrous mysteries to him. Even before he reached the age of fourteen he knew all the writings of the Ari ['the Lion', Isaac Luria] by heart. He is very modest, telling nothing of this even to his own father and obviously not to anyone else .... This is what happens. The angel speaks out of his mouth but we, his disciples, hear nothing. The angel begins to reveal to him great mysteries. Then my master orders Elijah to come to him and he comes to impart mysteries of his own. Sometimes Metatron,

the great prince, also comes to him as well as the Faithful Shepherd [Moses], the patriarch Abraham, Rabbi Hamnuna the Elder, and That Old Man and sometimes King Messiah and Adam .... To sum up, nothing is hidden from him. At first permission was only granted to reveal to him the mysteries of the Torah but now all things are revealed to him. (in Jacobs, 1978, 138)

When one of Gordon's letters came to the notice of Moses Hagiz, a Palestinian scholar and kabbalist, he warned the rabbis of Venice of the dangers of Luzzatto's activity. Although Luzzatto's teacher Isaiah Bassan came to the defence of his pupil, a bitter controversy raged and attacks were made on Luzzatto. In the opinion of various rabbis, Luzzatto was not suitable to receive such revelations since he was young and unmarried. A search was made of his house, and evidence of magical practices was uncovered. Eventually Luzzatto agreed to hand over his kabbalistic writings to Bassan, cease from recording the disclosures of the *maggid* and refrain from teaching *kabbalah* (mystical tradition). Yet despite such a commitment, the dispute about his activity continued and he was compelled to leave for Amsterdam in 1735. On arrival in Frankfurt, he sought the aid of Jacob ha-Kohen; however, instead of helping him, ha-Kohen forced Luzzatto to sign a document condemning the revelations of the *maggid* and stating that his mystical writings were false. Nonetheless, in Amsterdam Luzzatto continued to write about *kabbalah* but abstained from teaching. In 1743 Luzzatto went to Palestine and settled in Acre, where he and his family died in 1746, in a plague.

When Luzzatto propounded his kabbalistic theories, the mystical circle around him began to seek messianic redemption. A declaration from this group states that this study will not be regarded as a private *tikkun* (restoration) of the members nor will it be atonement for personal sins, but its only *kavvanah* (intention) will be wholly dedicated to the *tikkun* of the holy *Shekhinah* (Divine Presence) and all of Israel. According to these disciples of Luzzatto, the process of redemption had already begun and would soon be completed; in their opinion, they had a central part to play in the unfolding of this eschatological scheme. In this process Luzzatto had a crucial role: his marriage was seen as a mystical event in the heavenly heights. This earthly marriage was symbolic of the redemption of the *Shekhinah* and her union with a divine husband. Believing himself to be the reincarnation of Moses, Luzzatto was convinced he would redeem the Jewish people from exile.

Luzzatto's writings consist of works dealing with central mystical doctrines together with his own theories. His *Kelah Pithei Hokhmah* is a systematic presentation of the kabbalistic doctrines of Isaac Luria. In this study he minimized the mythological dimensions of Luria's theories, emphasizing instead the theosophical aspects of his writings. For Luzzatto, the idea of *tzimtzum* (divine contraction) is an act of divine justice representing God's intention to establish contact with creation. In another work, *Hoker u-Mekubbal*, Luzzatto defended kabbalistic study and sought to demonstrate that only Lurianic *kabbalah* is able to offer solutions to Judaism's most important religious problems. In his most important writing influenced by the *maggid*, entitled *Zohar Tinyana*, he utilized kabbalistic concepts to present his own views about messianic deliverance. In addition to such mystical studies, Luzzatto produced ethical works in which he instructed readers to abandon their sinful ways so they would be able to ascend to the heavenly domain.

In a letter to Rabbi Benjamin ben Eliezer ha-Kohen Vitale – kabbalist and father-in-law of Isaiah Bassan – Luzzatto defended his mystical claims. Beginning with an explanation of his reticence to disclose the source of his kabbalistic teachings, Luzzatto stated that God had revealed these mysteries to him:

All the God-fearing come daily to me to hear the new things the Lord tells me. The young men who had previously walked in the ways of youth's vanities, now, thank God, have turned from the evil way to return unto the Lord ... I have the obligation to encourage them until their feet have become firmly planted, as I hope, in the way of the Lord. (Ibid., 140)

In Luzzatto's view, the gates of divine grace were open when the Temple was standing, but the 'Other Side' took over its power when it was destroyed. From that time events have taken place in accord with the stages which require *tikkun*. Thus many *tikkunim* have been ordained for Israel during its exile: these are the *tikkunim* of the Mishnah (compendium of the Oral Law), the *Gemara* (talmudic commentary on the Mishnah) and the *midrashim* (rabbinic commentaries). But superior to all these is the Zohar (medieval mystical commentary on Scripture), which belongs to the category of the seminal drop which comes from *Yesod* (foundation–divine emanation). For this reason it is referred to as 'the brightness [*zohar*] of the firmament'. Because all providence proceeds by means of copulation, all things depend on the influence of this seminal drop. When it descends into the lower world everything is put right by means of a great *tikkun*. According to Luzzatto, Rabbi Simeon bar Yohai was worthy of becoming the channel through which this *tikkun* was performed; hence he composed the Zohar. However, the truth is that only part of that illumination has emerged – its purpose is to allow Israel and the world as a whole to survive during the exile. Yet for the real *tikkun* to be accomplished, it is necessary for it to become permanent and unceasing: in this way divine grace would constantly be renewed.

For Luzzatto, each *tikkun* depends on the preparation undertaken by its recipients. If there is a high level of supernatural illumination which those below are insufficiently prepared to receive, it will not be permanent; instead it departs, reserving the full *tikkun* for a later time. Thus, after Rabbi Simeon bar Yohai the illumination was blocked. But when new degrees of illumination were ready to appear, further *tikkunim* became necessary. Turning to his own religious experience, Luzzatto stated in a letter to Benjamin ben Eliezer ha-Kohen Vitale:

At this time the Lord, in his desire to be good to his people, wished to reveal a new light in the category of the Zohar, which, as mentioned previously, is the illumination provided by the seminal drop. For this, in his mercy, he chose me. If you ask me about the state of my preparation, what can I say? The truth is that it is by the Lord's grace alone and has little to do with the state of my preparation for it. However, it is also true that I have been assiduous for years in carrying out *yihudim* [unifications]. I perform a different *yihud* almost every quarter of an hour. The Creator now uses me as the instrument for the fulfilment of his purpose. (Ibid., 143)

Continuing the account of his revelations, Luzzatto described an experience that occurred when he was performing a certain *yihud*:

I fell into a trance. When I awoke, I heard a voice saying: 'I have descended in order to reveal the hidden secrets of the Holy King.' For a while I stood there trembling but then I took hold of myself. The voice did not cease from speaking and imparted a particular secret to me. At the same time on the second day I saw to it that I was alone in the room and the voice came again to impart a further secret to me. One day he revealed to me that he was a *maggid* sent from heaven, and he gave me certain *yihudim* that I was to perform in order for him to come to me. I never saw him but heard his voice speaking in my mouth .... Then Elijah came and imparted his own secrets to me. And he said that

Metatron [Divine agent], the great prince, will come to me. From that time onwards I came to recognize each of my visitations. Souls whose identity I do not know are also revealed to me. I write down each day the new ideas each of them imparts to me. (Ibid.)

References

L. Jacobs, *Jewish Mystical Testimonies*, New York, 1978

Luzzatto's major writings

N. Ben-Menahem, *Kitvei Rabi Mosheh Hayim Lutsato*, Jerusalem, 1951

See also in this book

Luria

Further reading

Y. Bindman, *Rabbi Moses Chaim Luzzatto*, Northvale, NJ, 1995
B.Z. Bokser, *The Jewish Mystical Tradition*, Northvale, NJ, 1993
L. Jacobs, *Jewish Mystical Testimonies*, New York, 1978
Encyclopaedia Judaica, vol. 11, Jerusalem, 1971

SOLOMON MAIMON

Born in Sukoviboeg, Poland, in 1753, Solomon Maimon married at the age of eleven, becoming a father three years later. At first he supported his family by serving as a tutor locally. Alongside his rabbinic studies, he concentrated on Jewish philosophy and mysticism. Because of his veneration of Maimonides, he adopted the name 'Maimon'. By attempting to illustrate that kabbalistic teaching is based on philosophic principles, he was regarded as a sceptic by the early *Hasidim* among whom he associated. Subsequently Maimon travelled to Berlin where he intended to devote himself to secular learning. When he arrived at the gates to the city, however, he was turned away by officials of the Jewish community, and he went to Posen (now Poznań) where he received assistance from Rabbi Zvi Hirsch ben Abraham. For two years he taught there, but eventually became disenchanted with the religious conservatism of the religious establishment. He then returned to Berlin where he was permitted to enter the city.

In Berlin Maimon became a disciple of Moses Mendelssohn, yet several years later he was abandoned by his patron because of his wayward lifestyle. In consequence he moved to Hamburg where he sought to convert to Christianity despite his inability to accept the central doctrines of the faith. When this request was rejected, Maimon moved to nearby Altona, where he studied at the local *gymnasium* through the financial aid provided by several benefactors. Poverty-stricken, he returned to Berlin, and later to Breslau (now Wrocław); in 1786 he moved back to Berlin where he studied Kantian philosophy, composing a treatise, *Versuch über die Transzendentalphilosophie*. The manuscript was sent to Marcus Herz and forwarded to Immanuel Kant who remarked in a letter to Herz that Maimon's study was of great value. Kant's response was of considerable importance, establishing Maimon's reputation as a significant philosopher. Maimon then published his book as well as several articles. From 1790 to 1795 he was supported by Count Adolf Kalkreuth; under his patronage, Maimon spent his final years at residences near Berlin and Freistadt, Silesia. After his death in 1800, he was buried outside the Jewish cemetery as a heretic.

Although trained in rabbinics, Maimon contributed to the development of neo-Kantian philosophy rather than Jewish thought. In his writings, Kant argued that there is a fundamental distinction between things-in-themselves and things as perceived through human comprehension. According to Kant, ultimate reality is unknowable since it lies outside the reach of the understanding. Maimon's major contribution to Kant's investigation concerns this issue. Agreeing with Kant that cognition must have a cause which guarantees the objectivity of human knowledge, Maimon maintains that such a cause exists within the mind rather than as an external source. Utilizing the Kantian distinction between sensibility and understanding, Maimon contends that the concepts of the understanding arise from perceptions of sensibility. These, he continues, are the same for every person and therefore ensure their objectivity. In addition, Maimon argues that sensibility is itself a form of understanding, but more limited in scope. In his view, the thing-in-itself is the final goal of cognition. Although our knowledge is inevitably fragmentary, it can become greater as it approaches ideal knowledge.

Even though Maimon rejects Kant's conception of the thing-in-itself as the source of knowledge, he is concerned to provide a solution to the question of how knowledge is related to the external world. Maimon's solution to this dilemma is to assume that human sensibility is simply an imperfect expression of intellectual reality. Thus the objects of the external world which are presented to sensibility are conceptual in character. In proposing this hypothesis, Maimon asserts that there is an infinite intellect which is the basis of human comprehension. As finite beings we are able to understand only a relatively small portion of this rational structure of reality.

Such a notion enables Maimon to bridge the gap that exists between intra-mental and extra-mental worlds. Yet the infinite intellect does not receive concepts from external objects; rather it creates them from within itself. As Maimon writes: 'We posit . . . an infinite intellect . . . which creates out of itself all possible kinds of relations of things. Our intellect is the very same intellect' (*Encyclopedia Judaica*, 1971, vol. II, 743).

In presenting this neo-Kantian position, Maimon seeks to describe the mode of thinking of the infinite intellect, and asks: How do its concepts cohere to produce the structure of the rational world? This is accomplished by what Maimon refers to as the law of determinability. This notion is based on Kant's distinction between analytic and synthetic judgements: analytic judgements (such as A=A) are tautological in character and are incapable of producing knowledge, unlike synthetic judgments (such as A=B). According to Maimon, Kant was mistaken in believing that synthetic judgments are certain because their subjects and predicates are not the same. Differing from Kant, Maimon formulates a third type of judgement which he refers to as the law of determinability. Such a judgement, he believes, is both analytic and synthetic. The proposition 'the colour is blue', for example, implies that the subject (colour) can exist without the predicate (blue). Thus, the relation between subject and predicate is synthetic. However, the predicate (blue) cannot exist independently – therefore it is analytic.

Despite the rationality of his philosophical system, Maimon adopts a sceptical stance with regard to metaphysics. Although he contends that the existence of an infinite intellect and the law of determinability provide the framework for perceiving the world as a rational structure, he refrains from claiming that that it is possible to know that this rational structure exists in reality. Philosophy, he maintains, is only capable of offering a rational explanation for what exists – it cannot demonstrate that its hypotheses are true in fact.

In addition to his philosophical writings, Maimon published an autobiography which provides a vivid account of European Jewish existence at the end of the nineteenth century. Throughout this work he provides insights into the various currents of Jewish life and thought. Typical among these observations is his account of the extreme asceticism he witnessed in his youth:

Two or three instances of which I was myself an eyewitness, will be sufficient to show what I mean. A Jewish scholar, well known on account of his piety, Simon of Lubitsch, had undergone the severest exercises of penance. He had already carried out the *teshuvat ha-kana* – the penance of *kana* – which consists in fasting daily and avoiding for supper anything that comes from a living being (flesh, milk, honey, etc.). He had also practised *galut*, that is, a continuous wandering in which the penitent is not allowed to remain two days in the same place; and, in addition, he had worn a hair shirt next to his skin. But he felt that he would not be doing enough for the satisfaction of his conscience unless he further observed the *teshuvat ha-mishkal* – the penance of weighing – which requires a particular form of penance proportionate to every sin. But, as he found by calculation that the number of sins was too great to be atoned for in this way, he took it into his head to starve himself to death. (Maimon, 1954, 81–2)

Although Maimon's ideas had little influence on the course of Jewish thought, his conceptions had a powerful impact on Johann Fichte and through him on German idealist philosophy. During the nineteenth century Maimon was largely neglected, but in this century interest in his writing revived, and in recent years a number of books have been published dealing with his philosophical notions. As far as his autobiographical reflections are concerned, his description of eighteenth-century Jewish life continues to provide a vitally important background to our understading of the development of Judaism in the age of the Enlightenment.

References/Maimon's major writings

Encyclopaedia Judaica, Jerusalem, 1971
Solomon Maimon, *Autobiography of Solomon Maimon*, London, 1954

See also in this book

Further reading

S. Atlas, *From Critical to Speculative Idealism*, The Hague, Netherlands, 1964
S. Atlas, in *Encyclopedia of Philosophy*, vol. 5, New York 1967
S.H. Bergman, *The Philosophy of Solomon Maimon*, Jerusalem, 1967
N.I. Jacobs, 'Solomon Maimon's Relation to Judaism', *Yearbook of the Leo Baeck Institute*, 8, London, 1963

MAIMONIDES

Born in Cordoba, Spain, in 1135, Moses ben Maimon (Maimonides) was the son of the *dayyan* (rabbinical judge) of Cordoba. Owing to the conquest of Cordoba by the Almohads in 1148, Maimonides left Cordoba with his family; for the next eight or nine years they wandered from town to town in Spain, eventually settling in Fez in north Africa in 1160. During this period Maimonides began a commentary on the Mishnah, wrote short treatises on logic as well as the Jewish calendar, and completed notes for a commentary on several tractates of the Talmud as well as a legal code. In Fez Maimonides studied under Judah ha-Kohen ibn Susan, and continued working on his commentary on the Mishnah in addition to other projects. After the martyrdom of his teacher, Maimonides together with his family fled from Fez to Acre where they stayed for several months. The family then left for Egypt; after a short stay in Alexandria, they took up residence in Fostat (Cairo).

After his father's death, Maimonides was supported by his brother David who imported precious stones; at this stage he devoted himself to writing and acting as a religious leader of the community. However, when his brother drowned in the Indian Ocean on a business trip, Maimonides worked as a doctor, eventually becoming one of the physicians to the ruler of Egypt. During this period Maimonides wrote his legal code, the *Mishneh Torah*, and his philosophical work, the *Guide of the Perplexed*. In a letter written to the translator of the *Guide*, Samuel ben Judah ibn Tibbon, Maimonides describes his busy life at this time:

> My duties to the sultan are very heavy. I am obliged to visit him every day, early in the morning ... I do not return to Misr [Fostat] until the afternoon. Then I am almost dying with hunger ... I find the antechambers filled with people, both Jews and gentiles, nobles and common people, judges and bailiffs, friends and foes – a mixed multitude who await the time of my return. I dismount from my animal, wash my hands, go forth to my patients, and entreat them to bear with me while I partake of some slight refreshment, the only meal I take in the twenty-four hours. Then I go forth to attend to my patients, and write prescriptions and directions for their various ailments. Patients go in and out until nightfall, and sometimes even, I solemnly assure you, until two hours or more in the night.(*Encyclopedia Judaica*, Jerusalem, 1971, vol. 11, 758)

In his major philosophical treatise, the *Guide of the Perplexed*, Maimonides draws on the great Muslim expositors of Aristotle such as Avicenna and al-Farabi. In line with Islamic teaching he argues that reason and faith are harmoniously interrelated, yet he criticizes various features of Muslim Mutazilite and Asharyite philosophy. The central aim of the *Guide* is to reconcile the Torah with a number of central tenets of Aristotelianism. As Maimonides explains in his introduction to this work, the *Guide* was deliberately written for an intellectual elite. His book was thus intended only for those whose study of logic, mathematics, natural science and metaphysics had led them to a state of perplexity about seeming contradictions between the Torah and human reason.

The first part of the *Guide* begins with a discussion of the anthropomorphic terms in the Hebrew Scriptures. A literal reading of these passages implies that God is a corporeal being, but according to Maimonides this is an error: such descriptions must be understood figuratively. In this connection, he argues – as did Abraham ben David Halevi ibn Daud in the *Exalted Faith* – that no positive attributes can be predicated of God since the Divine is an absolute unity. Hence when God is depicted positively in the Bible, such ascriptions must refer to His activity. The only true attributes, Maimonides contends, are negative ones – they lead to a knowledge of God because in negation no plurality is involved. Each negative attribute excludes from God's essence some imperfection. Therefore, when one says that God is incorporeal, this means He has no body. Such negation, Maimonides believes, brings one nearer to the knowledge of the Godhead.

Turning from God's nature to prophecy, Maimonides points out that most people believe that God chooses any person He desires and inspires him with the prophetic spirit. Such a view is opposed by the philosophers who contend that prophecy is a human gift requiring ability and study. Rejecting both positions, Maimonides states that prophecy is an inspiration from God which passes through the mediation of the Active Intellect and then to the faculty of imagination. It requires perfection in theoretical wisdom, morality and development of the imagination. On the basis of this conception, Maimonides asserts that human beings can be divided into three classes according to the development of their reasoning capabilities. First, there are those whose rational faculties are highly developed and receive influences from the Active Intellect but whose imagination is defective – these are wise men and philosophers. The second group consists of those where the imagination alone is in good condition, but the intellect is defective: these are statesmen, lawgivers and politicians. Third there are the prophets, those whose imagination is constitutionally perfect and whose Active Intellect is well developed.

Maimonides insists that God withholds prophetic inspiration from certain individuals, but those whom he has selected teach speculative truth and adherence to the Torah. Unlike the other prophets, who only intermittently receive prophecy, Moses prophesied continuously and was the only one to give legislation. The purpose of the body of Mosaic law is to regulate society and provide for spiritual well-being and perfection. As far as ceremonial law is concerned, Maimonides argues that the purpose of a number of ritual commandments was to prevent Israel from participating in pagan cultic practices which could lead to idolatry. Sacrifice, he suggests, was a concession to the popular mentality of the ancient Israelites since the nation could not conceive of worship without sacrificial offerings.

The problem of evil is also a central theological topic in the *Guide*. Maimonides contends that evil does not exist as an independent entity; rather it is a privation of good. What appears evil, such as human immorality, is frequently due to the fault of human beings and can be corrected through good government. Likewise, personal suffering is often the result of vice. Physical calamities – earthquakes, floods and disease – are not the result of human failing but are part of the natural order. To complain that there is more evil than good in the world results from an anthropomorphic conception of humanity's place in the universe – God's final purpose cannot be known. Unlike Aristotelian philosophers, Maimonides conceives of God's providence as concerned with each individual. For him such providential care is proportionate to the degree that a person has activated his intellect. In this regard, Maimonides argues that the ideal of human perfection involves reason and ethical action. To illustrate his view, Maimonides uses a parable about a king's palace. Those who are outside its walls have no doctrinal belief; those within the city but with their backs to the palace hold incorrect positions; others wishing to enter the palace not knowing how to do so are traditionalists who lack philosophical sophistication. But those who have entered the palace have speculated about the fundamental principles of religion. Only the person who has achieved the highest level of intellectual attainment can be near the throne of God.

Such philosophical attainment, however, is not in itself sufficient: to be perfect, a person must go beyond communion with God to a higher state. Quoting Jeremiah 9:23–4, Maimonides proclaims:

Let not the wise man glory in his wisdom, let not the mighty man glory in his might, let not the rich man glory in his riches; but let him who glories glory in this, that he understands and knows me, that I am the Lord who practise steadfast love, justice and righteousness in the earth; for in these things I delight, says the Lord.

Just as God is merciful, just and righteous, so the perfected individual should emulate God's actions in his daily life. Here then is a synthesis of the Aristotelian emphasis on intellectualism and Jewish insistence on the moral life. Such a philosophical exposition of the Jewish faith not only influenced Jewish writers, but also had an impact on medieval Christian scholars such as Albertus Magnus and Thomas Aquinas.

By the time of his death in 1204 Maimonides' writings – along with works by other medieval Jewish philosophers – had been translated into Hebrew by Jews living in southern France. As a result of this scholarly activity, Jews in Spain, Provence and Italy produced a variety of philosophical and scientific writings including commentaries on Maimonides' *Guide*. Though Maimonides was admired as a legal authority, some Jewish scholars were troubled by his views. In particular, they were dismayed that he appeared not to believe in physical resurrection;

that he viewed prophecy, providence and immortality as dependent on intellectual attainment; that he regarded the doctrine of divine incorporality as a fundamental tenet of the Jewish faith; and that he felt that knowledge of God should be based on Aristotelian principles.

For these sages, Maimonides' theology was seen as a threat to Judaism and to rabbinic learning. In 1230 some of those opposed to the Maimonidean philosophical system attempted to prevent the study of the *Guide* as well as the philosophical sections of Maimonides' legal code, the *Mishneh Torah*. The bitter antagonism between Maimonideans and anti-Maimonideans came to an end when Dominican inquisitors in France burned copies of Maimonides' writings – both sides were appalled by such an action. Yet opposition to Maimonides continued throughout the century. In 1300 anti-Maimonideans issued a ban against studying Greek philosophy before the age of twenty-five, but the conflict subsided when many Jews were expelled from France in 1306.

References

Encyclopedia Judaica, Jerusalem, 1971

Maimonides' major writings

Moses Maimonides, *Mishneh Torah: The Book of Knowledge* (trans. M. Hyamson), Jerusalem, 1962
Moses Maimonides, *The Guide of the Perplexed* (trans. S. Pines), Chicago, 1963
Moses Maimonides, *Rambam: Readings in the Philosophy of Moses Maimonides* (trans. E. Goodman), New York, 1976

Further reading

F.G. Bratton, *Maimonides, Medieval Modernist*, Boston, 1967
A. Cohen, *Teachings of Maimonides*, New York, 1968
M. Fox, *Interpreting Maimonides*, Chicago, 1990
A. Heschel, *Maimonides: A Biography*, New York, 1991

O. Leaman, *Moses Maimonides*, London, 1990
L. Roth, *Spinoza, Descartes and Maimonides*, Oxford, 1924

IGNAZ MAYBAUM

Born in Vienna in 1897, Ignaz Maybaum served as a rabbi in Bingen (on the Rhine), Frankfurt-am-der-Oder, and Berlin. During the years before the Second World War, he was actively involved in providing support for the Berlin Jewish community. In 1939 he moved to London where he subsequently became the rabbi of Edgware Reform Synagogue; in 1956 he helped found the Leo Baeck College in London to train Reform and Liberal rabbis. As a disciple of Franz Rosenzweig, Maybaum sought to interpret his teacher's philosophy for a post-Holocaust world. Throughout his life (he died in 1976) Maybaum published a number of theological works dealing with Jewish faith in modern society – pre-eminent among these studies is his investigation of the religious implications of the Holocaust: *The Face of God after Auschwitz*.

In this study Maybaum maintains that God has an enduring covenantal relationship with Israel, that he continues to act in history and that Israel has a divinely sanctioned mission to enlighten other peoples. According to Maybaum the Holocaust is the result of God's providential activity. It is not a punishment, but rather the unfolding of God's plan for his chosen people. In presenting this view, Maybaum uses the crucifixion of Jesus as a model for comprehending Jewish suffering during the Holocaust. Just as Jesus was an innocent victim whose death offers a means of salvation for all human beings, so the deaths of the victims of the Holocaust were a sacrificial offering. Maybaum argues that the Jews were murdered by the Nazis because they were chosen by God for this sacrifice. In this way God's purposes can be fulfilled. 'The

Golgotha of modern mankind is Auschwitz', he writes. 'The cross, the Roman gallows, was replaced by the gas chamber' (Maybaum, 1965, 36).

In Maybaum's view, Jewish history has been scarred by three major catastrophes which he designates by the Hebrew word *churban*, a term referring to an event of massive destructiveness. For Maybaum each *churban* was a divine intervention which has had decisive significance for the course of history. Each *churban* is thus an act of creative destruction brought about by divine providential decree. The first of these cataclysmic events was the destruction of Jerusalem in 586 BCE which resulted in the diaspora of the Jewish community. This uprooting of the Jewish population was a major calamity, yet it did inaugurate the Jewish mission to bring the knowledge of God and His laws to other nations outside Israel's borders. In this respect the first *churban* was a manifestation of creative destructiveness. The second *churban* was the Roman devastation of the second Temple in Jerusalem, which brought about the creation of the synagogue as the central focus of dispersed Jewish life where study and prayer took the place of sacrifice. For Maybaum such activity is of a higher order than the sacrificial system of the Biblical period.

The final *churban*, Maybaum continues, was the Holocaust, an event in which the Jewish people were sacrificed so that God's purposes could be realized. In Maybaum's opinion, God used the Holocaust to bring about the end of the Middle Ages. In this context, Hitler should be understood as an instrument of God's will. In Scripture, Nebuchadnezzar is depicted as the destroyer of Jerusalem; nonetheless he is referred to as 'Nebuchadnezzar, my Servant' (Jeremiah 27:6). Again, Isaiah proclaimed that Ashur who destroyed Samaria had been used by God to do His will. Similarly, Maybaum contends that Hitler was a servant of the Lord. Though Hitler was himself unworthy and contemptible, God used this instrument to purify a sinful world. The six million died an innocent death because of the sin of others. Thus Western man must say of the Jew what Isaiah said of the servant of God: 'Surely our diseases he did bear, and our pain he carried . . . he was wounded because of our iniquity'. (Isaiah 53:4–5)

For Maybaum the third *churban* brings about progress through sacrifice. But what kind of development took place? Maybaum insists that this catastrophe brought about an end to the medieval period. The structure of medieval society which survived for centuries in Europe was eliminated. Hitler did what should have been accomplished by others. The old order of Eastern European Jewry was exterminated in the gas chambers; after Auschwitz this large segment of the Jewish people who lived an essentially medieval lifestyle came to an end.

In the Middle Ages lord and vassal were bound together by an authoritarian hierarchy. This system of social differentiation formed a pyramid in which inequality became the primary social binding force. In this environment there was no place for Jewry: Jews were branded Christ-killers and thus perceived as providentially destined to be punished for their sin. Hitler was viewed by many as a crusader – Auschwitz was the place where the directors of the Inquisition did their work in the midst of the twentieth century. Yet Hitler accomplished what the progressives should have done: he destroyed the old order.

The end of the Middle Ages means the cessation of Jewish submission. It is not merely small isolated groups of the Jewish people who have been liberated, but the entire community. Jewry can now emancipate itself from the enforced compliance of Jewish religious life and dismiss the medieval mentality which separated one community from another, giving rise to the quest for a Jewish homeland. In Western democracies Jew and Christian meet as equals; they are to be treated in the same fashion before the law. Such equality breaks down barriers between Jew and non-Jew and provides them both with an opportunity to enrich the world in different ways. Now that the third *churban* has taken place, the Jewish people live outside the community-imposed legal system of past centuries. Jews today are compelled to make personal decisions about which aspects of the Jewish tradition are spiritually meaningful under the conditions of democracy and Western civilization.

Maybaum points out that there are some Jews who are unhappy about this transformation of Jewish life and view the Middle Ages nostalgically. They portray the poverty and unhygienic narrowness of European ghetto and *shtetl* (Jewish village) life in positive terms, romanticizing such conditions as a Jewish paradise with saintly piety. But Maybaum insists that no one would actually wish to return to such a state of affairs:

> Sometimes I feel I want to ask these writers the question, would you like to leave your Manhattan flat or your cosy British suburban home and live under the conditions in which your parents and grandparents lived, in the dire straits and humiliating status of civic inequality? The honest answer is obvious. Nobody wants to go back and everybody must admit the benefits from what can only be described as progress. Progress has taken place, the progress from the Middle Ages to the modern age of Western civilisation and democracy. (in Cohn-Sherbok, 1989, 35)

In replacing the medieval with the modern approach, contemporary Jewish historiography put an end to the notion of history as a long-drawn-out story of miracles and a continuous chain of legends about saintly individuals. The medieval dream has ended, and Western man now takes history seriously. In this regard, human beings have moved closer to the Hebrew Bible than was possible in a medieval context. Western man now has a dominant place on the stage of history. The remnant of the Jewish nation – the survivors of the third *churban*

– have become increasingly Westernized, and with the development of Western civilization the Jew will arise too. Out of the depths into which the horrors of our time plunged the Jewish people, there is hope for the future.

It is now the prophetic task of the Jewish nation to interpret the Holocaust as an awful portent (*mophet*) in the exodus from the past into the future. In the post-*churban* age, Western civilization can be the mediating force which brings to humankind what God has planned: justice, kindness and peace. Through the Jewish enlightenment movement (*Haskalah*), Zionism and socialism, Jews previously sought to bring Western ideas and the blessings of a Western way of life to east European Jewry. However, this task failed. Yet the terrible efficiency of Auschwitz achieved this end. As Jews say farewell to the long tradition of the Jewish people in the Middle Ages, they must be sustained by prophetic faith. Archaic traditions cannot serve them on their journey into the future. Only listening to God, Maybaum states, can aid them after the collapse of their faithfully preserved heritage. In the hour of the *churban*, the great and awful destruction of the medieval world, God calls the Jewish people as he did in ancient times: 'Prepare to meet thy God, O Israel' (Amos 4:12).

References/Maybaum's major writings

Ignaz Maybaum, *The Sacrifice of Isaac*, London, 1959
Ignaz Maybaum, *The Face of God after Auschwitz*, Amsterdam, 1965
Ignaz Maybaum, *Creation and Guilt*, London, 1969

See also in this book

Rosenzweig

Further reading

D. Cohn-Sherbok, *Holocaust Theology*, London, 1989

S. Katz, *Post-Holocaust Dialogues: Critical Studies in Modern Jewish Thought*, New York, 1983
N. de Lange, 'Ignaz Maybaum and His Attitude to Tradition' in Brian D. Fox, *Tradition, Transition and Transmission*, Cincinnati, OH, 1983

MOSES MENDELSSOHN

The principles of rational investigation propounded by Baruch Spinoza and others in the seventeenth century continued to dominate the intellectual climate of the next century. During the period of the Enlightenment, political and religious reformers pressed for the application of reason to all spheres of inquiry. From France this spirit of rationalism spread throughout Europe to the United States. In Germany the Jewish thinker Moses Mendelssohn spearheaded a revolution in Jewish life and thought. Born in Dessau in 1729, Mendelssohn suffered from a disease as a child which left him with a curvature of the spine.

As the son of a Torah scribe, he received a traditional Jewish education under David Fraenkel, the rabbi of Dessau. Later he settled in Berlin where he gained a broad secular knowledge under such teachers as Israel M. Zamosz, Abraham Kisch and A.S. Gumpertz. During this period he befriended the dramatist and literary critic Gotthold Ephraim Lessing who was the leading advocate of enlightened toleration in Germany. In 1750 Mendelssohn served as a teacher in the house of Isaac Bernhard who was the owner of a silk factory; four years later he became the book-keeper of the firm and subsequently a partner. Right up to his death in 1786, he worked as a merchant while engaging in literary activity.

Initially Mendelssohn published a number of philosophical works. In 1763 he was awarded first prize by the Prussian Royal Academy of Sciences for a philosophical study; his later philosophical works included *Phaedo* (1767) and *Morning Hours* (1785). In

1769 he was engaged in a dispute about the Jewish faith, and most of his works subsequently dealt with Jewish topics. To bring about the modernization of Jewish life, Mendelssohn also translated the Pentateuch into German so that Jews would be able to learn the language of the country in which they lived, and oversaw the production of commentary on Scripture (*Biur*) which combined Jewish scholarship with secular thought.

Prior to his friendship with Mendelssohn, Lessing had written a play portraying a Jew of exceptional qualities – for Lessing and others Mendelssohn represented such a person. With Lessing's assistance Mendelssohn published a series of philosophical essays in which he argued for the existence of God and creation, insisting that human reason is capable of discovering the reality of God, providence and immortality. At the height of his career, Mendelssohn was challenged by the Christian apologist John Casper Lavater to defend the superiority of Judaism over Christianity. From 1769 he engaged in Jewish apologetics, and in 1783 published his major work on the Jewish faith, *Jerusalem or On Religious Power and Judaism*.

In this study Mendelssohn maintains that no religious institution should use coercion; neither the Church, nor the state, he argues, has the right to impose its religious views on the individual. Addressing the question whether Jewish law sanctions coercion, he emphasizes that Judaism does not coerce the mind through dogma:

> The Israelites possess a divine legislation – laws, commandments, statutes, rules of conduct, instruction in God's will and in what they are to do to attain temporary and eternal salvation. Moses, in a miraculous and supernatural way, revealed to them these laws and commandments, but not dogmas, propositions concerning salvation, or self-evident principles of reason. These the Lord reveals to us and

as well to all other men at all times through nature and events, but never through the spoken or written word. (Mendelssohn, 1969, 61)

The distinction Mendelssohn makes between natural religion and the Jewish faith is based on three types of truth:

1 logically necessary truth;
2 contingent truths such as the laws of nature; and
3 the temporal truths that take place in history.

In this regard he writes:

> Whenever God intends man to understand a certain truth, his wisdom provides man with the means most suited to this purpose. If it is a necessary truth, God provides man with whatever degree of reason he requires for its understanding. If a natural law is to be disclosed to man, God's wisdom will provide him with the necessary capacity for observation; and if a historical truth is to be presented for posterity, God's wisdom authenticates its historicity by establishing the narrator's credibility beyond any doubt. (Ibid., 64–5)

In Mendelssohn's view, all human beings are capable of discovering religious truth. However, Judaism is different from other religions in that it contains a revealed legal code. The Jewish people did not hear God proclaim that he is an eternal, necessary and omniscient being who rewards and punishes humanity; rather, the *mitzvot* (commandments) were revealed to His chosen people:

> The voice that was heard at Sinai on the great day did not proclaim, 'I am the eternal, your God, the necessary autonomous being, omnipotent and omniscient, who rewards men in a future life according to their deeds.' This is the universal religion of mankind, not Judaism, and this kind of universal religion – without which man can become neither virtuous nor happy – was not and, in fact,

could not have been revealed at Sinai. For who could have needed the sound of thunder and the blast of trumpets to become convinced of the validity of these eternal verities. (Ibid., 68–9)

Rather at Mount Sinai the Jewish people heard the historical truth, 'I am the Lord your God who brought you out of the land of Egypt' – a statement introducing the legal code which is binding on the Jewish nation.

For Mendelssohn the purpose of ceremonial law is to bring all peoples to a belief in ethical monotheism:

And now I am finally at the point where I can elucidate my hypothesis about the purpose of the ceremonial law in Judaism. Our people's patriarchs – Abraham, Isaac and Jacob – had remained faithful to the Eternal and tried to preserve pure religious concepts free of all idolatry, for their families and descendants. And now these descendants were chosen by Providence to be a nation of priests, that is, a nation which, through its constitution and institutions, through its laws and conduct, and throughout all changes of life and fortune, was to call wholesome and unadulterated ideas of God and his attributes continuously to the attention of the rest of mankind. It was a nation which through its mere existence, as it were, would unceasingly teach, proclaim, preach and strive to preserve these ideas among the nations. (Ibid., 89)

Yet despite this universal mission, Jews are not at liberty to divorce themselves from their cultural connections with the countries where they dwell. Rather, they must engage in civic life while remaining faithful to their religious heritage:

Adopt the mores and constitution of the country in which you find yourself, but be steadfast in upholding the religion of your fathers, too. Bear both burdens as well as you can. True, on the one hand, people make it difficult for you to bear the burden of civil life because of the religion to which you remain faithful; and, on the other hand, the climate of our time makes the observance of your religious laws in some respects more burdensome than it need be. Persevere neverthless; stand fast in the place which Providence has assigned everything which may happen, as you were told to do by your Lawgiver long ago. (Ibid., 104–5)

At the end of *Jerusalem*, Mendelssohn argues for the individuality of all religious traditions. Rejecting the idea that all faiths should be merged into one universal creed, he maintains that the existence of many different religions is fundamental. In Mendelssohn's view, human reason serves as a means by which all people can arrive at universal truths about the nature of God and His activity in the world. In this sense all religions have the capacity to discover the reality of God, divine providence and the immortality of the soul. Yet as far as Judaism is concerned, the Jewish people are the recipients of a divine revelation consisting of ritual and moral law. This supernatural dispensation is what distinguishes Judaism from other faiths, and serves to impel the nation toward their universal mission for all humanity.

References/Mendelssohn's major writings

Moses Mendelssohn, *Judaism and Other Writings*, New York, 1969

Moses Mendelssohn, *Moses Mendelssohn: Selections from his Writings* (trans. E. Jospe), New York, 1975

Further reading

A. Altmann, *Moses Mendelssohn: A Biographical Study*, London, 1973

A. Arkush, *Moses Mendelssohn and the Enlightenment*, Albany, NY, 1994

E. Cassirer, *The Philosophy of the Enlightenment*, Boston, MA, 1955

M.H.Z. Meyer, *Moses Mendelssohn Bibliographie*, Berlin, 1965

H. Walter, *Moses Mendelssohn, Critic and Philosopher*, New York, 1930

CLAUDE MONTEFIORE

Claude Montefiore was born in 1858 into a prominent Anglo-Jewish family. After studying at Balliol College, Oxford, where he came under the influence of Benjamin Jowett, he was a student at the *Hochschule* in Berlin. There he encountered Solomon Schechter whom he brought back to England to be his private tutor in rabbinics. In 1902 Montefiore founded the Jewish Religious Union which led to the creation of the Liberal Jewish Synagogue in 1911. An ardent opponent of Zionism, Montefiore stressed the importance of a universalistic Jewish outlook; in his capacity as president of the Anglo-Jewish Association, he sought to prevent the signing of the Balfour Declaration. His death came in 1938.

Throughout his writings Montefiore sought to provide a positive appraisal of Christianity. Influenced by biblical criticism, Hegelianism and the theory of evolution, Montefiore believed in progressive revelation and the eventual enlightenment of humanity. Viewing the New Testament from a Jewish perspective, he sought to introduce the Christian tradition to the Jewish community. Nevertheless, he was aware that such inquiries would in all probability evoke suspicion and hostility:

> The teaching of Jesus has not been much discussed and appraised as a whole. And where it has been so discussed, the line has been rather to depreciate or to cheapen. Jewish writers have looked for parallels or for defects. Considering what Judaism and Jews have had to suffer at Christian hands, this Jewish treatment of the Gospels is not astonishing. (Montefiore, 1927, xxi)

Despite such a negative response, Montefiore was determined to reappraise Christianity. This quest, he states, would fall primarily on Liberal Jews. 'Liberal Judaism', he writes, 'does not believe that God has enabled the human race to reach forward to religious truth so exclusively through a single channel' (Montefiore, 1918, 78). As a consequence, other religions need to be examined in order to gain knowledge of God's disclosure. Because Montefiore felt most capable of exploring Christianity, he was committed to this enterprise.

In Montefiore's view, Liberal Jews are obliged to understand and gain an appreciation of the Christian heritage as part of their own religious background. The New Testament, he emphasizes, belongs to Judaism:

> It is a book which, in very large part, was written by persons who were born Jews. Its central hero was a Jew. Its teaching is based throughout – sometimes indeed by way of opposition – upon the teaching of the Old Testament. (Ibid., 80)

Because of this conviction, Montefiore became an apologist for the Christian faith, seeking to present the best of the Christian past to a Jewish audience. Writing about the New Testament, he states:

> The Liberal Jew at any rate will not be deterred from gaining all the good he can from the Gospels (or from the rest of the New Testament) because there are many things in it which he holds to be erroneous. It also contains a lower and a higher. So too the Prophets, but he does not therefore reject them. (Montefiore, 1927, cxliii)

In his discussion of Jesus' ministry, Montefiore rejects the miraculous features of the New Testament account. Instead, he focuses on the parallels between Judaism and Christianity. In *Rabbinic Literature and the Gospels Teachings* as well as *The Synoptic Gospels*, he traces these connections. Given such links between Christian sources and Judaism, Montefiore argues that Jews should be inspired by the teachings of Christianity:

> We have ... brought together in words of striking simplicity and power in the pages

of the Gospels. Shall we admire and cherish, and learn from, these exquisite stories, or shall we sniff and sneer at them and pass them by? (Montefiore, 1918, 86)

Montefiore views Jesus as part of the prophetic tradition:

If Jesus resembled the prophets in the cause and occasion of his preaching, still more did he resemble them in his temper of mind, and therefore in one great feature and characteristic of his teaching . . . . The inwardness of Jesus, the intense spirituality of his teaching, need not be insisted on here. I only emphasize it now to show his connection and kinship with the Prophets. (Montefiore, 1910, 19)

For Montefiore, Jesus' sayings should be understood in the context of the prophetic tradition. According to Montefiore, Jesus did not seek to violate Jewish law:

It is even doubtful whether, except perhaps in cases of moments of stress and conflict, he sought or desired or intended to put his own teaching in direct contrast with, or substitution for, the teaching of those around him, or the teaching of the law. (Montefiore, 1927, 80)

Rather like the prophets, Jesus sought to affirm the importance of the moral law:

Jesus . . . had to hark back from the Law to the Prophets. His teaching is a revival of prophetic Judaism, and in some respects points forward to the Liberal Judaism of today. (Ibid., cxxxiv)

Discussing Jesus' statements, Montefiore asserts that in certain cases his sayings – such as 'Love thy enemies' – were by necessity intentionally exaggerated. This fact, he believes, has not been recognized by the Jewish community. In Montefiore's opinion, Jesus' utterances were totally consistent with traditional Jewish thought. For example, when Jesus referred to the Kingdom of God, he did not separate himself from previous

teaching. Moreover, in areas of philosophy and theology, Montefiore contends that Jesus added little that was new. It was only later that Christian writers reinterpreted and expounded his message.

The feature that Montefiore admires most in the Gospels is Jesus' heroism:

That heroic element seems to show itself in a certain grand largeness of views and in a certain grand simplicity. Taken as a whole, this heroic element is full of genius and inspiration. We must not always take it literally, and squeeze out of it too literal an application. The letter of even the prophet's teachings may kill; here too we must sometimes look only to the spirit. (Montefiore, 1918, 103)

Regarding the Christian doctrines of the Incarnation and the Trinity, Montefiore stresses Jesus' nobility:

We seem to see, through the mist of eulogy and legend, the sure outlines of a noble personality. Here we have a deeply religious nature, filled, as perhaps few before or after have been filled, with the love of God and the consciousness of his presence. A teacher stands before us who is not only a teacher, but a hero, strong, sometimes even passionate, fervent, devoted, brave. . . . He is filled with a true Jewish idealism, for there is no more idealistic race than that of Israel . . . . He has no ambition except one: to do the will of his Father in Heaven, and to serve the people to whom he has been sent. (Ibid., 126)

Despite such an assessment of Jesus' character, Montefiore perceived various inconsistencies in his teaching: these, however, were of minor significance. Nevertheless, it was largely because of these defects that Montefiore was unable to accept the Christian understanding of Jesus' nature: 'I would not deny that the dogma of the Incarnation of God as Jesus has had its effects for good as well as evil', he writes. 'But Liberal Jews do hold that it rests on a confusion, the confusion of a man with God (Montefiore, 1927, xxv).

In evaluating Paul's contribution to the development of Christianity, Montefiore attempts to explain his views in the context of first-century Judaism. In contrast with other Jewish scholars, he was not troubled by Paul's teaching:

In spite of his amazing forgetfulness of the Jewish doctrine of repentance and atonement, in spite too of the remoteness for us of his opposition 'law versus Christ', we may still admire the profundity and genius and adopt many true and noble elements of his religious and ethical teaching. (Montefiore, 1923, 114)

For Montefiore, Paul's attitude toward the Law has been widely misunderstood: the form of Judaism he attacked was not the rabbinic tradition. This form of Judaism was 'poor, more pessimistic . . . it possessed these inferiorities just because it was not Rabbinic Judaism, but Diaspora Judaism' (Montefiori, 1914, 93). The form of Judaism that Paul knew was solely that of the Diaspora; hence it is an error to regard him as an enemy of the rabbinic establishment. According to Montefiore, the greatness of Paul is attested by the autobiographical passages of the epistles: 'There is always something inspiring in the picture of a great man, convinced of his cause, and pursuing his straight course in the face of constant opposition and trial. Paul not only rises superior to his sufferings, but he exults and rejoices in them.' (Ibid., 179)

In his writings, Montefiore sought to present Christianity in the most positive light; in his opinion, the New Testament contains various truths which are of crucial importance for Jewry. In Jesus, he believes, Jews can discover a prophetic figure of great significance. Similarly, Paul stands out as a figure of central importance. Committed to the belief in the progressive revelation of God's will, Montefiore was convinced that God was at work in the lives of these two major figures of the Christian heritage.

References/Montefiore's major writings

Claude Montefiore, *Some Elements of the Religious Teaching of Jesus According to the Synoptic Gospels*, London, 1910
Claude Montefiore, *Liberal Judaism and Hellenism and Other Essays*, London, 1918
Claude Montefiore, *Outlines of Liberal Judaism*, London, 1923
Claude Montefiore, *The Synoptic Gospels*, London, 1927

Further reading

N. Bentwich, *Claude Montefiore and His Tutor in Rabbinics*, Southampton, Hampshire, 1966
L, Cohen, *Some Recollections of C.G. Montefiore*, London, 1940
W. Jacob, *Judaism* 19, no. 3, 1970
W.R. Matthews, *Claude Montefiore, the Man and His Thought*, Southampton, Hampshire, 1956
V.E. Reichert in *Central Conference of American Rabbis Yearbook* 38, 1928

NAHMAN OF BRATZLAV

Born in 1772 in Medzibezh, Nahman of Bratslav was the great-grandson of Israel ben Eliezer Baal Shem Tov on his mother's side, and the grandson of Nahman of Horodenka on his father's side. Brought up in a hasidic environment, he married at an early age, living in the home of his father-in-law. After his father-in-law's second marriage, Nahman moved to Medvedevka in the province of Kiev – there he was the leader of a circle of devoted followers. In 1798 Nahman travelled to Israel accompanied by his disciple Simeon; during this period he visited Haifa, Jaffa, Tiberius and Safed, meeting Jacob Samson of Shepetovka and Abraham ben Alexander Katz of Kalisk. When Napoleon invaded the country, Nahman fled after a stay of only a few months.

In Medvedevka, Nahman was embroiled in a local conflict and developed the theory that controversy about him was inevitable. In the summer of 1800 he moved to Zlatopol near Shpola in the province of Kiev. After his arrival he engaged in controversy with Aryeh Leib of Shpola, the aged hasidic leader who exerted an important influence on Jewry in Podolia and other parts of what is now the Ukraine. In Aryeh Leib's opinion, Nahman's teachings contained Shabbatean and Frankist heretical views; in addition, he was critical of Nahman's moral behaviour. In 1802 Nahman left for Bratslav in Podolia, where the *zaddikim* (spiritual leaders) came into conflict with him (with the exception of Levi Isaac of Berdichev). In 1810 Nahman left Bratslav and settled in Uman (Kiev province) where he died the following year.

Nearly all of the existing Bratslav literature was compiled by Nathan ben Naphtali Hertz Sternhartz, Nahman's scribe and disciple who joined his small circle of followers in 1803. Initially he was not a member of Nahman's innermost circle; it was only after his master's death that he assumed a central role. The first volume of Nahman's theological writings, *Likkutei Moharan*, was published during his lifetime; the second volume – *Likkutei Moharan Tinyana* – appeared posthumously. The stories Nahman related during the last years of his life were collected in *Sippurei Maasiyyot*. The manuscript of his most esoteric writing, *Sefer ha-Nisraf* (The Burned Book) was destroyed in accordance with Nahman's wish in 1808. Another esoteric text appears to have survived in manuscript form among the Bratslav *Hasidim*, and was entitled *Sefer ha-Ganuz* (The Hidden Book). Nathan Sternhartz also edited another work entitled *Likkutei Tefillot* in which he transformed Nahman's teachings into a series of prayers.

Although Nahman asserts that his teaching is based on tradition, his theories contain numerous innovations. In his view, the *Ayn Sof* (Infinite) sought to reveal its mercy by creating the world which it rules in accordance with its absolute will. Thus divinity inheres in all things, even in the demonic realm. Hence, even if a person is evil, he can find God and repent of his sins. For Nahman, the Lurianic notion of *tzimtzum* (divine contraction) gives rise to a paradox: it postulates the withdrawal and disappearance of the Divine so as to create a vacuum while simultaneously assuming divine immanence. According to Nahman, *tzimtzum* can be achieved only in the future, yet he is less concerned with this contraction than with the space which is devoid of the divine presence. This, he believes, generates doubts regarding the existence of the Creator. Thus the formation of a question (*kushya*) serves as an important feature of his doctrine, depending on the first created act in relation to human beings. In Nahman's view, even though human beings may be vexed by doubt, it is possible to rise beyond such hesitation – this is the ultimate purpose of humankind's fall.

In addition to the question that arises in connection with the *tzimtzum*, there is another further difficulty regarding the 'breaking of the vessels'. In line with his dualist understanding of Lurianic *kabbalah*, Nahman contends that the *kelippot* (realm of evil) emerged as a result of the breaking of the vessels, denoting a separate realm for their destructive action. Further, he argues that they serve as the source of secular studies and hence of heretical questioning. Nonetheless, because the holy sparks fell into this sphere, it is possible to find salvation and arise from that place, thereby establishing a solution to heresy. The most important questions, he continues, arise out of the vacuum and through silence: this answer is the holy silence of the faithful. Rational reflection, he asserts, cannot resolve the ultimate questions of faith.

Faith, Nahman maintains, is able to rise above all doubts; it is much more paradoxical and complex than the questions it seeks to answer. Rational certainty, on the other hand, is not a matter of faith – it is arguably its worst enemy. For Nahman, the faith of those who believe is an expression of free will, which is not based on logic or conditional upon it. In *Lukkutei Moharan*, he writes:

The main purpose and perfection of man is the worship of God in naïveté and with no crafty side thoughts . . . only by faith and through the practical *mitzvot* performed according to the Torah in simplicity and naïveté . . . because this can be done by every man, thereby achieving his ultimate objective. (*Likkutei Moharan*, part 1, 19)

For this reason, Nahman is highly critical of the study of philosophy; faith, he believes, is one of the highest religious ideals. The recognition that human logic differs in principle from divine reasoning forms a series of paradoxes which only faith can overcome. Faith begins where reason ends, he writes. Where something cannot be grasped through the intellect, faith is required. In his opinion, the exile exists because of the lack of such religious commitment.

Discussing the concept of the *zaddik* (spiritual leader), Nahman argues that such a figure provides redemptive force to the prayers of the Jewish people; in addition, reflection on heretical questions by the *zaddik* can bring about spiritual illumination for those who have been overwhelmed by doubt. Likewise the hasidic melody sung by the *zaddik* can exert a spiritual influence on the faithful. It is necessary, he continues, to believe in the *zaddik* despite one's doubts, to recognize that the *zaddik* simulates the Creator, and that through his teachings the *zaddik* is able to instruct the Holy One, Blessed be He, how to deal with humanity. When the *zaddik* rises above the level of *Ayin* (Nothingness), he is close to human beings and is able to supervise them. The *zaddik* lives, as it were, eternally, regardless of where he dwells – an individual must travel to the *zaddik* so that he can hear words from his mouth. Further, Nahman stresses that one should confess before the *zaddik* and praise him. Because the *zaddik* embodies all that is taking place in the terrestrial and celestial domain, communication with him contributes to the process of *tikkun* (cosmic restoration).

Despite these conceptions of divine reality, Nahman's religious conceptions are largely pessimistic in character. For Nahman, there are many obstacles in one's path. It is as if a person were suspended by a thread over a raging sea. Yet, Nahman firmly rejects dspair: the rafts to cling to in life are faith, joy, melody, dance, self-criticism, communication with the *zaddik*, and the quest to know God. For this reason prayer plays a central role in his religious system – it is defined as a dialogue between human beings and the Divine. In this regard Nahman taught a form of meditation in which the mystic was able to concentrate on an external object such as a name or a mantra.

In his view such prayers should arise spontaneously and bring about the loss of self:

You must make yourself in God's unity, which is the imperative existence. You cannot be worthy of this, however, unless you first nullify yourself. It is impossible to nullify yourself, however, without *hitbodedut* (mental self-seclusion) meditation. When you meditate and express your spontaneous thoughts before God, you can be worthy of nullifying all desires and evil traits. You will then be able to nullify your entire physical being, and become included in your root. The main time to meditate is at night . . . it is also necessary that you meditate alone. This is a time when the world is free from mundane concerns. Since people are involved in the mundane, by day, you will be held back and confused, so that you will not be able to attach yourself to God and include yourself in Him . . . it is also necessary that you meditate in an isolated place. You must therefore be alone, at night, on an isolated path, where people are not usually found. Go there and meditate, cleansing your heart and mind of all worldly affairs. You will then be worthy of a true aspect of self-nullification. (in Kaplan, 1982, 309)

References

A. Kaplan, *Meditation and Kabbalah*, York Beach, ME, 1982

Nahman's major writings

M. Levin, *Classical Hassidic Tales: Marvellous Tales of Rabbi Israel Baal Shem and of His Great-grandson, Rabbi Nachman*, New York, 1975
Nahman of Bratslav, *Rabbi Nachman's Wisdom* (trans. A. Kaplan), Brooklyn, NY, 1973
Nahman of Bratslav, *The Chambers of the Palace*, Northvale, NJ, 1993

Further reading

M. Buber, *The Tales of Rabbi Nachman* (trans. M. Friedman), Atlantic Highlands, NJ, 1988
G. Fleer, *Rabbi Nachman's Fire*, New York, 1972
G. Fleer, *Rabbi Nachman's Foundation*, New York, 1976
A. Green, *Tormented Master: The Life and Spiritual Quest of Rabbi Nahman of Bratslav*, Woodstock, VT, 1992
A. Kaplan, *Until the Mashiach: Rabbi Nachman's Biography*, Jerusalem, 1985

NAHMANIDES

Born in Gerona, Catalonia, in 1194, Moses ben Nahman (known as Nahmanides) was a descendant of Isaac ben Reuben, a contemporary of Isaac ben Jacob Alfasi; his mother was the sister of Abraham, father of Jonah ben Abraham Gerondi. His teachers included Judah ben Yakar who established a *yeshivah* (rabbinical academy) in Barcelona and Meir ben Isaac of Trinquetaille. From these scholars he received the tradition of the tosafists (medieval talmudists) of northern France as well as the methods of close study used in the *yeshivot* (rabbinical academies) of Provence. According to tradition, Nahmanides earned his livelihood as a physician, and it appears that he headed a *yeshivah* in Gerona. After the death of Jonah ben Abraham Gerondi in 1264, Nahmanides served as chief rabbi of Catalonia until he

emigrated to *Eretz Israel*. In later generations the Spanish rabbis regarded him as their great teacher, referring to him as 'the trustworthy rabbi'.

When the Maimonidean controversy raged in Montpellier in 1232, Nahmanides sought to bring together the opposing camps even though he agreed with Solomon ben Abraham of Montpellier and his disciples who condemned the way Maimonides' writings had been used by various philosophers. In letters sent to leaders of Aragon, Navarre and Castile, he attempted to prevent them from taking measures against the extremists of Montpellier. However, he also requested the rabbis of France to annul the *herem* (edict of excommunication) they had proclaimed against Maimonides' works. To avert a split between the opposing factions, he designed a detailed programme which would suit the different conditions in France and Spain, and would regulate the study of sciences to meet the needs of the local populations. This plan failed, however, because of the influence of the extremists on both sides.

Nahmanides exerted a considerable influence in public life in Catalonia; he was even consulted by King James I, and in 1232 on the advice of Nahmanides the King rejected the claims of the Alconstantini family to the position of *dayyan* (judge) over all the Jews in the kingdom. In 1263 the King persuaded Nahmanides to participate in a public disputation in Barcelona with a Jewish apostate, Pablo Christiani – this disputation was held in July in the presence of the King and the heads of the Dominicans and Franciscans. At the request of the bishop of Gerona, Nahmanides later summarized his arguments. Subsequently the Dominicans who had initiated the disputation summoned Nahmanides to stand trial for his alleged abuses of the Christian faith. Before the tribunal Nahmanides explained that he had been promised freedom of speech by the King, and that he had written his views at the bishop's request. When the King extricated Nahmanides from the trial, the Dominicans sought the assistance of Pope Clement IV who requested that the King penalize him. In the light of these events, Nahmanides escaped from Spain and settled in the Holy Land.

Arriving in Acre in 1267, Nahmanides went to Jerusalem. In a letter to his son Nahman he describes the ruins of the city after the Tartar invasion which had occurred seven years previously. In Jerusalem he found a few Jews whom he succeeded in organizing; they erected a synagogue in a derelict house, and Nahmanides seems to have founded a *yeshivah* there. Quickly, reports of Nahmanides' activities circulated in the country, and other Jews came to Jerusalem. In 1268 Nahmanides settled in Acre where he served as the spiritual leader of the community, succeeding Jehiel ben Joseph of Paris, until his death in 1270. The site of his tomb is not certain: some believe he was buried at the foot of Mount Carmel; others contend that he was buried in Haifa beside the tomb of Jehiel ben Joseph of Paris; while others assert he was interred in Acre.

Approximately fifty of Nahmanides' works survive as well as others which have been attributed to him – the majority are novellae on the Talmud and *halakhah* (Jewish law). Nahmanides also composed a number of books and letters, various poems and prayers, and a commentary on the narrative and legal parts of Scripture. In addition to these writings, Nahmanides' record of the Barcelona Disputation of 1263 provides a graphic picture of his public activities. This confrontation was the most important disputation between Jews and Christians in the Middle Ages. At the beginning of the encounter, Nahmanides stated that he wished to discuss those matters which are fundamental to the Jewish and Christian tradition. As Nahmanides writes:

> We agreed to speak on whether the Messiah was truly active, or entirely human, born from a man and a woman. And after that we would discuss whether

the Jews still possess the true law, or whether the Christians practise it. (in Maccoby, 1982, 103)

Following this scheme, those representing the Christian side – primarily Pablo Christiani – sought to demonstrate that Jesus is the Messiah on the basis of rabbinic sources. In reply Nahmanides attempted to illustrate that such texts had been incorrectly interpreted. Countering the assertion that Jesus is the Messiah, Nahmanides stated that Jesus never had any power; instead, during his lifetime he could not even save himself from crucifixion. Further, he stressed that the prophetic predictions in Scripture had not been fulfilled:

> The prophet says that in the time of the Messiah, 'And no longer shall each man teach his neighbour and each his brother, saying, "Know the Lord", for they shall all know me' (Jeremiah 31:34); also, 'The earth shall be full of the knowledge of the Lord as the waters cover the sea' (Isaiah 11:9); also, 'They shall not lift up sword against nation, neither shall they learn war any more' (Isaiah 2:4). Yet from the days of Jesus until now, the whole world has been full of violence and plundering. (Ibid., 121)

Further Nahmanides stressed that Jesus did not fulfil the messianic task of bringing about the return of the exiles, the rebuilding of the Temple and the messianic kingdom:

> But even your Messiah, Jesus, did not gather one man of them, and did not even live in the time of the Exile. It is also the task of the Messiah to build the Temple in Jerusalem, but Jesus did not carry out anything in connection with the Temple, either building or destruction. Also the Messiah will rule over the peoples, and Jesus did not rule even over himself. (Ibid., 132)

Regarding the question whether Jesus is God Incarnate, Nahmanides maintained that such a belief is irrational: 'The doctrine in which you believe', he stated, 'and which is the foundation of your faith cannot be accepted by reason,and nature affords no ground for it, nor have the prophets ever expressed it. Nor could even the miraculous stretch as far as this' (Ibid., 120). In Judaism, he continued, the Messiah is conceived as completely human – if Jesus were in fact born by the Spirit of God, he would not fulfil Isaiah's prophecy in 11:1 ('And there shall come forth a rod out of the stem of Jesse'). Even if he were lodged in the womb of a woman who was the seed of Jesse, he would not inherit the Kingdom of David because neither daughters nor their progeny have this right.

Responding to such criticisms, the King cited Psalm 110:1 ('A Psalm of David; the Lord said to my Lord: Sit thou at my right hand'). Referring to this verse, Pablo Christiani asked who King David was referring to other than a divine personage. How, he asked, could a human being sit at the right hand of God? In reply Nahmanides maintained that King David composed the Psalms so they could be sung by the Levites before the altar of the Lord; hence he was compelled to write the psalm in a style which was suitable for a Levite:

If he had said, 'The Lord said to me', the Levite would have been uttering a falsehood; but it was fitting for a Levite to say in the sanctuary: 'The Lord said to me; "The Lord said to my Lord [that is, King David]: Sit at my right hand"' – the meaning of this 'sitting' is that the Holy One, blessed be He, would guard him all his life . . . . And this is what is meant by 'the right hand of God'. (Ibid., 135–6)

On the Sabbath following the disputation, the King and the Preaching Friars visited the synagogue; the Christian scholar Raymond of Peñaforte preached a sermon about the Trinity. After he had finished, Nahmanides declared:

Hearken and listen to my voice, Jews and Gentiles. Fra Paul [Pablo Christiani] asked me in Gerona whether I believed in the Trinity. I said, 'What is the Trinity? Does it mean that the Deity has three physical bodies such as those of human beings?' Said he, 'No'. 'Does it mean, then, that the Deity has three refined entities, such as souls or angelic beings?' Said he, 'No'. 'Does it mean one entity derived from three, as bodies are derived from the four elements?' Said he, 'No'. 'If so, what is the Trinity?' Said he, 'Wisdom, will and power'. So I said, 'I agree that God is wise and not foolish, that he wills, and is not inert, that he is powerful, and not powerless; but the expression "Trinity" is a complete mistake.' (Ibid., 144–5)

After Nahmanides finished speaking, Pablo Christiani stood up and affirmed that he believed in a perfect Unity, and together with it the Trinity. Yet he asserted it is a matter so deep that even the angels and the powers on high do not understand it. In response, Nahmanides disagreed: 'It is obvious', he proclaimed, 'that a person cannot believe what he does not know; which means that the angels do not believe in the Trinity' (Ibid., 146).

References

Hyam Maccoby, *Judaism on Trial*, London, 1982

Nahmanides' major writings

Nahmanides, *Commentary on the Torah* (trans. C.B. Chavel), New York, 1971–6
Nahmanides, *Writings and Discourses* (trans. C.B. Chavel), New York, 1978
Nahmanides, *The Disputation at Barcelona* (trans. C.B. Chavel), New York, 1983

Further reading

R. Chazan, *Barcelona and Beyond: The Disputation of 1263 and Its Aftermath*, Berkeley, CA, 1992
H. Chone, *Nachmanides*, Nuremburg, 1930
D. Novak, *The Theology of Nahmanides Systematically Presented*, Atlanta, GA, 1992

I. Twersky (ed.), *Rabbi Moses Nahmanides (Ramban): Explorations in His Religion and Literary Virtuosity*, Cambridge, MA, 1983
Y. Unna, *R. Moses ben Nahman*, Jerusalem, 1954
A. Yeruham, *Ohel Rahel*, New York, 1942

PHILO

At the end of the first century CE, the city of Alexandria was one of the most important centres of Greek philosophical tradition. Numerous schools flourished there including the Stoics, Epicureans, Sceptics and Aristotelians. Although these Hellenistic philosophers are cited by Greek and Latin writers, the major source for this period is the collected works of the Jewish philosopher and theologian, Philo of Alexandria. A representative of Hellenistic culture and Alexandrian Judaism, Philo was in all likelihood born c. 20 BCE; in 40 CE he travelled to Rome to intercede with the Emperor Caligula on behalf of the Alexandrian Jewish community.

During his lifetime Philo produced a wide variety of treatises. These writings were exclusively in Greek and it is not known whether Philo knew Hebrew; yet it appears that he had some familiarity with midrashic literature, even though he quoted the Bible in the Greek translation (Septuagint). Despite his centrality in the history of Jewish philosophical reflection, Philo's work was largely ignored by later Jewish thinkers and his views had hardly any impact on medieval writers. The Christian community, however, was deeply influenced by his thought, and Philo's ideas affected generations of Christian theologians.

In particular his attempt to harmonize Scripture with Greek culture served as a model for later Christian speculation. Because Philo's writings are largely exegetical in character, it is difficult to present a systematic treatment of his thought; further, Philo is frequently inconsistent. This is not entirely surprising since Philo's aim was not to provide a unified philosophical system – instead he sought to explain how the Torah and philosophy can be reconciled. Philosophy, he believed, is synonymous with the commandments contained in Scripture. His aim is to explain such congruence. In attempting to harmonize the Bible with Greek thought, Philo maintains that the wisdom of the Greeks and others was based on Jewish teaching – the original Jewish philosophical treatises were lost during the Exile, but the ideas they contained were transmitted first to the Chaldeans and Persians and later to the Greeks and Romans.

Philo's writings consist primarily of three series of works. The first is an exposition of the Pentateuch beginning with *On Creation*. Here he argues that, although the Pentateuch is primarily a law code, it begins with the story of Creation – this demonstrates that laws in the Five Books of Moses are consonant with the laws of nature. This is followed by biographies of Abraham, Isaac and Jacob as well as Joseph: all of these figures are perceived as living embodiments of the Torah. In another biography intended as a separate unit, Philo presents a profile of Moses as lawgiver, priest and prophet. This is followed by a treatise (*On the Decalogue*) dealing with the Ten Commandments. In a concluding treatise (*On the Special Laws*), Philo categorizes all biblical ordinances under the headings of the various commandments of the Decalogue.

A second series of writings (*Allegorical Interpretation*) consists of a philosophical interpretation of the Five Books of Moses: this consists of eighteen exegetical treatises. Here Philo sets aside the narrative content of the Torah; instead he allegorizes these stories into abstract philosophical ideas. In the final treatise of this series, *On Dreams*, Philo focuses on the dream narratives of Scripture.

A third series – *Questions and Answers on Genesis* and *Questions and Answers on Exodus* – takes the form of Hellenistic commentary in which each paragraph begins with an exegetical question followed by a short literal interpretation and a lengthy allegorical exposition. In addition to these works, Philo composed a number of separate studies dealing with a variety of philosophical topics, two books on history concerning the onslaught on Alexandrian Jewry in 38 CE and his mission to Rome two years later, and a study of the contemplative life.

In these various works Philo adopts the Platonic distinction between the higher, spiritual realm and the lower, material world. In his view, it is only in the upper intelligible realm that truth can be attained; but in the earthly realm one can seek to attain the contemplative life whereby one is freed from bodily pleasures. In portraying this process, Philo argues that not only does the soul long to ascend to God, God also descends into the human soul. There is thus an interplay between God and man.

Ascending to the Ultimate, humans must strip themselves of earthly bonds. In presenting this doctrine, Philo repeatedly utilizes the scriptural narrative; hence the three patriarchs are presented as so many stages of the journey to God. In this context Philo writes that Abraham proceeded from erudition (symbolized by Hagar) to virtue (symbolized by Sarah). In formulating this scheme Philo appeals to the concept of divine intermediaries. These intermediaries present themselves to the ascending soul as stages on its way to the Divine. Although the soul cannot advance to God by itself, it can reach one of his powers. Such an idea is illustrated by an analogy of the six towns of refuge in Numbers 35 which are interpreted as a sequence of stations on the way to God.

In presenting his conception of the spiritual journey, Philo stresses that God is the highest reality. For Philo, God is utterly transcendent – He surpasses virtue, knowledge, and even the good itself. As such, He is unknowable and without name. This does not mean that human beings should cease from striving to comprehend the Divine; rather,

it is impossible to apprehend God's true essence. Such an emphasis on transcendence, however, is balanced by Philo's insistence that God is immanent in the world through intermediary powers.

According to Philo, all matter is evil and therefore God, who is good, is located outside the physical universe. Yet even though God is not directly involved in the created order, Philo believes that He is able to have contact with the world through divine agencies. In his work *On Dreams* he writes that God, not condescending to come down to the external senses, sends his own words (*logoi*) for the sake of all those who love virtue. In *Allegories of Sacred Laws*, Philo identifies the *logoi* with angels. In his view angels represent the Deity – angelic beings or *logoi* symbolize God in action: men pray to be nourished by the word (*logos*) of God. But Jacob, raising his head above the world, says that he is nourished by God Himself:

The God in whom my father Abraham and Isaac were well pleased; the God who has nourished me from my youth upwards to this day; the angel who has delivered me from all evils, bless these children . . . for the good things which he has previously mentioned are pleasing to him, in as much as the living and true God has given them to him face to face, but the secondary good things have been given to him by the angels and by the word of God. (in Cohn-Sherbok, 1994, 18)

For Philo these angelic beings are 'incorporeal souls' rather than material in form. This understanding serves as the basis for his interpretation of Jacob's dream in Genesis 28:12 ('And he dreamed that there was a ladder set up on the earth, and the top of it reached to heaven; and behold, the angels of God were ascending and descending on it') in *On Dreams*.

The air is the abode of incorporeal souls since it seemed good to the Creator of the universe to fill all parts of the world with living creatures. For the Creator of the universe formed the air so that it should be the habit of those bodies which are immovable, and the nature of those which are moved in an invisible manner. (Ibid.)

Such a notion of 'incorporeal souls' is akin to the Aristotelian doctrine of 'intelligences' or 'intermediate beings' between the Prime Mover and the material world.

In explaining the nature of God's creation, Philo provides an elaborate theory of human nature: man, he believes, is composed of body (connecting him with matter) and soul (connecting him with God). As a result, human beings are compelled to make fundamental decisions about the directions of their lives. In formulating this thesis, Philo argues that Adam's sin in the Garden of Eden should be understood allegorically – it is a drama of the Fall. Here lust is represented as a snake who appeals to the senses (Eve) rather than reason (Adam), thereby subduing intellect. Therefore Genesis 2:24 ('Therefore a man leaves his father and his mother and cleaves to his wife, and they become one flesh') is given an allegorical interpretation: a man leaves his father (God) and his mother (wisdom) and clings to his wife (sensuality) so that they become one.

It might be thought that such a stress on abstract philosophical ideas would lead to a neglect of earthly duties. Philo, however, is emphatic about the importance of Jewish law. In his view the legal code was inspired by God. Appealing to the philosophically educated, who regard the law as symbolic, he argues that Scriptural prescriptions should not be set aside. Although admitting that the fulfilment of these obligations is simply the outward requirement of the law, Philo insists on the superior value of Mosaic legislation. Concerning the Oral Law, however, he is less demanding – possibly this was due to his Alexandrian upbringing. But in any case, Philo's strict adherence to the legal tradition illustrates his loyalty to the Jewish heritage despite his philosophical orientation.

References

Dan and Lavinia Cohn-Sherbok, *Jewish and Christian Mysticism*, New York, 1994

Philo's major writings

Philo, *The Works of Philo: Complete and Unabridged* (trans. C.D. Yonge), London, 1854–5
Philo, *Complete Works* (12 vols), Loeb Classical Library, Cambridge, 1953–63

Further reading

J. Abelson, *Jewish Mysticism*, Brooklyn, NY, 1969
E.R. Goodenough, *An Introduction to Philo Judaeus*, Lanham, MD, 1986
S. Lieberman, *Hellenism in Jewish Palestine*, New York, 1962
S. Sandmel, *Philo's Place in Judaism*, New York, 1972
S. Sandmel, *Philo of Alexandria: An Introduction*, New York, 1979
V. Tcherikover, *Hellenistic Civilization and the Jews*, Philadelphia and Jerusalem, 1959
H.A. Wolfson, *Philo: Foundations of Religious Philosophy in Judaism, Christianity and Islam*, Cambridge, 1947

LEON PINSKER

Among the early supporters of a Jewish homeland, Leon Pinsker played a pivotal role in the development of Zionist ideology. Born in Tomaszów, Poland, in 1821, Pinsker studied at his father's school, becoming one of the first Jews to attend Odessa University. At first he studied law, but when he discovered that as a Jew he had no opportunity to become a lawyer, he enrolled at the University of Moscow to study medicine. On his return to Odessa in 1849, he was one of the founders of the first Russian Jewish weekly *Razsvet* (*Dawn*), to which he contributed various articles; the aim of this journal was to encourage Jewish readers to become acquainted with Russian culture and to learn the Russian language.

Subsequently Pinsker became an editor of the Russian language publication *Sion* which took the place of *Razsvet*; he was also an active participant in the Odessa branch of the Society for the Dissemination of Enlightenment among Jews. During this period Pinsker contributed to the Russian-language weekly *Den* (*Day*) which was founded by the society, encouraging Jewish assimilation to modern culture. However the pogroms that took place from 1881 in Odessa deeply affected those Jews who had been encouraging Jewish reform. In the ensuing years, Pinsker concentrated on medicine, publishing a work on the medicinal value of the sea and the Liman spa at Odessa. In addition, he became a prominent figure in public affairs. When the Odessa Branch of the Society for the Dissemination of Enlightenment was reopened, Pinsker served on its committee.

However, when Jews were massacred in the Russian pogroms of 1881, Pinsker left the Society, convinced that a more radical solution was required to solve the plight of Russian Jewry. In 1882 he published *Auto-emancipation*, a tract parallelling themes contained in Moses Hess' writings on Jewish nationalism. Later he became the leader of the new *Hibbat Zion* (Love of Zion) movement, and in 1884 convened its founding conference. He died in 1891. In *Auto-emancipation* Pisker argues that the Jewish problem is as unresolved in modern times as it was in previous centuries. In essence, the dilemma concerns the unassimilable character of Jewry. 'The Jewish people', he writes, 'has no fatherland of its own, though many motherlands; it has no rallying point, no centre of gravity, no government of its own, no accredited representatives. It is everywhere a guest, and nowhere at home' (Pinsker, 1932, 6).

Among the nations of the world, Pinsker continues, the Jews are like a nation long dead – they are the dead walking among the living. This eerie, ghostly existence is unique in human history, and has given rise to current Judeophobia. The prejudice against Jews has become rooted in society and naturalized among all peoples. As a psychic aberration, it has become hereditary; as a disease transmitted for thousands of years, it is incurable. Such Jew-hatred has given rise to numerous charges against Jewry: throughout history Jews have been accused of crucifying Jesus, drinking the blood of Christians, poisoning wells, exacting usury and exploiting the peasantry. Invariably such accusations are groundless; they were trumped up to salve the conscience of Jew-baiters. Hence Judaism and anti-Semitism have been inseparable companions through the centuries, and any struggle against this aberration of the human psyche is fruitless.

Unlike other peoples, the Jew is inevitably an alien. Having no home, he can never be anything but a stranger. He is not simply a guest in a foreign environment – he is more like a beggar and a refugee. The Jewish community consists of aliens, he writes, who have no representatives because they have no fatherland. Because their home has no boundaries behind which they can entrench themselves, their misery also has no bounds. It is an error to think that the legal emancipation of Jewry will bring about social emancipation. This is impossible because the isolation of the Jew cannot be removed by a form of official emancipation. In summary he writes:

> For the living, the Jew is a dead man; for the natives, an alien and vagrant; for property holders, a beggar; for the poor, an exploiter and a millionaire; for patriots, a man without a country; for all classes, a hated rival. (Pinsker, 1969, 188)

Such antagonism between Jew and non-Jew has given rise to a variety of reproaches directed by both parties at one another. From the Jewish side, appeals to principles of justice have frequently been made to ameliorate the condition of the Jewish population. In response, non-Jews have attempted to justify their negative attitudes by groundless charges. A more realistic approach, however, would involve the recognition that the Jewish people have no option but to reconstitute themselves as a separate nation. In recent times, Pinsker declares, there has been an increasing awareness of the need for a Jewish homeland:

Nowadays, when in a small part of the earth our brethren have caught their breath and can feel more deeply for the sufferings of their brothers; nowadays when a number of other dependent and oppresed nationalities have been allowed to regain their independence, we, too, must not sit even one moment longer with folded hands; we must not admit that we are doomed to play on in the future the hopeless role of the 'wandering Jew' . . . it is our bounden duty to devote all our remaining moral force to re-establishing ourselves as a living nation, so that we may finally assume a more fitting and dignified role. (Ibid., 191)

The Jewish quest to reach this goal has an inherent justification that belongs to the struggle of every people that is oppressed. Even though this endeavour may be opposed by various segments of the population, the battle must continue. The Jewish people have no other way out of their desperate situation. There is a moral obligation to ensure that persecuted Jews wherever they reside will have a secure home of their own. In this respect, it is a serious danger for Jews to attach themselves only to the Holy Land. What is required is simply a place where Jews can reside in peace:

We need nothing but a large piece of land for our poor brothers; a piece of land which shall remain our property, from which no foreign master can expel us . . . . Perhaps the Holy land will again become ours. If so, all the better, but first of all, we must

determine . . . what country is accessible to us, and at the same time adapted to offer the Jews of all lands who must leave their homes a secure and unquestioned refuge which is capable of being made productive. (Ibid., 194)

According to Pinsker, the present moment is decisive for the revival of national aspirations. History seems to be on the side of world Jewry in its desire for a national homeland. Even in the absence of a leader like Moses, the acknowledgement of what the Jewish nation needs most should encourage a number of energetic individuals to accept positions of responsibility. Already, he observes, there are societies which are pressing for the establishment of a Jewish state. They must now create a national congress, and establish a national directorate to bring about the completion of these plans: 'Our greatest and best forces – men of finance, of science, and of affairs, statesmen and publicists – must join hand with one accord in steering toward the common destination' (Ibid., 196). Inevitably not all Jews wil be able to settle in such a commonwealth, yet it could serve as a refuge for those who seek to flee from oppression and misery.

In conclusion, Pinsker maintains that Jews are despised because they do not constitute a living nation. It is a mistake to believe that civil and political opportunities will raise Jewry in the estimation of other peoples. Rather, the only proper remedy for the Jewish problem is the creation of a Jewish nation, of a people living on its own soil. Jewry must reassert their national self-respect, and cease to wander from one place to another. At the present time there are forces helping to realize this goal, and the international Jewish community should work toward achieving this vision. No sacrifice, he states, will be too great to achieve this aim which will assure that the Jewish nation's future is secure.

References/Pinsker's major writings

Leon Pinsker, *Autoemancipation*, London, 1932,
Leon Pinsker, *Autoemancipation* in A. Hertzberg
(ed.), *The Zionist Idea: A Historical Analysis and
Reader*, New York, 1969

See also in this book

Hess

Further reading

B. Netanyahu (ed.), *Road to Freedom: Writings
and Addresses by Leo Pinsker*, New York, 1944
M. Yoeli, *J.L. Pinsker*, Tel Aviv, Israel, 1960

FRANZ ROSENZWEIG

Born in Kassel, Germany, in 1886, Franz
Rosenzweig studied Hebrew under a private
tutor and attended the local *gymnasium*.
Subsequently he studied medicine at the universities of Gottingen, Munich and Freiburg,
and later philosophy, theology, art, literature
and classical languages at the universities of
Berlin and Freiburg. In 1912 he completed his
doctoral dissertation on Hegel's political
theory. After being drafted into the army,
Rosenzweig studied jurisprudence at the
University of Leipzig. Although he sought to
convert to Christianity, in the end he did
not do so. After attending High Holy Day
services in an orthodox synagogue in Berlin,
he devoted himself to studying Hebrew texts,
and composed a critique of contemporary
Jewish and Christian theology.

Later Rosenzweig volunteered for the
German army, serving in Berlin, France,
the Balkans and near Warsaw. During this
period he wrote *It is Time*, a work addressed
to the German Jewish philosopher Hermann
Cohen on the need to improve Jewish education; in addition, he published a tract dealing
with Schelling's plan for a unified system of
German idealism. In 1918, while confined
to hospitals in Leipzig and Belgrade, he
composed his systematic religious philosophy, *The Star of Redemption*. On his return
home, Rosenzweig dedicated himself to
establishing the Freies Jüdisches Lehrhaus
in Frankfurt, an institution dedicated to
bringing Jews back to the faith; its faculty
included such figures as Martin Buber, Erich
Fromm, Leo Strauss, Walter Birnbaum,
Gershom Scholem, Ernst Simon and Leo
Baeck. In 1921 Rosenzweig became partially
paralysed, but continued his writing; in the
last year of his life he prepared a second
edition of *The Star of Redemption*. He died
in 1929 of a fatal illness.

In this work, Rosenzweig explores the
ways in which theology complements philosophy. In his view, God confronts human
beings through the process of revelation –
what is revealed is God's presence and
through the experience of divine love God's
creatures are commanded to love God in
return. In propounding this view, Rosenzweig distinguishes between commandments,
which are directed to individuals, and laws
for humanity – revelation results in
commandments rather than laws. This relationship between God and human beings is
supplemented by creation which relates the
individual to the world. Creation, Rosenzweig argues, establishes the dependence
that all creatures have on God's power. A
third relationship is provided by redemption,
which links humans and the world. For
Rosenzweig, through redemption it is
possible to overcome isolation because of
God's command to love one's neighbour.
Throughout history, redemption has per-
vaded the world through acts of loving
kindness, bringing about the unification of
the world and man with the Divine. These
three themes – revelation, creation and
redemption – are thus viewed as central
aspects of God's plan of cosmic restoration.

Rosenzweig was also concerned with
the relationship between Christianity and
Judaism with regard to God's Kingdom. As
a Jew, Rosenzweig believed that he could
view Christianity impartially; Christians,

however, could not be equally objective about Judaism because of their missionary zeal. Nonetheless, Rosenzweig felt that the modern period offers new opportunities for both religious communities to reach a greater degree of understanding. Given this situation, he sought to explain the nature of the Jewish faith to his newly converted friends. Yet he recognized that this is not an easy task:

> I realize that everything I wrote about is beyond my power to express to you. For I should now need to show you Judaism from within ... just as you would have to show Christianity to me, an outsider. Just as you cannot do this, neither can I. The soul of Christianity lies in its expressions; while Judaism shows only its hard, protective shell to the outer world; only within can one speak of its soul. (Rosenzweig, 1935, 688)

Despite such obstacles Rosenzweig was anxious to compare the two traditions. These faiths, he argues, have a special status granted to no other religion. Paganism, he maintains, contains no valid approach to the Divine; Judaism and Christianity, on the other hand, share God, revelation, prayer and final redemption. These eternal verities constitute their common ground. Rosenzweig represents this shared basis symbolically with Israel as the star and Christianity as the rays:

> The truth, the entire truth, belongs neither to them nor to us. We bear it within ourselves, precisely, therefore, we must first gaze within ourselves, if we wish to see it. So we will see the star, but not its rays. To encompass the whole truth one must not only see the light but also what it illumines. They, on the other hand, have been eternally destined to see the illuminated object, but not the light. (Rosenzweig, 1930, vol. iii, 200)

On this view truth appears only in divided form: the Jewish and the Christian way. However, before God it is united. For Rosenzweig, the roles of Judaism and Christianity are symbolized by the image of a star burning at its core and sending out rays. Judaism's self-absorption is represented by the burning core whereas Christianity's worldliness is symbolized by the rays sent forth from the star's centre. Following this image, the burning star does not require its rays – it continues to burn even if the rays are blocked in the process of radiation. The rays, on the other hand, require the continuous burning of the star's core. Christianity is thus dependent on Judaism, but not vice versa. On this view, Christianity has not overcome the Jewish traditon. Rather, Judaism must continue to nurture the Christian faith.

This astronomical image is used by Rosenzweig to illustrate the different roles of these two faiths in God's eternal plan. Creation, Rosenzweig argues, is constituted as God's relationship with man; and redemption as the final reconciliation between God-related human beings and a God-related world. This final stage will result in the direct relationship of everything with God. In this process Jews and Christians hold fast to their different traditions. Judaism, he maintains, constitutes the basic relationship between God, humanity and the world. Christianity, on the other hand, has the unique function of including all nations in the revealed relationship with the Divine. Because of its own particularistic nature, Judaism is unable to perform this redemptive function; if it were to do so, it would lose the unique intensity of its relationship with God. Hence Jewry must acknowledge the indispensable universalistic ministry of Christianity for the sake of the final redemption.

In Rosenzweig's view, Jewish identity is dependent on birth and brings with it covenantal obligation. The Christian, however, is not a Christian by birth, but only by accepting a set of beliefs. Such personal commitment is necessary for the Jews: 'We possess what the Christian will one day experience ... we have it from the time of our birth and through our birth it is in our blood. The antecedent of the experience goes back beyond our birth to the antiquity of our people' (Rosenzweig, 1935, 356). Because Jews are born into this special relationship with God, Rosenzweig contends that it is impossible for a Jew to convert to Christianity. Such a state of affairs has crucial implications for Jewry in their relationship to Christianity as well as other faiths.

Despite Rosenzweig's positive evaluation of the Christian faith, he was critical of the doctrine of the Incarnation. The Christian way into the land of God, he explains, is divided into two paths – a dualism which is incomprehensible to the Jew, but nevertheless forms the basis of the Christian life. The Christian has no hesitation in approaching the Son with the sort of piety Jews display toward the Father:

> Only by holding the hand of the Son, does the Christian dare to approach the Father; he believes that he may only come to the Father through the Son. If the Son had not been a man, then he would be useless to the Christian. He cannot conceive that God Himself, the only God, could descend far enough for his needs. (Rosenzweig, 1930, vol. III, 114)

For Rosenzweig such a conception is unacceptable. In the end of days the Christian will come to see that such ideas no longer hold sway and that all peoples will acknowledge the Jewish doctrine of God. At this time there will be a universal acceptance that the Jewish God is the Lord of history. Then one will approach the Father only through him. This is currently the situation of the Jewish people, but in time it will become a universal truth. Thus, despite Rosenzweig's conviction that the entire truth belongs neither to Jews nor to Christians, he endorses the classic Jewish view that Judaism will be the final form of the religion of humanity: inherent in Rosenzweig's theology is the conviction that the Christian faith would ultimately lead to a universal form of Judaism for all people.

References/Rosenzweig's major writings

Franz Rosenzweig, *Der Stern der Erlösung*, Heidelberg, 1930
Franz Rosenzweig, *Briese*, Berlin, 1935

See also in this book

Baeck, Buber

Further reading

J.B. Agus, *Modern Philosophies of Judaism*, New York, 1941
S.H. Bergman, *Faith and Reason*, New York, 1963
E. Freund, *Franz Rosenzweig's Philosophy of Existence*, The Hague, 1979
N. Glatzer, *Franz Rosenzweig: His Life and Thought*, New York, 1953
S. Schwarzchild, *Franz Rosenzweig: Guide of the Reversionists*, London, 1960

RICHARD RUBENSTEIN

Born in 1924, Richard Lowell Rubenstein was ordained a Conservative rabbi at the Jewish Theological Seminary in New York in 1952 and obtained a doctorate from Harvard in 1960. His most important work, *After Auschwitz*, was published in 1966, evoking a hostile response from the religious establishment. In 1970 he became a professor at Florida State University; subsequently he published a major study of the Holocaust, *Approaches to Auschwitz*, with the Christian scholar, John K. Roth.

In his writings Rubenstein argues that it is no longer possible to sustain a belief in a supernatural Deity after the events of the Nazi era. This view was precipitated by a meeting with the Dean of the Evangelical Church in East and West Berlin, Heinrich Grüber, in August 1961. Rubenstein had planned a trip to West Germany, but on 13 August the wall between East and West Berlin was erected. Rubenstein decided to postpone his visit until two days later. When he arrived in Bonn, he was invited by the Federal Republic to fly to Berlin where he attended a mass rally addressed by Willy Brandt, the major of Berlin; in addition, he made a trip to East Berlin. In this turbulent atmosphere, Rubenstein interviewed Dean Grüber at his home in West Berlin.

During the war Grüber had helped baptize Jews and opposed the anti-Jewish policies of the Nazis. As a result he was incarcerated in Sachsenhausen concentration camp. In 1961 he was the only German who testified at Adolf Eichmann's trial. In his conversation with Rubenstein, Grüber affirmed that God was ultimately responsible for the death of six million Jews. Quoting Psalm 44:22 ('For thy sake are we slaughtered every day'), the Dean explained that for some reason it must have been part of God's providential plan that the Jews perished. Comparing the events of the Nazi regime with contemporary circumstances, he stated:

At different times, God uses different peoples as His whip against His own people, the Jews, but those whom He uses will be punished far worse than the people of the Lord . . . . I know that God is punishing us because we have been the whip against Israel. In 1938 we smashed the synagogues; in 1945 our churches were smashed by the bombs. In 1938 we sent the Jews out to be homeless; since 1945 fifteen million Germans have experienced homelessness. (Rubenstein, 1992, 10)

Grüber was convinced Hitler's actions were immoral and that he would be punished. Though the Dean did not explain the reason why the Jews had been punished, Rubenstein concluded that Grüber believed it was because of their unwillingness to accept Jesus as Lord. This was the view of the German Ecumenical Church three years after the war: in 1948 the Church asserted that the Holocaust was a divine punishment visited upon the Jews and they urged them to change their minds.

Although Rubenstein was shocked by

Grüber's words, he acknowledged that there was nothing new in this attempt to view history as the unfolding of God's plan. A similar interpretation of history was held by the biblical prophets, the rabbis and the Church Fathers. Nonetheless, Rubenstein had never before heard the argument applied to current events. Yet, as he notes in *After Auschwitz*, such an argument was theologically coherent:

Given the Judeo-Christian conception, so strong in Scripture, that God is the ultimate actor in the historical drama, no other theological interpretation of the death of six million Jews is tenable . . . . If one views all time and history through the perspective of the Christ, one would ultimately have to assert that God caused the Jews to be exterminated by the Nazis because of their continuing failure to confess and acknowledge the Christ. If one shared Rabban Johanan ben Zakkai's view, one would be drawn to assert that the Jewish people had been exterminated because of their failure to comply with the Lord's commandments as these had been enjoined in the Torah. (Ibid., 17)

When Rubenstein left Grüber's house, he was persuaded that he could not avoid the issue of God's relation to the Holocaust. Even though Grüber's conception of God was in harmony with Scripture, Rubenstein could not believe in such a divine being. It was incomprehensible to him that Jewish theologians still subscribed to the belief in an omnipotent, beneficent God after the tragedy of the Holocaust. Traditional Jewish theology asserts that God is ultimately responsible for whatever occurs – it interprets all tragedies as God's punishment for Israel's sinfulness. But Rubenstein was unable to see how such a view could be maintained with seeing Hitler as an instrument of God's will:

The agony of European Jewry cannot be likened to the testing of Job. To see any purpose in the death camps, the traditional believer is forced to regard the most demonic, anti-human explosion of all history as a meaningful expression of God's purposes. The idea is simply too obscene for me to accept. (Rubenstein, 1966, 153)

For Rubenstein a void now exists where once the Jewish people experienced God's presence. Such a revision of the Jewish heritage is, he argues, recognized in contemporary Jewish life even if it is not made explicit in Jewish theology. In the diaspora as well as in Israel the myth of an omnipotent God of history is effectively rejected in the lives of most Jews. After the Nazi epoch, life is lived and enjoyed on its own terms without any reference to the Deity.

Yet even though Rubenstein rejects the concept of God in the Hebrew Bible, he stresses that it would be an error to construe his position as atheism. What he wishes to demonstrate is that human beings now live in the time of the death of God. Rubenstein is compelled to use such an expression because it conveys the contemporary Jewish experience of God's absence. 'When I say we live in the time of the death of God', he writes, 'I mean that the thread uniting God and man, Heaven and earth, has been broken. We stand in a cold, silent, unfeeling cosmos, unaided by any powerful power beyond our own resources. After Auschwitz, what else can a Jew say about God?' (Ibid., 151–2).

In *Approaches to Auschwitz*, Rubenstein's most recent study of the Holocaust, he emphasises that his religious views today are akin to mystical religion. No longer does he regard the universe as cold and unfeeling. When he wrote *After Auschwitz*, his position was understandably bleak; yet now he would balance the elements of creativeness and love in the cosmos more evenly with those of destruction and hate than he was prepared to do in 1966. Rubenstein's initial response to Auschwitz was that the demise of Judaism's theological underpinnings would

not entail an end to the psychological or sociological functions of the tradition. Aware that many Jews remained loyal to the community despite a loss of faith, he argued that religion is more than a system of belief – it comprises shared rituals, customs and folk-memories. For Rubenstein, religion is not so much dependent on belief as upon practices related to life-cycle events. Hence he wrote in *After Auschwitz* that Judaism is the way in which Jews share the decisive times and crises of life through the traditions of their inherited community – the need for such sharing is not diminished in the time of the death of God.

In abandoning the biblical and rabbinic conception of God, Rubenstein expressed his belief in the immanence and transcendence of God. For Rubenstein, the cosmos is the expression of a single unifying source; furthermore, if human beings are perceived as an integral feature of the universe – which is the expression of this divine ground – then deity is capable of thought, reflection and feeling at least in its human manifestation. Such a notion of the Divine found in religious mysticism served as the basis for Rubenstein's understanding of God, his conception of nature paganism, and his perception of the Jewish people's aspiration to return to Zion.

According to Rubenstein, after the Holocaust and the return to Israel the God manifested in and through nature should become the God to whom Jews turn. For this reason, Rubenstein endorsed a modified form of Canaanite nature paganism in place of the worship of the God of Scripture. As the years passed however this endorsement of nature paganism, which was linked to the land of Israel, receded in importance in his thought – it became increasingly clear that the majority of the world's Jewish population did not regard Israel as their home. Most Jews simply did not wish to emigrate to the Holy Land. Rubenstein thus came to the realization that despite the challenge of the death camps, most religious Jews would continue to accept the biblical notion of God.

Moreover, those who lived in Israel had little interest in the nature paganism he had previously endorsed.

This altered situation led Rubenstein to revise his earlier position. As he came into contact with the civilizations and religions of the Far East, Rubenstein began to espouse a mystical theology similar to the mysticism found in Buddhism. In mysticism Rubenstein found a God whom he could affirm after the Holocaust. This view replaced his earlier stress on the silence of the cosmos. Such a notion of the Godhead, he insists, is meaningful after the death of the God-who-acts-in-history. It is an ancient understanding with deep roots in Western and Oriental mysticism. On this view, God is the Holy Nothingness. As such He is the ground and source of everything. He is not a void. Rather such a God is an individual *plenum*, so rich that all existence is derived from his essence. He is superfluidity of being rather than an absence of being.

Rubenstein's use of the term 'Nothingness' is due in part to the ancient observation that all definitions of finite entities involve negation. The infinite God cannot be defined: He is in no sense a thing resembling finite beings. Through the ages mystics have also spoken of God as the dark unnameable abyss out of which the world emerged; in the major world religions, sages have attempted to communicate the divine mystery by using similar images. 'Perhaps the best available metaphor for the concept of God as the Holy Nothingness', Rubenstein writes, 'is that God is the ocean and we are the waves. In some sense each wave has its moment in which it is distinguishable as a somewhat separate entity. Nevertheless, no wave is entirely distinct from the ocean which is the substantial ground' (Rubenstein, 1987, 316).

In mysticism then, Rubenstein has found the God whom he can affirm after Auschwitz. Not surprisingly Rubenstein's views were widely repudiated by the religious establishment, yet his writings have had a profound impact on contemporary Jewish religious thought and continue to provide a serious challenge to those who accept the traditional understanding of God and the events of the Holocaust.

References/Rubenstein's major writings

Richard L. Rubenstein, *After Auschwitz*, IN, 1966, 1992
Richard L. Rubenstein and John K. Roth, *Approaches to Auschwitz*, London, 1987

Further reading

D. Cohn-Sherbok, *Holocaust Theology*, London, 1989
B. Rogers Rubenstein and M. Berenbaum, *What Kind of God: Essays in Honour of Richard L. Rubenstein*, London, 1995

SAADIAH BEN JOSEPH GAON

In the Hellenistic period the Jewish philosopher Philo attempted to integrate Greek philosophy and Jewish teaching into a unified whole. By applying an allegorical method of interpretation of Scripture, he explained the God of Judaism in Greek philosophical categories and reshaped Jewish notions about God, man and the world. Philo was the precursor of medieval Jewish philosophy which also attempted to combine alternative philosophical systems with the received biblical tradition.

The beginnings of this philosophical development took place in ninth-century Babylonia during the height of the Abbasid caliphate when rabbinic Judaism was challenged by Karaite scholars who criticized the anthropomorphic views of God in midrashic and talmudic sources. Added to this internal threat was the Islamic contention that Muhammad's revelation of the Qu'ran superseded the Jewish faith. In addition, Zoroastrians and Manichaeans attacked monotheism as a viable religious system.

Finally, some gentile philosophers argued that the Greek scientific and philosophical world view could account for the origin of the cosmos without reference to an external Deity.

In combating these challenges, Jewish writers were influenced by the teachings of Muslim schools (*kalam*) of the eighth to the eleventh centuries; in particular the contributions of one school of Muslim thought, the Mutazilite *kalam*, had a profound effect on the development of Jewish thought. These Islamic scholars maintained that rational argument was vital in matters of religious belief and that Greek philosophy could serve as the handmaiden of religious faith. In their attempt to defend Judaism from internal and external assault, rabbinic authorities frequently adapted the Mutazilite *kalam* as an important line of defence.

The earliest philosopher of the medieval period, Saadiah ben Joseph al-Fayyumi was born in Pithom, Upper Egypt, in 882 CE. At the age of twenty he published a Hebrew dictionary; three years later he issued a polemic against Karaism (a Jewish sect opposed to rabbinic Judaism). After living in Palestine and Aleppo, Syria, he settled in Babylonia where he engaged in a bitter dispute with the Palestinian *gaon* (head of a Babylonian academy) Aaron ben-Meir about fixing the dates of the Holy Days. Subsequently he was appointed *gaon* of the Babylonian academy at Sura which had fallen into decline. Under Saadiah, Sura underwent a major revival, attracting students from throughout the Jewish world. In time, however, Saadiah became embroiled in a controversy with the *exilarch* (leader of Babylonian Jewry) David ben-Zakkai, who had appointed him. When David ben-Zakkai sought to replace Saadiah as *gaon*, Saadiah appointed a different *exilarch*. The quarrel between these two leaders split Baghdad Jewry, but seven years later the elders of the community arranged a reconciliation and Saadiah was reinstated.

As *gaon* of the Babylonian academy, Saadiah wrote treatises on a wide range of subjects: he produced grammatical and lexicographical studies, translated almost the entire Bible into Arabic, composed a book of prayers as well as liturgical poems, introduced a scientific methodology and a new interpretation of the study of the Talmud, defined and codified numerous questions of Jewish law, expounded important decisions in response to questions from diaspora communities, composed talmudic commentaries, wrote works on the calendar and on biblical and rabbinic chronology, and elaborated a rational theology, up until his death in 942.

In his major philosophical work, *The Book of Beliefs and Opinions*, Saadiah attempts to refute the religious claims of Christians, Muslims and Zoroastrians. Basing his approach on the teachings of the *kalam*, he argues that there are four sources of knowledge: sense experience, intuition of self-evident truths; logical inference and reliable tradition. This fourth category, reliable tradition, is derived from the first three and is the mainstay of civilization – it was given by God to human beings to provide guidance and protection against uncertainty since the vast majority of humanity is incapable of engaging in philosophical speculation.

Only the Torah, Saadiah maintains, is of divine origin – it was revealed by God to the prophets and transmitted in written and oral form. Adapting the teaching of the Mutazilites, Saadiah argues that religious faith and reason are fully compatible. On this basis, he attempts to demonstrate that God exists since the universe must have had a starting point. Time, he believes, is only rational if it has a beginning because it is impossible to pass from an infinite past to the present. The divine Creator, he asserts, is a single incorporeal Being who created the universe out of nothing.

In connection with God's unity, Saadiah – like the Mutazilite philosophers – assumes that if God has a plurality of attributes, this implies He must be composite in nature. Thus, he argues, such terms as 'life', 'omnipotence' and 'omniscience' should be understood as implications of the concept of God as Creator rather than attributes of the Deity. We are forced to describe God by means of these descriptions because of the limitations of language, but they do not in any way involve plurality in God. In this light Saadiah argues that the anthropomorphic expressions in the Bible must not be taken literally since this would imply that God is a plurality. Hence, when we read in the Bible that God has a head, eye, ear, mouth, face or hand, these terms should be understood figuratively. Similarly, when human activity is attributed to God or when He appears in a theophany, such depictions should not be interpreted in a literal way.

Turning to the nature of human beings, Saadiah contends that men and women possess souls which are substances created by God at the time when bodies are brought into being. The soul is not pre-existent nor does it enter the body from the outside; rather, it uses the body as an instrument for its functions. When it is connected to a corporeal frame the soul has three central faculties (reason, spirit and desire), yet it is incapable of activity if it is divorced from the body. As for the sufferings which the soul undergoes because of its bodily connection, some are due to its negligence, whereas others are inflicted for the soul's own good so that it may later be rewarded.

In order to lead a fulfilled life, humans have been given commandments and prohibitions by God, and these consist of two types. The first type embraces acts which reason recognizes as good or bad through a feeling of approval or disapproval which has been implanted in human beings: we perceive, for example, that murder is wrong because it would lead to the destruction of humanity and would also frustrate God's purpose in creating the world. The second group of ordinances refers to acts which are intrinsically neither right nor wrong, but are made so by God's decree. Such traditional laws are imposed on human beings

essentially so that we may be rewarded for obeying them. Nevertheless, these laws are not arbitrary; they have beneficial consequences as well. For instance, laws of ceremonial purity teach humility and make prayer more precious for those who have been prevented from praying because of their ritual uncleanliness.

Since these traditional laws are not inherently rational in character, divine revelation is necessary to supplement humanity's rational capacity. In addition, divine legislation is needed to clarify the moral principles known by reason. According to Saadiah, the corpus of Jewish law cannot be abrogated; it is valid for all time. Though God rewards those who keep His commands and punishes those who violate His law, people have free will. Thus the Bible declares: 'I have set before you life and death ... therefore choose life' (Deuteronomy 30:19). Likewise, the rabbis proclaimed: 'Everything is in the hands of God except the fear of God.' God's foreknowledge is not the cause of a person's action – rather God simply knows beforehand the outcome of one's free deliberation.

Discussing Jewish beliefs concerning the afterlife, Saadiah asks why the righteous suffer and the wicked prosper. Here he summarizes the traditional solutions to this problem: the pious suffer as a punishment for their transgressions; the suffering of the righteous is a test and mode of purification. Yet because there is more suffering than happiness in the world, divine justice requires that the soul should be immortal so that there can be a proper recompense in the hereafter. In Saadiah's view, the soul is a pure, luminous substance that acts through physical embodiment. For this reason the body is not impure – it will be resurrected together with the soul so that the entire person can enjoy bliss in the World-to-Come. For Saadiah, since God created the world *ex nihilo*, there is no logical difficulty in believing that God can recreate the bodies of those who have died.

In Saadiah's scheme there are two final stages of human existence. The messianic period will be inhabited by the remnant of the righteous of Israel who wil be allowed to participate in the restoration of the monarchy. At this stage poverty, oppression and conflict will disappear. Eventually the World-to-Come will be established. The dead of all nations will be rewarded and recompense will take place through the medium of the divine light – the righteous will be illuminated with joy whereas the wicked will be consumed by fire. In presenting these theories Saadiah was the first Jewish thinker to offer a systematic treatment of rabbinic theology. Throughout his writing the central doctrines of Judaism were defended on biblical and rabbinic grounds; like the Mutazilites, he was determined to provide a rational interpretation of the faith.

Saadiah Gaon's major writings

Saadiah Gaon, *The Book of Beliefs and Opinions*, New Haven, CN, 1948
Saadiah Gaon, *The Book of Doctrines and Beliefs* in A. Altmann, *Three Jewish Philosophers*, New York, 1969

See also in this book

Philo

Further reading

B. Cohen (ed.) *Saadia Annniversary Volume, Proceedings of the American Academy of Jewish Research*, 1943
L. Finkelstein (ed.), *Rav Saadia Gaon: Studies in His honor*, New York, 1944
A.J. Heschel, 'The Quest for Certainty in Saadia's Philosophy', *Jewish Quarterly Review* 33, 1942–3
H. Malter, *Saadia Gaon: His Life and Works*, New York, 1929
E.I.J. Rosenthal (ed.) *Saadya Studies*, Manchester, 1943

SOLOMON IBN GABIROL

Beginning in the eleventh century there appeared a number of Jewish writers in the Mediterranean West who made major contributions to the history of Jewish thought. The first Spanish Jewish philosopher, Solomon ben Judah ibn Gabirol produced an influential work in the Neoplatonic tradition, *The Fountain of Life*, as well as a religious poem, *The Kingly Crown*, which had an important impact on later Jewish as well as Christian thinkers. Born in 1021 most probably in Malaga, ibn Gabirol lived at Saragossa where he was educated. When he was a child, his father died, followed by his mother in 1045.

In his poetry, ibn Gabirol provides a self-description: he was, he states, small, sickly, ugly and of a disagreeable disposition. The most important of his friends appears to have been Jekuthiel ben Isaac ibn Hasan whom he praises for his erudition and worldliness. However Jekuthiel, because of his courtly connections, was assassinated in 1039. In consequence Gabirol's financial position deteriorated, and he was unable to find other patrons in Saragossa. It seems that he attempted to settle in other towns including Granada and Valencia, where he died at an early age, in 1057.

Ibn Gabirol's philosophical treatise, *The Fountain of Life*, contains no biblical quotations or allusions to the Jewish religious tradition except for scattered references to the early mystical work, the *Sefer Yetsirah* (Book of Creation). Like other Neoplatonic works, *The Fountain of Life* is written in the form of a dialogue, no doubt in imitation of Plato. However, in contrast with the Platonic dialogues, the personalities of the master and his pupil are de-emphasized – philosophical doctrines are explained by the master and the pupil's role is solely to put relevant questions to his teacher which provide the opportunity for an extended response.

Written in Arabic, *The Fountain of Life* is divided into five treatises dealing mainly with the principles of matter and form. In the first treatise, Gabirol discusses matter and form as they exist in objects perceived by the senses as well as the underlying qualities of corporeal existence; the second contains a depiction of the spiritual matter that underlies corporeal form; the third deals with the existence of simple substances; the fourth concerns the form and matter of simple substances; the fifth treats universal form and matter as they exist in themselves. In expounding this metaphysical scheme, Gabirol adopts a Neoplatonic framework – in his view, God is the First Essence. Next in descending order of being is the divine will, followed by universal matter and form, the simple substances (intellect, soul and nature), and then the corporeal world.

In presenting his cosmological theories, Gabirol argues that both spiritual and corporeal substances are composed of two elements – form and matter – and this duality leads to the differences between various substances. In some passages of *The Fountain of Life*, it appears that the forms are responsible for differentiating one substance from another, whereas in other sections matter seems to be the cause. In any event, Gabirol contends that matter is the substratum underlying the forms. All distinctions in the various substances are due to the differences between universal matter and form, which are the first created beings. Gabirol, however, appears to offer two different accounts of their creation: in one case universal matter is described as coming from the essence of God and form as coming from the divine will; elsewhere both principles are described as the product of the divine will. Further, in some passages Gabirol contends that universal matter exists independently, but in other sections he argues in accordance with Aristotelianism that matter is akin to privation and exists only in potentiality.

Turning to the doctrine of forms, Gabirol suggests that all forms are contained in universal form. Matter and form do not exist independently: their first compound is intellect, which is the initial spiritual substance from which emanates the soul, which is similarly composed of matter and form. All spiritual or simple substances, he continues, emanate forces that give existence to substances below them in the order of being. Hence soul is emanated from intellect and is of three types: rational, animate and vegetative. There are also cosmic principles which exist in human beings. Nature is the last of the simple substances and emanates from the vegetative soul – from it emanates corporeal substance which is below nature in the chain of being. Corporeal substance is the substratum underlying nine of the ten Aristotelian categories; the tenth category – substance – is universal matter as it appears in the corporeal world, and the nine other categories are universal form as it appears in the corporeal world.

In order for souls to be linked to bodies, a mediating principle is needed: the principle which joins the universal soul to the corporeal world is Heaven; the principle combining the rational soul with the body is the animal spirit. The relation of the human body to the soul is like the relation between form and matter – the soul comprehends the forms but not matter, since matter is unintelligible. The forms which always exist in the soul are intelligible; however, since the soul was deprived of knowledge because of its union with the body, these forms exist only in potentiality. Therefore God created the world and provided senses for the soul by means of which it can conceive concrete forms and patterns. It is through the comprehension of the sensible forms that the soul is able to apprehend ideas which in the soul emerge from potentiality to actuality.

In Gabirol's view all forms exist in a more subtle and simple fashion in the intellect than in the soul – there they are combined in a spiritual union. Intellect, he argues, consists of universal form and matter, and is at a lower plane – it is capable of conceiving of universal form and matter only with difficulty. Above the knowledge of form and matter there is a knowledge of the divine will which is identified with divine wisdom and divine *logos*. This will in relation to its activity should be conceived as identical with the divine essence yet, when considered with respect to its activity, it is separate. In its essence, the will is infinite, but with regard to its action, it is finite. Hence it is the intermediary between divine essence and matter and form even though it penetrates everything.

In terms of its function, it is the efficient cause of all things, uniting form with matter; the will, however, which is the cause of all movement, is in itself at rest. The First Essence, or God, cannot be known because it is infinite and lacks any similarity with the soul; nonetheless its existence can be demonstrated. For Gabirol, the highest aspiration is to attain knowledge of the purpose for which human beings were created: such knowledge can be achieved through an apprehension of the will as it extends to all form and matter as well as through an understanding of the will as it exists in itself. Such an awareness brings about release from death and attachment to the source of all things.

Such theoretical speculation about form and matter, and the process of emanation, is reflected in Gabirol's religious poem, *The Kingly Crown*. Here he provides a description of the three worlds that present themselves to human thought: the divine world, the created universe, and man. Beginning with praise of God, the poem continues with a depiction of the hidden secrets of the divine:

This is the mystery of power, the secret and the foundation.
Thine is the name that is hidden from the wise, the strength that sustains the world over the chaos, the power to bring to light all that is hidden.
Thine is the mercy that rules over Thy creatures and the goodness preserved for those who fear Thee.
Thine are the secrets that no mind or thought can encompass, and the life over which decay has no rule, and the

throne that is higher than all height, and the habitation that is hidden at the pinnacle of mystery.
Thine is the existence from the shadow of whose light every being was made to be and we said, 'Under His shadow we shall live'.
Thine are the two worlds between which Thou didst set a limit, the first for works and the second for requital.
Thine is the reward which Thou has set aside for the righteous and hidden, and
Thou sawest that it was good, and has kept it hidden. (*The Kingly Crown*, 1961, 27–8)

The end of the first part of the poem concludes with a series of statements about the topics dealt with in *The Fountain of Life*: God and his wisdom; the will; matter; form; and the combination of the two which forms all creation:

Thou art wise; and wisdom, the fountain of life, flows from Thee, and every man is too brutish to know Thy wisdom.
Thou art wise, pre-existent to all pre-existence, and wisdom was with Thee at nursing.
Thou art wise, and Thou didst not learn from any other than Thyself, nor acquire wisdom from another.
Thou art wise, and from Thy wisdom Thou didst send forth a predestined Will, and made it as an artisan and a craftsman,
To draw the stream of being from the nothingness as the light is drawn that comes from the eye.
To take from the source of light without a vessel, and to make all without a tool and cut and hew and cleanse and purify.
That Will called to the nothingness and it was cleft asunder, to existence and it was set up, to the universe and it was spread out.

It measured the heavens with a span, and
its hand coupled the pavilion of the
spheres,
And linked the curtains of all creatures
with loops of potency; and its strength
reaches as far as the last and lowest
creature – 'the uttermost edge of the
curtain in the coupling'. (Ibid., 32-3)

Because Gabirol did not deal with the issue
of the relationship between philosophy and
faith and also since his work lacks Jewish
content, his writings did not have a major
impact on subsequent Jewish thought.
Nonetheless, *The Fountain of Life* was quoted by such twelfth-century Jewish scholars as
Moses ibn Ezra, Joseph ibn Zaddik, and
Abraham ibn Ezra; in addition, his views
were bitterly criticized by another twelfth-
century thinker, Abraham ibn Daud. In time,
however, Gabirol's Neoplatonic theories
were largely neglected by Jewish thinkers.

References/ibn Gabirol's major writings

Solomon ibn Gabirol, *The Kingly Crown* (trans. B.
Lewis), London, 1961
Solomon ibn Gabirol, *The Fountain of Life* (trans.
H.E. Wedeck), London, 1963

See also in this book

Abraham ibn Daud

Further reading

F. Brunner, *Platonisme et Aristotélisme – la critique
d'Ibn Gabirol par St. Thomas d'Aquin*, Louvain,
1965
I. Davidson, *Selected Religious Poems of Solomon
ibn Gabirol*, Philadelphia, 1924
R. Loewe, 'Ibn Gabirol's Treatment of Sources in
Keter Malkhut' in A. Altmann (ed.), *Jewish
Medieval and Renaissance Studies*, Cambridge,
1967
R. Loewe, *Ibn Gabirol*, New York, 1990
J. Schlanger, *La Philosophie de Salomon Ibn-
Gabirol*, Leiden, 1968

BARUCH SPINOZA

The roots of Jewish thought during the
Enlightenment go back to seventeenth-
century Holland where a number of Jewish
thinkers sought to interpret the Jewish tradition in the light of the new scientific understanding of the world. The greatest of these
Dutch Jewish thinkers was Baruch Spinoza
who was born in Amsterdam in 1632 of a
former Marrano family. Initially Spinoza was
exposed to Hebrew, the Bible and the Talmud
as well as medieval Jewish philosophy; subsequently he engaged in the study of natural
science and contemporary philosophy.

At the age of twenty-three he was questioned by the leaders of the Amsterdam
Jewish community about his religious
beliefs, and offered a stipend if he would
remain silent and conform to Jewish practice.
When he refused to comply, he was excommunicated. The rabbinical proclamation
declares:

The chiefs of the council make known to
you that having long known of evil opinions and acts of Baruch de Spinoza, they
have endeavoured by various means and
promises to turn him from evil ways. Not
only being unable to find any remedy, but
on the contrary receiving every day more
information about the abominable here-
sies practised and taught by him, and
about the monstrous acts committed by
him, having this from many trustworthy
witnesses who have deposed and borne
witness on all this in the presence of said
Spinoza, who has been convicted; all this
having been examined in the presence of
the rabbis, the council decided, with the
advice of the rabbis, that the said Spinoza
should be excommunicated and cut off
from the Nation of Israel. (*Encyclopaedia
Judaica*, 1971, vol. 15, 276)

For the rest of his life, Spinoza lived in
various towns in Holland where he supported
himself by grinding and polishing optical

lenses. During this period he attracted a wide circle of admirers and was offered a professorship at the University of Heidelberg in 1673 which he declined. In 1661 he began work on his *Treatise on the Correction of the Understanding*. Two years later he embarked on his *Ethics*, and in 1670 he published his philosophical work, *Tractatus Theologico-Politicus* which evoked a hostile response from orthodox theologians. In 1677, at the age of forty-five, he died at The Hague.

In the first section of his *Tractatus Theologico-Politicus*, Spinoza maintains that prophecy is of an imaginative – as opposed to philosophical – character. In his view, the biblical prophets were philosophically untrained, indeed they were ignorant of the causes of natural events. Rejecting Maimonides' belief that Hebrew Scriptures were addressed in different ways to both the masses and the intellectuals, Spinoza maintains that the Hebrew Scriptures were directed solely to a general audience. God is presented as a lawgiver to appeal to the multitudes. The function of biblical law is to ensure social and political stability – hence its prescriptions are not of divine origin. In addition, Spinoza asserts that the biblical laws are suitable only to ancient times; they have no relevance for subsequent ages.

Concerning miracles, Spinoza contends that God's nature and activity cannot be known through miraculous events, but only from the order of nature and from clear self-evident ideas. Unlike medieval Jewish philosophers such as Maimonides, who believed that miracles transcend the natural order, Spinoza argues that nothing can occur outside natural law. In this light, Spinoza insists that the Bible must be regarded in the same way as any work of ancient literature – the biblical books should be interpreted only according to their author's intentions. Such a conviction led Spinoza to the view that the Torah as a whole was not written by Moses and that the historical books are compilations assembled by many generations. Ezra, he concludes, was

responsible for harmonizing the various discrepancies found in Scripture.

For Spinoza, the function of religion is to provide a framework for ethical action. Philosophy, on the other hand, is concerned with truth, and philosophers should be free to engage in philosophical speculation unconstrained by religious opinions:

Faith, therefore, allows the greatest latitude in philosophical speculation, allowing us without blame to think what we like about anything, and only condemning as heretics and schismatics, those who teach opinions which tend to produce obstinacy, hatred, strife and anger, while, on the other hand, only considering as faithful those who persuade us, as far as their reason and faculties will permit, to follow justice and charity. (Spinoza, vol. I, 1956, 189)

According to Spinoza, it is a usurpation of the social contract and a violation of the rights of man to legislate belief. On the basis of this view, Spinoza propounded a metaphysical system based on a pantheistic conception of nature. Beginning with a belief in an infinite, unlinked self-caused Substance – which he conceives as God or Nature – Spinoza argues that God and Nature are one. For Spinoza God is totally immanent; hence all interconnections within the one divine system are logical relations. By knowing the truth about the whole system, one is able to comprehend the logical connections between each part. These connections are necessary – there is nothing contingent within the vast complex. 'In the nature of things nothing contingent is admitted, but all things are determined by the necessity of divine nature to exist and act in a certain way' (Spinoza, 1963, part I, prop. 29). According to Spinoza, although God or Nature is self-creating and thereby free, within nature all things are determined and everything is deducible from the concept of God.

As far as Divine Reality is concerned, Spinoza maintains that God has an infinity of attributes, but limited human understanding can conceive of things only in terms of thought and extension. In other words, human beings are capable of thinking of the universe as a system of minds or thoughts, or as a system of physical objects. Extension, Spinoza states, is essential to corporeal things and therefore is fundamental to the Substance we call God. But it would be a mistake to believe that thought and extension are separate bases of all that exists; rather they are simply different facets of the one Substance. A further aspect of Spinoza's philosophy concerns what he refers to as 'Modes' – a modification of Substance. Any body is a mode of the attribute of extension, an arrangement of particles which is differentiated from the rest of matter. A human mind is simply a mode of the attribute of thought, a mental aspect of the Substance of which the body is its material dimension.

Even though human beings are not distinct substances, each person endeavours to persist in its own being, a desire Spinoza calls 'conatus'. As thought, 'conatus' denotes the wish to maintain one's existence. Yet since all acts are linked in a causal chain, everything is what it is of necessity and cannot be anything else. Such a notion follows from Spinoza's idea of God as one Substance which is self-caused and immanent:

> There is no mind absolute, or free will, but the mind is determined for willing this or that by a cause which is determined in its turn by another cause, and this one again by another, and so on to infinity. (Ibid., part ii, prop. 48)

Even God's freedom seems to be limited by what is possible for a Perfect Being:

> All things depend on the power of God. That things should be different from what they are would involve a change in the will of God, and the will of God cannot change (as we have most clearly shown from the perfection of God): therefore things could

not be otherwise than as they are. (Ibid., part i, prop. 33, note 2)

This philosophical system is grounded in Spinoza's concept of three grades of knowledge. The lowest form depends on sense perception, consisting of ideas linked together by association. These insights are of practical importance, but they are inadequate since they do not bring about an understanding of the reason and cause of things. The second grade consists of systematic knowledge; it is exemplified by mathematical thinking where propositions are deduced from axioms and postulates in a coherent and consistent fashion. Here Spinoza utilizes Euclidian geometry as his model in arranging the elementary truths of consciousness into a deductive system. The third and most important form of knowledge is intuitive reason based on scientific and logical thinking which can comprehend the interconnection of the whole.

The person who reaches this final stage is able to apprehend Reality as a unity and attain an active love of God through knowledge:

> The wise man . . . is scarcely at all disturbed in spirit, but being conscious of himself, and of God, and of things, by a certain eternal necessity . . . always possesses true acquiescence of his spirit. If the way which I have pointed out as leading to this result seems exceedingly hard, it may nevertheless be discovered. Needs must it be hard, since it is so seldom found. How would it be possible, if salvation were ready to our hand, and could without great labour be found, that it should be by almost all men neglected? But all things excellent are as difficult as they are rare. (Spinoza, 1956, vol. ii, 270–l)

Departing from traditional Judaism, Spinoza rejects the belief that there is a final purpose to creation. In his view God does not have a separate existence from the world; instead he is totally immanent as the uniformity and sum of all laws: He is the principle of law and its manifestation in both nature and thought. On such a basis, Spinoza envisages God as the totality of all bodies in the physical universe. Such a conception led Spinoza to the conviction that there is neither creation nor freedom. The whole of Reality is free only in the sense that it is self-caused. Human beings are free, however, when they love God and perceive that they are made of Him. Such freedom consists in the liberation from anxiety and care. For Spinoza, submission to the interconnection of all things brings about a feeling of serenity and peace. Happiness is therefore defined in terms of intellectual joy. Not surprisingly Spinoza's ideas were bitterly attacked by the Jewish establishment of his time and largely ignored by later Jewish thinkers, yet his writings had a profound impact on the history of Western philosophy.

References/Spinoza's major works

Encyclopedia Judaica, Jerusalem, 1971
Baruch Spinoza, *The Chief Works of Benedict de Spinoza* (trans. R.H.M. Elwes), New York, 1956
Baruch Spinoza, *Ethics* (trans. A Boyle), London, 1963
Baruch Spinoza, *Treatise on the Correction of the Understanding* (trans. A. Boyle), London, 1963

See also in this book

Maimonides

Further reading

H.E. Allison, *Benedict Spinoza: An Introduction*, New Haven, CN, 1987
J.A. Bennett, *A Study of Spinoza's Ethics*, Cambridge, 1984
S. Hampshire, *Spinoza*, Harmondsworth, Middlesex, 1951
E.E. Harris, *Spinoza's Philosophy: An Outline*, Atlantic Highlands, NJ, 1992
L. Strauss, *Spinoza's Critique of Religion*, New York, 1965
H.A. Wolfson, *The Philosophy of Spinoza*, New York, 1958

SOLOMON LUDWIG STEINHEIM

Born in Bruchausen, Westphalia, in 1789, Solomon Ludwig Steinheim later qualified as a doctor in Altona. Subsequently he settled in Rome. In addition to his writings on medicine and natural science, he composed a number of theological works including his four-volume study, *Doctrine of the Synagogue*, published between 1835 and 1865. He died in 1866. In this study he argues that Judaism should not be confused with philosophical speculation. Critical of the German reform theologians Samuel Hirsch and Solomon Formstecher for their dependence on von Schelling and Hegel, Steinheim also attacked the German advocate of Jewish emancipation, Moses Mendelssohn, for his conviction that natural religion is the source of theoretical truth and that revelation consists of a corpus of law. For Steinheim, the knowledge obtained from Scripture consists of beliefs rather than legal prescriptions.

Following Kant's view that religion is incapable of comprehending things-in-themselves, Steinheim maintains that human reason is unable to construct on *a priori* grounds the concrete reality that is perceived through ordinary experience as well as scientific discovery. Ordinary perception and natural science, he insists, provide empirical knowledge that cannot be derived from thought. Revelation, on the other hand, is the source of suprarational insights that can be validated by the recognition that one is a free moral agent. Hence the content of revelation is not drawn from reason, but can subsequently be confirmed by it.

In line with Moses Maimonides, Steinheim stresses that the central issue of theology is whether God is a free creative being. In this context, he distinguishes between natural and revealed religion. Natural religion, he asserts, is based on the assumption that all things are caused and that nothing can come from nothing. Natural religion, however, is untenable because these two ideas are incompatible. Natural religion defines God as First Cause. Yet, if everything has a cause, then matter must have a cause – as a consequence, something can come from nothing. On the other hand, if nothing can come from nothing, there is no need to explain the existence of material reality. On this account, God is not required as First Cause. According to Steinheim, the only way out of this difficulty is to appeal to the revealed doctrine of *creatio ex nihilo*. Only revealed religion, he believes, can offer a basis for the freedom which is attested by ethical consciousness.

Turning to Christianity, Steinheim contends that the Christian faith has been in danger of degenerating into paganism:

Let all those who have counterfeited our pure concept of revelation, and have adulterated it with pagan philosophical elements, rebuke as an enemy of Christianity the individual who has accused them of neglect of duty and unfaithfulness in the stewardship of their precious talent. This will not cause him to shrink back; he will rather accept this title if they speak of their own mixture as a kind of Christianity .... A Christianity which is not as much based upon revelation pure and simple as upon myth and philosophy is not worthy of the name! ... Let it not be called revelation and the teaching of Christ, but the very opposite, apostasy from it. It leads to the gods of Meru and Mount Olympus but not to God, who revealed Himself to Moses upon Sinai, the God who instructed Christ and the Apostle to the Gentiles. (Steinheim, 1863, vol II, xii)

In making this allegation, Steinheim seeks to illustrate how pagan beliefs have penetrated into the Christian tradition. True revelation, he argues, is always an auditory experience whereas false revelations are visible. For Steinheim, Jesus stood completely within the sphere of true revelation; paganism,

however, was introduced into the faith by John through the doctrine of the Trinity. As Christianity spread to other countries, such pagan elements gained wide acceptance, and through the ages Christian theologians have been more interested in these features of the faith than in Jesus' teaching and ministry. For this reason, Christianity has deteriorated from its original Jewish purity.

This adulteration, Steinheim states, is a tragedy since the core of the Christian tradition is of profound religious significance. In the life of Jesus, the Jew can recognize God's providence:

We have guarded ourselves categorically against the charge or the suspicion of harbouring hostile feelings against the sublime founder of the new brotherhood, the man who unlocked the sanctuary for the pagans. However we distinguish sharply ... we are completely and sincerely convinced of its providential character and value as a means of attracting and overcoming paganism and dogmatic rationalism in all its forms. (Ibid., 76)

According to Steinheim, the mission of the Jews in ancient times was to struggle against natural religion; in modern times the Jewish faith must avoid succumbing to the fashions of philosophical rationalism. But unlike Judaism, Christianity has become adulterated – it is a conglomeration of biblical truth and pagan ideas.

For Steinheim, the history of Christianity is an extended struggle, with paganism continually triumphant. On some occasions the pagan features of the faith have virtually destroyed its authentic religious core; it was only because of the Reformation that human progress became a possibility. This was, however, not Luther's primary aim in the quest to reform the Church, and Steinheim offers a critical analysis of Luther's handling of Scripture as well as an attack on Luther for fostering anti-Semitic attitudes. Nonetheless, Steinheim regards Luther's writings as of vital importance in the evolution of Christianity. 'Blessed be the memory of Luther', he writes, 'despite every way in which he may have erred in word and deed! His memory shall also be holy for us' (Ibid., 246).

The Reformation, Steinheim maintains, was an important step on the way to human progress: it has granted human beings freedom. Yet it has not done much for revelation itself despite such contributions:

> In the midst of the circle of idolatry, which matches that of paganism in extent and intensity, amidst all the helpers, intercessors and representatives of the miserable outcast, there suddenly arose a spark which had been excluded by the Reformation. (Ibid., 244)

For Steinheim, then, the Reformation has moved too slowly, failing to bring about the religious advances he advocated.

Unlike other thinkers of the Enlightenment, Steinheim did not share the same optimism about modern thought; rather he viewed natural science and contemporary philosophical reflection as a return to paganism. In this light he criticized Jewish emancipationists such as Moses Mendelssohn as well as contemporary philosophers such as Schelling and Hegel. Although Steinheim was in the minority, he was not deterred:

> What leads us into the struggle with these powers? – us who are weak into battle with men, into the struggle of the spirits. Let me be permitted to respond to this question with a thought of the great reformer [Luther]: 'Only when the day of universal redemption is at hand would it dawn on me to see whether I could possibly reinstate Moses again and to lead the little brooks to the right spring and river'. (Ibid., 335)

In his writing, Steinheim views Jesus' ministry as a central part of God's revelation to humanity, condemning Christianity for adulterating his message and thereby descending into pagan belief. Christians, he believes, must engage in the quest to reform their heritage. Jews, on the other hand, have the responsibility to refute natural religion in all its manifestations: as the superior faith, this should be Judaism's task in the modern world.

References/Steinheim's major writings

Solomon Ludwig Steinheim, *Die Offenbarung nach dem Lehrbegriff der Synagogue*, Leipzig, 1863

See also in this book

Formstecher, Samuel Hirsch, Maimonides, Mendelssohn

Further reading

J. Haberman, *Philosopher of Revelation: The Life and Thought of S.L. Steinheim*, Philadelphia, 1990

HAYYIM VITAL

Born in *Eretz Israel* in 1542, Hayyim Vital was the son of Joseph Vital Calabrese who originated from Calabria, in southern Italy. After studying in *yeshivot* (rabbinical academies) in Safed, he began to study the *kabbalah* (Jewish mysticism) in 1564 through the system of Moses Cordovero. He was also drawn to other disciplines, spending the years 1563–5 in the practice of alchemy. After Isaac Luria's arrival in Safed, Vital became his principle disciple, studying under Luria until the latter's death in 1572. Subsequently, he began to arrange Luria's teachings in written form, producing his own kabbalistic theories. In this process Vital strove to prevent Luria's other disciples from expounding alternative interpretations of their teacher's ideas. In 1575 twelve of Luria's disciples signed a pledge to study Luria's doctrines only from Vital and to keep these mysteries from others

– this study group disbanded when Vital settled in Jerusalem where he served as a rabbi and head of a *yeshivah*.

In 1586 Vital returned to Safed; according to tradition, he became ill in 1587 and during a period of unconsciousness the scholars of Safed bribed his younger brother, Moses, who permitted them to copy Vital's writings and circulate them among a small group. In 1590 Vital was ordained rabbi by Moses Alshekh; three years later he travelled to Jerusalem, possibly staying there for three years. According to the tradition of the Jerusalem rabbis, he eventually moved from Jerusalem to Damascus where he was the rabbi of the Sicilian Jewish community. After a serious illness in 1604, Vital's sight was seriously impaired. Between 1609 and 1612 Vital assembled a collection of autobiographical notes entitled *Sefer ha-Hezyonot* (Book of Visions) containing stories and testimonies about himself and others. He died in 1620.

According to his son, Vital's major writings were collected into two works, *Etz ha-Hayyim* (Tree of Life) and *Etz ha-Daat* (Tree of Knowledge). The first volume contains Vital's elaboration of Luria's views and was organized into eight sections (gates): Gate One contains everything which had survived in Luria's handwriting; Gate Two contains the doctrine of emanation and creation; Gate Three contains Vital's commentaries on the Zohar (Book of Splendour) and talmudic tractates arranged according to Lurianic principles; Gate Four covers commentaries on the Bible; Gate Five explains mystical customs and meditations; Gate Six outlines the *mitzvot* (commandments) based on the Torah; Gate Seven deals with meditation, customs and acts of magical contemplation, and principles of physiognomy; Gate Eight discusses doctrines concerning the soul and its transmigrations. Throughout this work Vital stresses his indebtedness to Luria:

In [this book] I will explain mysteries that were not grasped by earlier generations that I received from the lips of the Holy Man, the angel of the Lord of Hosts, the godly Rabbi Isaac Luria of blessed memory. (Cohn-Sherbok, 1994, 52–3)

Although most of Vital's writings deal with kabbalistic theories as expounded by his master, there are frequent references to practical meditative kabbalistic techniques. In Lurianic teaching, meditative procedures are related to specific practices. Such meditation allegedly brings a person into the upper spheres by the use of divine names. The essence of Luria's meditative system consists of *yihudim* (unifications) in which manipulations of the letters of the name of God occur. As Vital explains:

I had asked my master [Isaac Luria] to teach me *yihud* so that I should gain enlightenment. He replied that I was not ready. I continued to press him until he gave me a short *yihud*, and I got up at midnight to make use of it. I was immediately filled with emotion, and my entire body trembled. My head became heavy, my mind began to swim, and my mouth became crooked on one side. I immediately stopped meditating on that *yihud*.

In the morning, my master saw me and he said, 'Did I not warn you? If not for the fact that you are a reincarnation of Rabbi Akiva, you would have [become insane] like Ben Zoma. There would have been no way to help you . . .'. On the day before the New Moon in *Elul*, he said to me, 'Now you are ready.' He then gave me a *yihud* and sent me to the cave of Abbaye.

I fell on the grave of Abbaye, and meditated with the *yihud* involving the mouth and I fell asleep; and when I woke up, I could see nothing. I then fell on Abbaye's grave once again, and made use of another *yihud* that I found in a manuscript actually written by my master. This *yihud* involved intertwining the letters YHVH and *Adonai* . . . when I did this, my thoughts became so confused that I could not integrate them. I immediately stopped meditating on this coupling.

It then appeared as if a voice in my mind was saying to me, 'Return in you!' over and over, many times . . . . Then I once again began meditating on this juxtaposition of letters, and I was able to complete the *yihud* . . . . I then began to tremble and all my limbs shuddered. My hands vibrated towards each other, and my lips also vibrated in an unusual manner. They trembled very strongly and rapidly. It seemed as if a voice was sitting on my tongue . . . . The voice literally exploded in my mouth and on my tongue, and over a hundred times it repeated, 'The Wisdom! The Wisdom! The Wisdom!' (in Kaplan, 1982, 219–20)

In addition to Vital's presentation of Lurianic *kabbalah* and his description of mystical meditation, his Book of Visions contains both his own dreams and visions and those of other individuals. In one passage he gives an account related to his preaching in Jerusalem:

On Sabbath morning I was preaching to the congregation in Jerusalem. Rachel, the sister of Rabbi Judah Mishan, was present. She told me that during the whole of my sermon there was a pillar of fire above my head and Elijah of blessed memory was there at my right hand to support me and that when I had finished they both departed. (in Jacobs, 1978, 125)

Again, he recounts that in Damascus this same individual had a vision:

She saw a pillar of fire above my head when I conducted the *Musaf* [additional] service in the Sicilian community on the Day of Atonement. This woman is wont to see visions, demons, spirits and angels and she has been accurate in most of her statements, from the time she was a little girl until now that she has grown to womanhood. (Ibid.)

On another occasion, Vital was visited by an Arab custodian of a mosque who claimed that he had seen him in a vision:

He was a Jew-hater yet he kissed my hands and feet and entreated me to bless him and to write in my own handwriting whatever two or three words I would choose so that he could hang them around his neck as a kind of amulet. I asked him why the sudden change of heart and he replied: 'I know now that you are a godly and holy man. For I am the custodian of a mosque. Last night at midnight I went out of the door of the mosque to relieve myself. The moon was shining so brightly at the time that it was as clear as noon. I raised my eyes and saw you flying through the air, floating for an hour above the mosque – you yourself, without any doubt.' (Ibid.)

In this work Vital also describes his own dreams which had particular significance. In one case he encountered Moses Cordovero, who stated that he would pray for him in Heaven:

I had a dream in which it was the day of Rejoicing of the Law and I was praying in the synagogue of the Greeks in Safed. Rabbi Moses Cordovero was there with another man, greater than he in degree. When I awoke I forgot whether it was the *tanna* [early rabbinic sage] Rabbi Phinehas ben Jair of blessed memory or our contemporary Rabbi Eleazar ben Yohai . . . . After the prayers Rabbi Moses Cordovero said to me: 'Why do you torment yourself to such a degree to grasp the wisdom of the Zohar [Book of Splendour] with utter clarity and why can you not be content with the comprehension of the Zohar I and the sages of previous generations have attained?' I replied: 'I shall continue to acquire as clear a comprehension as I can. If they do not wish it in heaven, what more can I do?' He said to me: 'If this is your desire to know the work to its very roots, more than the generations before you ever comprehended, I shall ascend to Heaven to pray for you with all my might.' (Cohn-Sherbok, 1994, 54)

References

D. and L. Cohn-Sherbok, *Jewish and Christian Mysticism*, New York, 1994
L. Jacobs, *Jewish Mystical Testimonies*, New York, 1978
A Kaplan, *Meditation and Kabbalah*, York Beach, ME, 1982

Vital's major writings

M. Benayahu, *Sefer Toledot ha-Ari*, Jerusalem, 1967

See also in this book

Luria

Further reading

L. Jacobs, *Jewish Mystical Testimonies*, New York, 1978
A. Kaplan, *Meditation and Kabbalah*, York Beach, ME, 1982
G. Scholem, *Major Trends in Jewish Mysticism*, New York, 1995

ELIE WIESEL

Born in Sighet, Romania, in 1928, Elie Wiesel was deported with his family to Auschwitz, where his mother and sister died; his father perished in Buchenwald. After liberation, Wiesel studied in France, becoming an American citizen in 1963. Over the years he received numerous awards and prizes including the Nobel Peace Prize in 1986. In his many literary works, he has become a major spokesman for religious protest. In his autobiographical novel, *Night*, he portrays the evolution of his despair. At the beginning of the novel the author describes himself as a youth preoccupied with God's mystery. As a student of Talmud and mystical lore in the Transylvanian town of Sighet, he confronts a madman who tells him about the destruction of the Jews.

Later in the novel he is transported to Auschwitz where his loss of faith begins. Shortly after his arrival, he questions God: 'Some talked of God, of His mysterious ways, of the sins of the Jewish people and of their future deliverance. But I had ceased to pray. How I sympathized with Job! I did not deny God's existence but I doubted His Absolute Justice' (Wiesel, 1960, 55–6) Later his religious rebellion deepens. He is shocked by the incongruity of the Jewish liturgy that praises God and the events of the camps that indict Him. Dismayed by the new arrivals who recite the Kaddish prayer when they recognize the nature of their plight, he is consumed with anger: '"Why should I bless His name?" he asked. "The Eternal, Lord of the Universe, the all-powerful and terrible was silent. What had I to thank Him for?"' (Ibid., 43).

As the novel progresses, Wiesel's anger intensifies. At the New Year service, he refuses to bless God and praise the universe in which there is mass murder: 'This day I had ceased to plead. I was no longer capable of lamentation. On the contrary, I felt very strong. I was the accuser, God the accused' (Ibid., 79). On *Yom Kippur*, he decides not to fast. 'There was no longer any reason why I should fast. I no longer accepted God's silence. As I swallowed my bowl of soup, I saw in the gesture an act. In the depths of my heart, I felt a great void' (Ibid., 80). This void is the loss of faith, the acknowledgement that God has betrayed His chosen people, leaving them to die in the elaborate machinery of the camps.

This theme of religious protest is the subject of one of Wiesel's later works, *The Trial of God*; here he draws together a number of themes from his previous writings. This play takes place in the village of Shamgorod in 1649 on the Jewish festival of *Purim*. Three Jewish actors have lost their way, and they arrive at the village. They soon discover that this is not a place for festivity since two years previously the town was devastated by a pogrom. Only two Jews survived: Berish the innkeeper and his daughter who was abused on her wedding night. In the region of Shamgorod, anti-Semitism is on the rise, and it appears that a pogrom may occur again. Nonetheless, the festival of *Purim* demands that a dramatic performance be enacted.

Berish urges that a play depict the trial of God. No one wants to speak for God except for a stranger, Sam, who enters the village unnoticed. Berish begins with his prosecution:

'I, Berish', he commences, 'accuse Him of hostility, cruelty and indifference. Either He dislikes His chosen people or He doesn't care about them – period! But then why has He chosen us – why not someone else, for a change? Either He knows what's happening to us, or He doesn't wish to know! In both cases He is ... He is ... guilty! Yes guilty! (in Cohn-Sherbok, 1989, 99)

In response Sam demands evidence that God is guilty. Berish points to himself and his daughter. Sam agrees that the suffering the village endured is sad. But he remains unconvinced that God was responsible. God's ways are mysterious, he emphasizes. Echoing the words of the prophets, Sam states that if God chooses not to explain His ways, He must have His reasons. God is God, and His will is unfathomable.

Berish is unmoved, however, and declares that he is unable to worship God. Sam tries to comfort Berish. He recounts the generations of Jews who mourned over the massacre of their relations. Yet they put their faith in God. So, too, Berish should trust the Lord. Throughout history Jews confessed their sins and looked to God for strength. In the chain of misery stretching back through time, Jews have remained loyal to God. God is just, Sam insists. He created the world and the task of human beings is to praise Him. Yet, as the play concludes, Sam reveals his

identity: he is Satan. And as he laughs in mockery at those who listened to his defence, the door to the inn is opened accompanied by deafening and murderous roars.

Here and elsewhere Wiesel expresses his bewilderment. God appears to be indifferent to the suffering of the Jewish people, and Wiesel castigates Him for his lack of interest in the fate of His faithful servants. The Jewish people seem to be no more than playthings who are abused by Satan. Yet despite such dismay at God's seeming lack of concern with the house of Israel, Wiesel refuses to abandon God, and in some of his other works he asserts that God suffers as His people face death and destruction.

In the cantata, *Ani Maamin*, for example, which was performed after the *Yom Kippur* War, Wiesel presents a dialogue between Abraham, Isaac and Jacob who have the responsibility of directing God's attention to Israel's suffering. As they witness the Holocaust, they turn to God who does not listen to their plea. After Abraham pleads to God, a voice responds:

The Master of the World
Disposes of the world.
His creatures
Do their creator's bidding.
Accept His laws
Without a question. (Wiesel, 1973, 65–7)

Abraham, however, is not convinced. He argues that if he was able to appeal for the inhabitants of Sodom, he has the same responsibility to speak on behalf of the one million innocent children. The answer is:

God knows
What He is doing –
That must suffice. (Ibid., 67)

Abraham refuses to be silenced, and extracts the promise of salvation. Yet even this is not sufficient. He asks:

But what kind of Messiah
Is a Messiah
Who demands

Six million dead
Before He reveals himself? (Ibid., 69–71)

The voice answers, echoing God's response
to Job:

God wills,
That is enough.
God takes
And God gives back,
That is enough.
God breaks
And God consoles,
That is enough. (Ibid., 71)

Abraham is not persuaded. Together with
Isaac and Jacob he maintains that the events
of modern Jewish history – the creation of a
Jewish state, the return from exile, the armies
of Israel – are no consolation for the tragedy
of the Nazi era. But instead of explaining
God's way, the voice attacks human beings
for what they have made of God's creation.
Again the patriarchs remain unconvinced.
The narrator then states:

What is the use of shouting that the future
corrects nothing? That it is pointless to
change the past? What is the use of
pleading? The Judge is avenger. There is
no hope. (Ibid., 77)

The patriarchs then decide to inform
humanity that there is no judge and that God
does not reveal Himself in history:

Abraham: Their battles will have been
            for nought –
            And so will ours.
Isaac: Let us go and tell them.
Jacob: They will die
            With their eyes open,
            Facing emptiness.
            They will perish
            As free men,
            Knowing,
            Aware,
            They will perish without
            regret. (Ibid., 79)

Abraham, Isaac and Jacob leave heaven and
visit earth. When Abraham sees mothers
and children being slaughtered, a little girl
declares: 'I believe in you [God]' (Ibid., 91).
The narrator comments that, unknown to
Abraham, a tear clouds God's eye. Isaac
also witnesses the massacre of the Jewish
community, yet its *dayyan* (judge) proclaims
his belief in God and the Messiah. Again,
God is moved by this declaration of faith, and
another tear is shed down God's sombre
countenance. Jacob, too, observes a Passover
celebration in the camps. The narrator
relates that, unknown to Jacob, 'God
surprised by His people, weeps a third time
– and this time without restraint and with –
yes – love. He weeps over His creation – and
perhaps over much more than His creation'
(Ibid., 97)

Despite God's inaction, the patriarchs are
deeply impressed by the faith of these individuals. Abraham praises Israel; Isaac blesses
the nation for such dedication despite the
cruelty it has endured; Jacob blesses Israel
for its loyalty. God does not remain silent.
He leaves heaven and accompanies the
patriarchs without their knowledge, weeping,
smiling, whispering, 'My children have
defeated me, they deserve my gratitude'
(Ibid., 105). The narrator concludes:

Thus He spake – He is speaking still.
The word of God continues to be heard,
So does the silence of His dead children.
   (Ibid.)

In this work Wiesel appears to have abandoned his initial conception expressed in
other writings of a God who is totally indifferent to human misery. Here God does not
treat His creatures as toys for His amuse-
ment. Rather, He is portrayed as a compassionate and consoling God who weeps for His
people in their distress and rejoices in the
faith of those who remain faithful despite
their suffering. Thus Wiesel is ambivalent
in his attempt to make religious sense of
the Holocaust: his tragic vision of a void in
which God is absent is counterbalanced by
the conception of God as a compassionate
comforter who sheds tears of sorrow for

those who remain loyal to him despite their pain and suffering.

References/Wiesel's major writings

D. Cohn-Sherbok, *Holocaust Theology*, London, 1989
Elie Wiesel, *Night*, New York, 1960
Elie Wiesel, *Ani Maamin*, New York, 1973
Elie Wiesel, *The Trial of God*, New York, 1977

Further reading

Michael Berenbaum, *The Vision of the Void: Theological Reflections on the Works of Elie Wiesel*, Middletown, CN, 1979
D. Cohn-Sherbok, *Holocaust Theology*, London, 1989

SHERWIN WINE

Born in 1928, Sherwin Wine was the founder of Humanistic Judaism. Ordained a rabbi at the Hebrew Union College in Cincinnati, Ohio, he served as a rabbi at the Birmingham Temple in Detroit, Michigan. In 1965 Humanistic Judaism emerged when the Birmingham Temple began to publicize its philosophy of Judaism. In l966 a special committee for Humanistic Judaism was established at the Temple to disseminate service and educational material with rabbis and laity throughout the United States. The following year several leaders of the movement met in Detroit, issuing a statement which affirmed that Judaism should be governed by empirical reason and human needs; in addition a new magazine, *Humanistic Judaism*, was created. Two years later Temple *Beth Or* in Deerfield, Illinois, and the Congregation for Humanistic Judaism in Fairfield County, Connecticut, were established. In 1969 the Society for Humanistic Judaism was founded in Detroit, and the next year the first annual conference of the Society took place. During the next ten years new congregations were established in Boston, Toronto, Los Angeles, Washington, Miami, Long Beach and Huntington, New York.

In subsequent years, Secular Humanistic Judaism under Wine's leadership became an international organization with supporters on five continents. The National Federation of the movement issued a proclamation stating its ideology and aims in 1986:

We believe in the value of human reason and in the reality of the world which reason discloses. The natural universe stands on its own, requiring no supernatural intervention. We believe in the value of human existence and in the power of human beings to solve their problems both individually and collectively. Life should be directed to the satisfaction of human needs. Every person is entitled to life, dignity and freedom. We believe in the value of Jewish identity and in the survival of the Jewish people. Jewish history is a human story. Judaism, as the civilization of the Jews, is a human creation. Jewish identity is an ethnic reality. The civilization of the Jewish people embraces all manifestations of Jewish life, including Jewish languages, ethical traditions, historic memories, cultural heritage, and especially the emergence of the state of Israel in modern times. Judaism also embraces many belief systems and lifestyles. As the creation of the Jewish people in all ages, it is always changing. We believe in the value of a secular humanistic democracy for Israel and for all the nations of the world. Religion and state must be separate. The individual right to privacy and moral autonomy must be guaranteed. Equal rights must be granted to all, regardless of race, sex, creed or ethnic origin. (Cohn-Sherbok, 1996, 156)

Such an ideology of Judaism is based on Wine's radical interpretation of the tradition as espoused in his major work, *Judaism beyond God*. According to Wine, the traditional conception of Jewish history is erroneous. In his view, Abraham, Isaac and Jacob never existed. Further, the Exodus account is a myth:

> There is no historical evidence to substantiate a massive Hebrew departure from the land of the Pharaohs. As far as we can surmise, the Hebrew occupation of the hill country on both sides of the Jordan was continuous. The twelve tribes never left their ancestral land, never endured 400 years of slavery, and never wandered the Sinai desert. (Wine, 1985, 35–6)

Moreover, Moses was not the leader of the Hebrew people, nor did he write the Torah. Thus, Wine maintains, it is a mistake to view the biblical account as authoritative. Instead, it is a human account of the history of the Israelite nation, an account whose purpose is to strengthen the faith of the Jewish people. Humanistic Judaism, however, rejects this fundamental assumption of the tradition, insisting that all Jews should be at liberty to exercise their own personal autonomy in determining which aspects of the Jewish heritage are spiritually significant.

Dedicated to Jewish survival, Humanistic Judaism stresses the centrality of Jewish festivals in fostering Jewish identity. Yet, for Humanistic Judaism, these celebrations must be detached from their supernatural origins and made relevant for the modern age. Thus Wine writes:

> The Jewish holidays have no intrinsic divine connection. They derive from the evolution of the human species and human culture . . . . For humanistic Jews the holidays need to be rescued from rabbinic tyranny and given a secular language and a secular story. (Ibid., 150)

Shabbat, for example, serves as a testimony to the human links which made survival a possibility – it should be a time when humanistic Jews celebrate the human support system: 'Our *Shabbat* dinner', Wine writes, 'is a tribute to the family that sits around the table. Our *Shabbat* service is a tribute to the

Jewish extended family that shares our history and social fate' (Wine, 1982, 154). Similarly, the High Holy Days can serve as an occasion to reflect on human needs: '*Rosh Hashanah* [New Year] and *Yom Kippur* [Day of Atonement] open our Jewish year with the most important message of Jewish history. Human dignity is not the gift of destiny. It is a human achievement, requiring courage and human self-reliance' (Ibid., 157).

Other humanistic themes are featured in the seasonal holidays: *Sukkot* (Festival of Booths), *Hannukah* and *Pesah* (Passover). A humanistic *Sukkot* should be a tribute to human culture – agricultural, pastoral and urban. *Hannukah*, too, celebrates human potential:

> If *Rosh Hashanah* and *Yom Kippur* are testimonies to the assumption of human responsibility for human life in the face of an absurd and indifferent universe, if *Sukkot* is the witness to the power of human ingenuity and creativity, then *Hannukah* is the celebration of human power, the increasing power of people to use the world to enhance the quality of human life. (Wine, 1985, 164)

Passover also celebrates human achievement – it commemorates the rediscovery of human dignity.

Such an interpretation of these holidays as well as others in the Jewish calendar provides a basis for extolling human capacities. So, too, does Humanistic Judaism's conception of life-cycle events. The ceremonies connected with these events stress the importance of group survival. Nonetheless, humanistic philosophy – based on the conviction that all individuals are equal – rejects male circumcision:

> A humanistic morality that defends female equality would have a hard time justifying a birth ritual that excludes women . . . . The *brit* [the covenant ceremony] is, by its very nature, inconsistent with a humanistic value system. (Ibid., 186)

In its place Humanistic Jews have substituted an occasion that grants equal status to boys and girls, dramatizing the relation between the child and the future of the family, the Jewish people and humanity.

Similarly, Humanistic Judaism advocates a humanistic maturity ceremony which reflects the ethical commitment of Humanistic Jews. Ensuring the equality of both sexes, such celebrations are designed to express the beliefs of the individual celebrants as well as the ideals of the community. Within such a framework, there is a variety of alternatives available: 'Presenting a lecture to an adult audience is only one of many options. Music, dance, humour, science and business are as much a part of Jewish culture as worship. (Ibid., 186)

As another important transitional event, marriage should also embody humanistic values. In Wine's opinion, the wedding should embrace the concept of a bride and groom publicly proclaiming their dedication to one another. The major feature of this ritual is the pledge made by the bride and groom in the presence of family and friends. Such a declaration should not be simply a ritualistic formula; rather it should be a personal statement accompanied by the exchange of rings or other gifts symbolic of their dedication to one another. Humanistic marriage ceremonies also include songs and poetry about love and loyalty, a marriage contract expressive of the couple's personal relationship, and a philosophical statement about the meaning of marriage.

Rituals connected with death should likewise be expressive of humanistic principles. For Humanistic Jews, mortality is an unavoidable event. Accepting this fact, it is possible to live with courage and generosity in the face of tragedy. As Wine states, 'A humanistc Jewish memorial service is an opportunity to teach a humanistic philosophy of life. Both the meditations and the eulogies must serve to remind people that the value of personal life lies in its quality, not in its quantity' (Wine, 1982, 182).

Humanistic Judaism, as understood by Wine, offers an option for those who wish to identify with the Jewish community despite their rejection of the traditional understanding of God's nature and activity. Wine's conception of Judaism thus fosters a radically new approach to the tradition. In his view, the Jewish heritage is relevant only in so far as it advances humanistic principles for the modern age. In proposing such a human-centred ideology, Wine sets aside traditional definitions and principles in the quest to create a Judaism consonant with a scientific world-view. Secular in orientation, Humanistic Judaism seeks to create a society in which the Jewish people are dedicated to the betterment of all humankind.

References/Wine's major writings

D. Cohn-Sherbok, *Modern Judaism*, Basingstoke, Hampshire, 1996
Sherwin Wine, *Judaism Beyond God*, Birmingham, MI, 1985
Sherwin Wine, *Celebration*, Buffalo, NY, 1988

Further reading

D. Cohn-Sherbok, *Modern Judaism*, Basingstoke, Hampshire, 1995
D. Cohn-Sherbok, *The Future of Judaism*, Edinburgh, 1994